D1019845

MY HOME SWEET HOME

SURVIVING AN ABUSIVE RELATIONSHIP

REVIEW

Every choice has a consequence. Hope resides even in situations which seem helpless. Courage comes in many packages.

These messages reverberate through Maxine Derr's book, My Home Sweet Home – Surviving an Abusive Relationship.

I had the honor of reading this book recently. As her story unfolded, I saw how her choices, both healthy and unhealthy, profoundly impacted the trajectory of her life. I discovered how Maxine's hope sustained her despite seemingly devastating circumstances.

Above all, I read of courage in a young woman whose life challenges would prompt many to throw in the towel.

Maxine's story needs to be heard.

Pastor Beth Armstrong
Anchorage Free Methodist Church
Anchorage, Alaska

To Wanda & Robert
"Enjoy"

MY HOME SWEET HOME

SURVIVING AN ABUSIVE RELATIONSHIP

MAXINE E. DERR

Maxine E. Derr

NORTHBOOKS
Eagle River, Alaska

Copyright © 2005 by Maxine E. Derr

All rights reserved. No part of this book may be reproduced in any form without permission except by a reviewer who may quote brief passages in a media review.

Photo Credits: Personal collection of author

Credits: U.S.Army Discharge Certificate, November 21, 1918
                  Bible quotations from King James Version

Published by:

ŊORCҺBOOKS

17050 N. Eagle River Loop Road, # 3
Eagle River, Alaska 99577

Printed in the United States of America

ISBN 0-9720604-5-6

Library of Congress Control Number: 2004118009

DEDICATION

To my four children....
Jack, Daniel, Mark, and Cynthia

This book is dedicated to my children who also experienced many of these trials in their lives during this time period. The respect they have always shown me is an example of their appreciation of the years I spent trying to raise them under stressful conditions.

God has blessed me with kind and thoughtful children, three of them having families of their own, having given me many grandchildren and great-grandchildren. I call them my fringe benefits of my senior years.

These four children have all the faith to go to other places to live and find their Home Sweet Home, also giving me the freedom to visit them in many places throughout the beautiful United States of America.

For life's greatest blessings, I thank Thee, Lord. Home is a foretaste of heaven.

ACKNOWLEDGMENTS

Pastors Beth and Jason Armstrong, Anchorage Free Methodist Church, for the encouragement they gave me to have this book published.

Ray and Jan Holmsen of Northbooks for editing and publishing this book when no one else would. They spent many hours editing the manuscript and patience while working with a new writer and having the faith in me to inspire me to finish this book and continue on to write a second one.

TABLE OF CONTENTS

PREFACE

The country was recovering from the Great Depression of the late twenties and early thirties, business was just beginning to pick up and the hope of the future was more prevailing among the majority of the population. The economic crisis was being solved by the New Deal for the "forgotten man" by the newly-elected President Roosevelt, and most everyone began to pull themselves literally up by their bootstraps. Although some of the forgotten men didn't even have boots, let alone the straps to hang on to, they had a new hope, a sparkle of light and courage given by a leader who knew what it was to overcome many obstacles. A new leader with a heart and soul for the down-and-out people, he was a God-fearing and loving man.

America, the melting pot of all nationalities, has many, many tales to be told of families and their struggles of how they triumphed over difficulties through the many years of peace and war; also, their own personal struggles with daily problems that arose and how they faced them by trial and error. It is as if our Heavenly Father knows each and every individual and their problems as they arise.

He does, because He made us, so He knows every hair on our heads, and there is no problem that He cannot solve, if we ask Him for His help. This story is one of thousands like it all over the world: of how God does live today and is able to help each and every individual, no matter what is wrong. But first, one has to have the faith to believe God's Word and that He is able to do that which is abundantly above all we may ask or think, through faith in the Lord Jesus Christ.

Christ was first to give equal status to women. He said there would be no difference between male and female, and it has taken many years for women to get the respect and equality men have. Although, even today, many males still have an old-fashioned idea about woman's place in the home and that she is inferior to men. Everyday common sense is an asset and very few people use it. Women who choose to stay home and raise their families, dedicating their lives to them by teaching their children to the best of their abilities, are to be commended for building a safe and secure foundation for their lives. They fill children with their love and understanding to be able to overcome bitterness, hatred, jealousy, and envy by being patient, sacrificing for their good with a joyful heart and receiving the peace that passeth all understanding of human nature.

The years of college education and experience for women and their struggles to hold many major positions in the private and corporate sector, as well as the political field, have proven that our Lord was so right about women, whom He knew were as capable as men. Even though many women have not had the opportunity or the finances to go on with their education and have had to struggle much harder through life, this does not mean they are not equal to their male counterparts.

Threads are woven to make cloth, some threads being much stronger then others, therefore, the strength of the thread will be the end results of the cloth and the wearing length of it. The same is true with people throughout life and their strength to cope with life and its ups and downs.

God gives us strength as we live our lives and by the decisions we make throughout life. Some are bad choices and we learn by them one way or another, and by the attitude we take realizing that we made the mistake and no one else is to blame. By asking God for forgiveness and believing He does forgive, we can go on with the gratitude of thanksgiving and the attitude of loving one another as God has loved us. Gratitude is the attitude to take and pass on to others throughout life.

The soul of a man or woman may rise from the deepest despair to heavenly heights but only by the Grace of God, which He gives us even though we do not deserve it. He loved us so much that He gave His only begotten Son Jesus Christ to die on the cross for all who will believe. When we are willing to believe and accept that God sent His only Son Jesus Christ to die on the cross for our sins, was buried and rose again to be at the right hand of His Heavenly Father making intercession for us to the Father by saying, "Father forgive them they do not know what they are doing; I died once and for all who will believe and receive your everlasting love, it is done, the debt has been paid in full," then as believers we shall rise up like eagles, run and not be weary, walk and not faint, be free to soar on heights unknown to many.

This is free for the asking and with faith believing that Christ is the only answer to help anyone to rise up from the deepest despair to a new life with Christ.

May the spiritual aspect of this story be the prevailing thought uppermost in your minds as you read this book, recording many of the trials and tribulations that have been a part of my life. The many people I have known who have touched my life and influenced many changes in my life throughout the years have been faithful and loving people, examples of what God can do for others and what He can do for you.

God has given me the inspiration to write this story and how it unveils the faith I have had in believing throughout my life that Salvation is for lost souls and only by the Lord Jesus Christ and His Love for those lost sheep, who was willing to die for them. I was lost but now I am found. Thank you, Lord, for saving my soul and thank you for making me whole.

Maxine E. Derr
January, 2005

MAXINE E. (BOHL) DERR – 1944

SIXTEEN YEARS OLD

CHAPTER ONE

A PROPHETIC DREAM

Dreams of great significance have been interpreted to mean something that will happen far into the future and does happen. In the Old Testament of the Bible there are some dreams recorded, their interpretations, and the results of those dreams affecting their lives and the lives of others.

Maxine was a very strong-willed lady, whose strong mind-set was on accomplishing what she believed was the best way to happiness and peace of mind. She tried extra hard, many times for so long relying on her own strength, determined she could, having been taught by her mother, "Can't never tried." She wouldn't stop trying.

Within the middle years of Maxine's life, she dreamed a specific dream, a dream that left her questioning the significance and the interpretation. As the years have gone by, the meaning of this dream has enlightened Maxine to just what God was trying to do for her in her life whenever she yielded her life to Him, letting Him have His way.

In this dream she kept banging herself against a big wall many times, trying over and over again, until she lost all of her strength and will to even try anymore. She fell helpless, letting go of her own will to succeed, her will to have it her way. Letting go, she rested helpless. God took control, He lifted her up and over that wall, so easy without any effort, this big wall of indifference, built upon natural man's (woman's) self-will. God's power of love lifted her above this huge wall, filling her life with love to soar above this world and its ways, to help accomplish what God has in store for his children: Love.

"Love lifted me, when nothing else could help, love lifted me," as the song goes. And so we know and rely on the love God has for us. God is love, whoever lives in love lives in God, and God in him. In this way, love is made complete among us so that we will have confidence on the day of judgment, because in this world we are to be like Him.

There is no fear in love. But perfect love drives out all fear, because fear has to do with punishment. The one who fears is not made perfect in love. We love because He first loved us. The wages of sin is

1

death, but the gift of God is eternal life (Romans 5:21). God so loved the world that he gave his only begotten Son, Jesus Christ, that who soever believes in Him, shall not perish, but shall have everlasting life (John 3:16).

This transformation took place in the unfolding of the years of Maxine's life. She finally realized after many years of trials and tribulations throughout her life the true significance of this dream she had and the meaning of it. The years of maturity were unveiling the truths of the lessons learned and the wisdom to be able to pass on to others who might be or have been in familiar situations. But, first and foremost, to be able to prevent others from ever making the bad choices Maxine made by not relying first on God's will instead of her own stubborn will.

The righteousness from God comes through faith in Jesus Christ to all who believe. All have sinned and come short of the glory of God (Romans 3:22-23). With Maxine's guilt and shame through many years of her own sins, she thought she deserved the punishment of an abusive relationship, until she heard and believed that, "Christ is the only answer."

Therefore, since we have been justified through faith, we have peace with God through our Lord Jesus Christ (Romans 5:1). A peace that only God can give and hope to be with the Lord Jesus Christ in heaven someday. A dream that God gave to Maxine.

And so, the story unfolds...

Chapter Two

The Early Years

The sun was peeping through the morning clouds and it was the beginning of a beautiful Easter Day; the family was awakening to greet the day with great expectations of celebrating Easter, especially the children as they began looking for their candy-filled baskets hidden by their mom and dad. With seven boys and girls scurrying about looking everywhere for the basket with his or her name on it, Dad always liked to hide them in difficult places to find. Soon the baskets were all found but little Toddie's (Maxine's nickname). She looked and looked and was getting very discouraged, but no one would help her or even give her a hint of the whereabouts of the basket. The other children were sampling their candy and teasing her that maybe she didn't get one, but she wouldn't give up looking for it. She tried so hard to find it, then finally Daddy took her by the hand and took her out to the old shed where they raised rabbits and pointed to a loose board on the floor. As she raised the board she could see the bright beautiful basket with her name on it. Oh what joy came over her as she lifted the basket up from the hiding place.

The day continued to be a beautiful day and the family celebrated and thanked God for our Lord Jesus Christ, who arose to be with His Father, the meaning of this day of celebration: new hope for the days ahead. The depression years had taken a toll on this family, but they did not lose their faith or love for each other and their God.

German born and eldest of four boys, Henry, the father of the family, was very strict with his five boys but pretty lenient with the two little girls. Although Toddie was afraid of her daddy (because she had seen the boys get severe spankings and surely did not want any of them, a fear that stayed with her for many years), she later changed to respect and to develop a deep love for her daddy.

The older boys sold papers on the street corners to help out and sometimes they got into trouble, so Dad did the only thing he knew to do: punish them. Sometimes they got into trouble at school, typical boys, especially the third son Harold. Mother had to go to school several times to see the principal. A few times, Harold came home with his shirt torn and Mother went to school and reported it to the principal, who in turn spoke to the teacher about using a different method of controlling Harold, and from then on there was no trouble.

Henry had gone into business with a German-born cousin, the only other relative to come to America, and they lost everything when the banks failed. The family home was taken and they had to move. They moved to a little town south of Jackson and things seemed to go pretty good for a while. Henry got a job at the state capital, Lansing, and was away from home a lot and Herman and Harold got into more trouble and were sent to a boy's reform school. Mother's legs were very bad with broken varicose veins and she had to stay off of them as much as possible, so the eldest son Snookie (a nickname for Henry Jr.) had to help around the house, as did Clara the elder girl, fourth from the eldest child.

Ernest, the next to the youngest, had pneumonia and brain fever when he was only six months old and it left him impaired, so he was quite a handful for the family. At the home in Vandercook Lake when Ernie was about six years old, he fell off the running board of the Model T Ford car Snookie was driving and got his leg run over and was in a cast for many months after, so the family all helped to care for him and entertain him with games and by reading to him.

The summers were very nice living there because there was a lake close by and the children could go swimming. There was a large slide and a roller coaster at the amusement park at the lake. The slide let you go into the water and it was so much fun, and the children had freedom to laugh out loud and holler out with such joy. It was such a relief from being so quiet and obedient in the home, since to be seen and not heard was the rule. Also, on Saturday nights there were free movies in the park. They took a blanket and watched them, it was such a treat for them, even if they had to sit on the ground. Looking back to those wonderful times of youth, it was precious, and home was such a haven. Even though times were hard, the children understood why their parents had it so hard, as many others did, too.

Once when the family was in need of food very bad, Mother accepted surplus food from welfare and when Father found out, he

4

was very irritated and went to the welfare office and paid for everything Mother had received. He was a very proud man and felt it was his job to support his family; from then on he was very careful to make sure there was enough to eat in the house while he was gone and to make sure there was money to buy whatever was needed for the family.

The neighbors next door were good neighbors. Ester, the mother was ill; she had water on the knee and couldn't walk for some time, so Clara and Toddie would go over to their house and help her with cleaning, cooking and taking care of their two little girls, Janice and Joan. This was an experience for them as well as earning money; Clara would baby-sit for the girls sometimes when Ester and Tom wanted to go somewhere. Toddie wasn't old enough to do that. Oh, by now they called her Maxine, her given name.

Maxine walked to school, usually by herself, and would pass the little white church on the corner and sometimes hear the choir practicing on her way home. She would stop and listen for a little while, but not for long because she had only so much time to get home because her mother had a time limit for her. Mother had warned her girls to never talk to strangers or accept a ride from anyone they did not know. One time, Maxine decided to go home with a friend and they rode the trolley car to her friend's home, which was quite a long way from the school, and Maxine's family was worried about where she was. The friend helped Maxine call the neighbors to go over and tell Mother where she was and that she would take the next trolley car back home. With her fear of getting lost and her fear of punishment, that was a long ride home. It was reason to never do that again, along with the punishment from Mother.

Two years had passed and the house they were renting was being sold, so they had to move; everyone pitched in and packed like little beavers to get the job of moving done, and cleaned the house for the new owners. Mother had gone and found a house to move into in Jackson and made arrangements for the family to move. The new house was a much bigger one than they had been in, and all eyes were so surprised at the size of it. It was on the corner, had an inside bathroom, a tub and extra bedrooms too. Oh, what joy came over them all as they went in and looked it over and ran from room to room.

Unpacking began and settling down to a different place and with new neighbors to meet and new friends to play with, what excitement and anticipation they all had as they proceeded with the work to be done. The children talked about the new schools they would attend and how far they were from the schools, and how they would miss the lake and all of its fun they used to have there, would they find anything around here that would replace that entertainment that was free and so much fun? Mother said, "Don't worry there will be many things to do around here when you meet new friends. They will show you things to do and places to go."

Living on the corner and just two blocks away from a K-6 grade school, called East Main, the younger children attended until the school board decided they should be attending the Trumble School, because they lived on the north side of the street. Trumble School was about eight or nine blocks away, much farther for them to walk, and for several months the children attended there until the school board decided they should go back to East Main School.

While in the fifth grade, Maxine came down with scarlet fever and rather than have the whole family quarantined, the doctor advised her to go to an isolation hospital for contagious diseases. She was so scared; Mother couldn't come into her room and had to look through a window in the door. The nurses asked Maxine if she had nightmares because her bed covers were so messed up in the morning, but she couldn't remember. After the required time away from home, it was safe to return back to school for classes but it was hard because she had been absent for such a long time. They held her back half a year to catch up, at that time the schools had half years, like 1A and 1B.

The school principal talked to Mother and advised her to send Ernie to an ungraded room at a school that was close to downtown, because his school did not have the teachers to teach handicapped children. So Maxine had to leave East Main in order to escort Ernie to Pearl School by way of the city bus. It was hard for her because she had to adjust to a new school and new teachers, plus the responsibility of seeing that Ernie got to his class every day. Maxine took Ernie to school faithfully every morning, and many times by the time she got back to her room he would have disappeared. He had a bad habit of running away, wandering is more the word for it. The police would be called and they would search for him, many times finding him miles away from home or school. This presented a big problem for Mother and the rest of the family. In his travels, he would steal milk bottles from peoples' front porches; this was, of course, when the milkman delivered milk to homes. Ernie would then go buy candy for the neighbor children with the money he received from the bottles he sold.

Mother was getting very discouraged about his running away from school and home, too. It was hard on her because Father had a job out of town and wasn't home too often because he had heart trouble and didn't travel well. They talked it over and one of Father's friends with influence helped to get Ernie into a state home for retarded children. This was very hard on all the family but it had to be done because Mother's health couldn't take the pressure of his wandering away from home so much.

Because of the illness when he was a baby, the doctors at the home said he would never mature beyond a twelve-year-old's mental capacity for learning. Sometimes he ran away from the state home and had to be punished. The last time he ran away they tied him to his bed for several days and he finally realized he had to stay within the boundaries of the home. They appointed him to do jobs, like dishes and laundry to keep him busy when he wasn't in school learning.

The family visited as often as a ride was available, because no one in the family had a car at this time, so friends would help out once in a while and take Mother up to visit Ernie. This was another experience for the younger children, especially Maxine. She was fearful of going to the home because so many of the residents there were physically impaired as well as mentally, and this made a bad impression on her mind. Each time she went it took a few days for her to get it out of her mind because it was very discouraging and so hard to understand why so many children were in such bad condition, and wondering if the people who took care of them were good to them. It scared her also because she was so concerned for her brother being there; she realized he wasn't nearly as bad off as many of the others.

Maxine did graduate from the sixth grade at Trumble School and was anticipating the new school year at East Intermediate School, which was seventh through the ninth grades, and was many more blocks away than Trumble School.

As time went by everyday chores, school and friends filled her mind with other things to think about, like learning new songs she heard on the radio and doing things like playing hop scotch, kick the can, hide and go seek; learning how to roller skate with the neighbor children's skates, playing soft ball in the street, climbing trees, playing horse shoes and many other games to keep busy and out of trouble. Maxine would also baby-sit the neighbor's children and earn money; plus Ester and Tom would come every Friday night and get her to baby-sit Janice and Joan on Saturday nights, then bring her back home on Sunday after-noon after they had gone visiting with friends and relatives. So she earned money to help buy her school clothes. Mother would go during the summer and pick out the clothes and put them on layaway and pay on them until it was time for school to start. Oh, how happy the children were when Mother brought home the new clothes for school; they were so thankful for the new things. Even though they didn't get to pick them out, they were new, and they'd think, "My, what will we wear the first day?"

Clark, the youngest son, had a paper route and he earned enough money to buy his bike and Maxine would help him deliver the papers to his customers. Clark was four years younger then Maxine but he was a very ambitious young boy and wanted things and knew he had to earn money in order to get them. Clark's nick name was Corky, and he was somewhat spoiled by Mother and all the older children because Dad was away from home so much during later years of his life and the discipline wasn't so harsh by this time.

Mother had friends who would come and visit her; one of them had a guitar and gave Maxine lessons on it, although not enough to be able to play well. Besides, she was an active child and was more inter-ested in physical activities than playing a guitar.

Mother did not visit with neighbors very much; she kept to herself a lot, except when friends and her sister or brothers would come to visit. She was a very private person. She told Maxine that people gossip and she didn't want any part of it. She was friendly enough to the neighbors whenever they were around, but would not go to their homes to visit. Sometimes, she would take Maxine and Corky to the Saturday matinee to see a movie. They would go by bus, and that was about the only entertainment she would have besides the radio; she would listen to *My Gal Sunday, Jack Benny, Amos and Andy, Fibber McGee & Molly, George Burns and Gracie Allen*, and *The Hit Parade*. There would be a contest between Frank Sinatra and Bing Crosby as to who had the most votes for best singer that week. Then, in the evening *The Lone Ranger* and *Inner-Sanctum* (The Squeaking Door) would be on and the children usually listened to those programs.

Mother would send the laundry out to be washed and it would come back wet and the girls had to hang it up on the clothesline outside. When it dried they took it down and folded it. The girls had to do the ironing also with so many boys in the house. They ironed many shirts and pants, plus their own clothes. They were thankful to have an ironer to iron the flat pieces like tablecloths and hankies. Many times the older boys would give Maxine money to press their good pants or to polish their shoes for them. The girls also did all the dishes and cleaned the house on Saturdays. They could not go anywhere until the housework was done and this taught them responsibility, which carried over to their adult lives. Maxine would clean the downstairs and Clara would clean the upstairs. While cleaning the downstairs Maxine would dance around and sing with such vigor and happiness; Mother would say if she would just do her work she would do it faster. But at least she did it willingly and with a good attitude, that was so much better then being grumpy about it.

At meals many times Snookie (Henry Jr.) would give Maxine a nickel to buy dessert, and she would go to the grocery store on the corner and buy a candy bar. The older boys would play tricks on Maxine; one time they sent her to the store to buy elbow grease, and she went to the store and asked for it and everyone there sure got a big laugh out of it. It sure embarrassed Maxine and made her very upset with her brothers.

CHAPTER THREE

FORMING THE FOUNDATION

One of the neighbors was a Christian lady and she invited Maxine, Clara, and Clark to go to Sunday school with her and her children. They went and enjoyed it very much. The Sunday school bus came every Sunday to pick them up and Maxine was so excited to go each Sunday to learn about God and Jesus; the teachers were kind and gentle and were so interested in the children. During the summers they would have Vacation Bible School and many children would attend; there was so much to do: they learned Bible verses and where to find them; they learned all the books in the Bible, and there would be quizzes on them and if you were first, you got a sticker for your Bible. It was so rewarding and made them happy when they were able to be first to recite or find the verses. Sometimes when another church had Vacation Bible School, Maxine would attend that one too. She loved to sing the songs about Jesus and His love.

Maxine accepted the Lord Jesus when she was twelve years old and was baptized. What a wonderful experience that was, nothing like that had ever happened to her before. All these experiences helped her grow in the knowledge of the Lord; they were positive experiences and brought joy to her. They preached that you should not drink alcohol, smoke, or go to the movies, if you do you will go to hell, and this left quite an impression on Maxine; she really believed it. She wanted to be good so she would go to heaven someday, she had never heard these things were sin before.

It was hard for a young lady her age to overcome the shame of having two brothers that got into trouble all the time, so embarrassing, but she would try to keep her feelings within herself, although it was hard because she didn't find many she could call friends at intermediate school; everyone seemed to be strangers, except the neighborhood friends. Whenever she would baby-sit she would do extra things, like pick up, do the dishes, and even sweep the floor if it needed it. She just wanted to be liked for herself and not for being one of the sisters of the bad boys. She tried so hard to be good and to be accepted for herself.

Maxine had only a few close friends, and was very quiet. As the years flew by, in her teen years, she would spend Saturday nights with some friends and go to a Shirley Temple movie with them and come out of the theater with a guilty conscience because she had been taught that if you go to movies you would go to hell, because you were of the devil. Later in life she realized the difference in movies and their content and how silly it was to feel such guilt. No one told her she could ask God's forgiveness, repent and say she was sorry, so she carried that guilt around for a long time. It gave her an inferiority complex, which showed up in school. She tried hard to study and get good grades at school but learning came hard for her. She did make it on the "B" honor roll a couple of times with extra hard study and encouragement from Mother.

Father had gone to Detroit, which was approximately eighty-five miles from home, and gone to work for the Ford Motor Company as a watchman and came home less and less, maybe once or twice a month. But when he did come home Maxine was so happy to see him she would spend as much time with him as she could. His heart was not good and it was hard on him to travel, the doctor advised him not to travel so much. The eldest son, Henry, was working in a factory and helping with household expenses. He was able to purchase an automobile, what a wonderful thing it was to have an automobile in the driveway, and the children got to go for a ride in it once in a while.

The older boys and Clara would go to the roller-skating rink and take Maxine with them once in a while. She really loved it. Herman liked a girl who was giving skating lessons, dance lessons such as waltz and tango, and she gave free lessons to Maxine. She would let Maxine be her partner whenever she wanted to demonstrate one of the dances, it was so much fun. Maxine would go whenever she could and practice. The music was live by an organist named Goldie; she did such a good job on all the types of music: waltzes, tangos and polkas. Goldie loved those who came to the roller rink and was so friendly, and she would play the songs anyone would request.

Going to the intermediate school, Maxine made some friends. One lived only two blocks away and her name was Arahbelle. She invited Maxine to come and stay overnight with her on Saturdays and go to the movies. Arahbelle had one sister and three brothers and she was the youngest. They had so much fun pretending to be different characters they had seen in the movies. After some time Maxine had stopped going to Sunday school because she didn't understand about forgiveness and felt she wouldn't be accepted anymore. Of course this was not true, but she somehow visualized this in her mind and would not attend. She buried this guilt by having fun with her friend Arahbelle.

Arahbelle let Maxine borrow her brother's ice skates, which were about four sizes too big for her. She tried to ice skate and really liked it, so she asked for a pair of skates for Christmas. She wanted figure skates so she could learn some tricks she had seen Sonja Henie do in the movies. They weren't as easy as they looked in the movies. So many times she fell down, but she would get back up and try again and again, with bruised knees and so tired, she would walk home with sore tired feet.

Summers were great too, the children in the neighborhood would play ball in the street and roller skate also, because there were not that many cars on the road at that time. There wasn't much money for entertainment but Mother would try to give them money whenever she could because they helped her so much with all the housework. Most of the neighbors were in the same boat, so to speak, and sometimes on the weekends they would all get together and play games, parents included. They would play kick the can, hide and go seek, and rover, rover who's going to cross over. Then the parents would just sit and talk for a while until it was time to go in.

Sometimes when it rained real hard the corner would flood and the basements would get water in them. Whenever it flooded the children would put on their swimsuits and have a good time wading and splashing through the water. Cars would try to go through the water and the drivers wouldn't realize it was so deep and the cars would stall. The kids would all get behind and push real hard to get them out – oh, what fun. Then the bus would go by and it would really splash and spray the kids. When the sewer was unplugged and the water drained away, it would leave a bunch of mud. What a mess: the sidewalks were muddy and had to be washed off and debris that had floated from other places had to be picked up.

During the summer the intermediate school was open for swimming classes and Maxine and one of her friends would go because it was so much fun. It was another activity to keep the children busy in the summer. It was great fun until someone stole Maxine's new tennis shoes and she had to go the summer wearing shoes with cardboard in them for soles. They didn't last long either, so she went barefoot most of the time.

Then there were times the kids would feel like being devilish, and would go up to the next corner and turn in a fire alarm and run like the dickens and hide under the front porch, which was all enclosed except for an opening big enough for them to get in. Or they would just mosey around in the front yard like they were so innocent, until they finally got caught at it and were punished by their parents who explained to them just how serious it would be if there was really a fire and the fire trucks weren't available to go and put out the fire.

When things were quiet and there was nothing to do in the evening, Maxine would sit on the lawn and look up at the sky and watch the stars, sometimes she would see a shooting star. She would think about God and her life, meditating and thinking deep thoughts of what the future may be like, it was a time to be alone and just wonder. She would think about the girl across the street, who was an only child and all the things she had to play with and how her parents were well to do, according to the rest of the neighbors; both parents worked and they had a nice car. But Maxine realized she had brothers and a sister and parents who loved her, and she would try not to think about those things she didn't have.

Maxine spent some time at her neighbor's, the friend who asked her to go to church. Francis and her children were friendly and always took time to talk and play games with her and she was always welcome to come in without knocking on the door. She would pitch in and help do dishes or help pick up after the children, they were very young and kept Fran very busy at times. Her husband had died so she had to go to work at a factory not far from where they lived and she asked Maxine to baby-sit for her during the summer months. The children, one boy and three girls, were good and were well behaved. They knew Maxine well and cooperated whenever she told them to behave. It was a joy to look after them.

On the weekend of December 6 and 7, 1941, Maxine was with the Baracloughs and they were at Ester's sister's house out on Moscow Road in Spring Arbor Township when the news came over the radio about the attack on Pearl Harbor and that President Franklin Roosevelt had just declared war on the Japanese. They all listened to his speech with much concern; the United States was now in the Second World War, and everyone was conscientious about being patriotic. They left to go home and were all concerned about Pearl Harbor.

Herman was the first one in line to sign up to go into the Navy, on December 8, 1941. Snookie (Henry Jr.) the eldest son, stayed home as long as he could to help out financially. But then the draft notice came and Snookie was inducted into the Army. Harold, the third oldest son, tried to join but was unable to go in because he was too young, only seventeen. Flags with big white stars were displayed in the windows of the families who had boys in the service, as they were in our window at home.

Everyone was saving tin cans, aluminum foil and scrap iron to be used for recycling. Cigarettes were in demand; silk stockings were hard to come by; gas, meat, and sugar were rationed; and people had to stand in line for many things that were scarce. But all Americans left at home pitched in and did their share to help. Women went to work in the factories in masses to help the war effort, they did many jobs they never thought of doing before. This was the beginning of women's release from the old-fashioned idea that a woman's place is in the home, even though it meant double duty for her, especially if she had children at home. "Rosie the Riveter" was a common saying about the women working in the factories, but they sure did their part to help win the war.

As the days passed by one by one, they waited anxiously for the mailman to bring news from the two boys in the service, and shared the news with all of the relatives, especially Grandma and Grandpa. The war was raging on and Henry was sent straight overseas without any leave to come home before he was shipped out. When they landed in Africa he drove supply trucks and one of the amphibian "Ducks" which he had been trained to do. During the long battles throughout Africa, he contracted a slight case of malaria and was treated for that. As the war

14

continued their units were shipped to Italy, they went through that campaign, and then up through Italy into Germany. These were long and hard battles. As the war continued Henry was faithful in sending letters home. Of course they were all censored and any letters that were sent to him were censored also, in case of any espionage that would cause any kind of trouble. A frequent saying was, "A slip of the lip will sink a ship." Mother would faithfully keep her letters going to the boys informing them about the daily activities and experiences. The boys looked forward to hearing from home and what was going on with the citizens' efforts to help win the war. Mother would also send CARE packages to them with homemade goodies.

Herman finished boot camp and was on a ship in the Pacific for a period of time, then was stationed in California after he had come home on a furlough. While at home he wasn't feeling well and went to the doctor and discovered he had contracted a disease while in the Pacific. Returning to California, he notified his commander of the doctor's written report, who had the Navy doctors examine him and they also verified his illness. He was then discharged from the Navy and came home and went to work in a factory.

Clara, the fourth from the oldest, quit school and went to work at a Rexall Drug Store to help out with expenses at home, and she was very active with her friends and did a lot of roller skating as well. She didn't have to help with the housework anymore because she had a job, so Mother thought that was enough for her to do along with her social life. Clara was very kind to Maxine and would buy her some new clothes for school, because Maxine would wear her things and when she went to get them they would be dirty and the laundry only went out once a week. So the deal was Maxine would help keep Clara's clothes washed and ironed, too, in exchange for the new clothes from her.

Maxine, by this time, was in intermediate school and kept herself busy with her homework, friends and baby-sitting on weekends. One hot summer day while sitting on the neighbor's front porch and visiting with Fran and her children, some of the neighbor children and their country cousins came by and were acting pretty smart and sassy. They began heckling Maxine and her friends saying snide remarks like, "Maxine has a big butt," and Maxine spoke up and said "At least I don't have buck teeth!" The young lady, Jackie, said in a distressed voice, "I can't help it if my father don't have the money to have my teeth fixed!" and Maxine replied wittingly, "And I can't help it if my father don't have the money to have my butt fixed either!" So that was the big joke in the neighborhood for some time. And later on Maxine and Jackie became real good friends for many years. They skipped rope, roller skated, played ball and practiced cheerleading in the back yard and also put together a tumbling act that they performed in front of general assembly at school for a talent show.

The neighborhood was generally very friendly, and incidents like this did not happen too often, in fact they were all willing to help each other whenever help was needed. Only the children would get in squabbles once in a while, and the mothers would tell them, "Just forget it; you will all be out there playing with each other in a few minutes anyway," so the mothers understood their petty differences and knew human nature.

Maxine tried out for cheerleading in the eighth grade because they needed three girls. She came in fourth place, which was a big disappointment, but at least she got to be a substitute a couple of times at the basketball games, so this helped smooth over the disappointment. Later on, her gymnasium teacher told her that she thought Maxine deserved to be one of the three chosen but because her mother didn't go to the parent/teachers meetings and wasn't involved with any of the activities put on by the PTA, she wasn't chosen. This was a lesson about politics and favoritism discovered in this stage of her life and she felt it was morally wrong.

Usually three times a week Maxine would have to walk up to the "day-old bakery," which was about five blocks the opposite way from home, to get bread to take home for the family. After she arrived home from school it was her job to go to the corner grocery store for whatever Mother would be fixing for supper that evening, then after supper she did the dishes, and while washing them she would sing a song from the sheet of music she had propped up in front of her, singing it over and over until she learned it by heart. Mother said, "If you put as much effort into doing the dishes as you do in singing you would get done faster." Maxine thought, "It doesn't seem like such an effort to do dishes when I am singing."

Homemaking class required the girls to work in the cafeteria for a semester at different jobs: clearing the tables, peeling potatoes, getting vegetables ready and working at the steam tables. This helped Maxine get over her shyness and being bashful. She studied very hard because lessons came hard for her and she would get discouraged and Mother would say, "Keep trying," and Maxine would almost cry and say, "I can't do it," and Mother would say, "Can't never tried!" She'd make her try again until she understood the problem and was able to do the lesson.

It was getting time for graduation from intermediate school and the excitement of graduation and shopping for a formal dress for the graduation ceremony was a new experience. Trying on formals was so much fun because always before Mother had done all the shopping for clothes, but this time Maxine got to help pick out her own formal. It was a red polka-dotted Swiss with puffy sleeves and gathered at the waist-line with a red ribbon. What fun they had shopping for new shoes, too. This was so wonderful going with Mother and picking the ones she wanted. She tried on the formal several times before graduation and would dance and whirl around the house and the dress would flare out – oh, such fun. Then the day arrived and Mother had bought a corsage for Maxine to wear. What a wonderful mother to make sure she did not have to go without a corsage at graduation exercises. At that time the school did not have proms; they eliminated them during the war years due to the expense of putting them on and out of patriotism.

Neighbors helped each other by sharing their rationing stamps; some would need more gas stamps, some would need more stamps for food and they would exchange for whatever they needed. This was a time when everyone was like a family to one another.

News of the war was getting worse and more and more human lives were being sacrificed for the country. With the rationing of gas, cigarettes, and other things, the nation was pulling together and show-ing their love for one another, under God Almighty's power, a genera-tion of people who believed in the United States of America, a place of life, freedom, liberty and justice for all, united in one effort to keep America free.

During that summer Maxine met the neighbor's cousin who lived on the same street about three blocks away. He would come over and sit and talk with her, sometimes they would go bike riding, climb trees and play horseshoes in the neighbor's backyard. His name was Mickey and he really liked her very much and was so much fun to be with. His family was Catholic and at this time of her life Maxine did not know the difference between Catholic and Protestant religions. He was a blond, blue-eyed very nice young man and Maxine liked him, but he moved away and she didn't see him much, only when he would visit his cousin, so that was her first encounter with a boy liking her. She had five brothers and could care less about boys except to be friends and talk to.

The war was raging on and Henry wrote to Mother and let her know he was in Germany and had been in the town Dad's family lived in, Neustadt/Weinstraff, and found their home. He went there, knocked on the door several times, but no one answered; he wrote to Mother and told her he tried to contact them. Later on they found out that an aunt and a thirteen-year-old female cousin were in the house but were fearful of opening the door to an American soldier. They had seen him, but did not know he was a relative as he did not call out and tell them who he was.

About the same time one of their cousins, Werner Bohl, was a German soldier and had been captured by the Americans and was brought to America as a prisoner of war. Werner, in letters from his family in Germany, learned that he had relatives living in Michigan and he was given the address. He wrote to Mother from the prisoner-of-war camp in Kansas and she sent him a radio and some cookies, and continued to correspond with him until he was shipped back to Germany after the war. He told Mother he was treated very kindly and appreciated how Americans treated their prisoners of war.

Father's cousin, Heindrich, also lived in Jackson, and he translated the letters Mother received from Cousin Werner. Sometimes, the children would go with mother to Heindrich's place of business, just two blocks from home, called The Rainbow Inn. He opened the beer garden after the business failure with Father that they had experienced earlier. Heindrich's family lived upstairs, and the children had so much fun playing around in the building and listening to Heindrich speak be-

18

cause it reminded them of their father's accent. Heindrich was kind to them and would give them a candy bar, which was a real treat for them at that time. Heindrich and his wife Hilda had two sons, Ronald and Richard. A few years after the war began they sold the Rainbow Inn and opened a new business, The Pattern Works, a business for building wood patterns.

CHAPTER FOUR
DOUBTS AND UNSETTLED CHANGES

Maxine decided to go back to church and Sunday school with her friend Dorene, after being gone for several years after she was first baptized. The altar call was given and Dorene went forward and so did Maxine. It was the First Baptist Church in downtown Jackson. They were asked if they wanted to be baptized and they both said yes. She believed that by being baptized the second time, she could have the bad; guilty feelings she had about going to the movies be taken away like the first time she was baptized after having gone to the movies. The baptism ceremony was scheduled for that evening. So she went home and told her mother about it and Mother said, "No, you've already been baptized once and your Father doesn't believe you need it twice." But Maxine was determined she was going to do it anyway and thought, "What does he care, he is never home anyway." So she took an extra pair of panties and clothes to put on after the baptism was over.

Their home had a sun deck off of the bathroom and there was a door going out on to it and a tree was growing up along the side of the sundeck, which they could climb up and down. Maxine went out that way with her clothes and went with Dorene to be baptized. Well, it surely didn't make her feel any different like it did before when she was twelve years old. The next day her brother Henry's (Snookie) fiancé, who went to church that night, called and talked to Mother and said, "We were sure happy to see that Maxine has accepted Christ and was baptized last night." Boy, Mother was very unhappy with Maxine and confronted her and said. "Did you expect to get away with that?" So there goes some more guilt piled up to burden her in later life. She was so susceptible to feelings of guilt. She thought, "I tried to experience the happy, wonderful and peaceful feeling I had the first time I was baptized," but said to her Mother, "I don't know, I am sorry." Her Mother added, "Your sins will find you out for sure, Maxine."

Harold, who did not go to war, had married Jeanne Shaw and they had a beautiful little girl in October 1943, the first grandchild in the family, and they named her Carol Jean. Father had looked forward to seeing Carol Jean but the doctor had warned him not to take the bus trip home because it was too much strain on his heart. So Harold and Jean took the Greyhound bus to Dearborn to see Father, where he had opened a servicemen's canteen, but at that time there was a race riot in Dearborn and they were not permitted to get off the bus, so they had to return home without Father ever seeing Carol Jean. What a disappointment that was for them, and for Father, when he found out what had happened.

On the fourth day of February, 1944, Jeanne went to get Carol Jean in the morning and she had died, a crib death. What a shock to the family, only five months old. Such a sad time; Father was notified and insisted on coming home for the funeral because he said, "In no way will they bury my granddaughter before I get to see her." The doctors insisted that it would be too hard on him if he went and that he would be taking a risk of a heart attack. He had to climb a long set of stairs to be able to see Carol Jean in her casket. After the funeral he went back to Dearborn to continue his work at the servicemen's canteen.

Father was a member of the American Legion and he opened a servicemen's canteen to help service men and women in the Dearborn and Detroit area who came for a visit and wanted some place to go for entertainment. They had meals, music, and dancing with young ladies they called hostesses. They also had sing-a-longs with anyone who could play the piano. It was just a happy place to spend the evening. As a veteran of the First World War, Father knew what it was like to be lonely and not have a place to go for good clean entertainment. His being from Germany and not being able to speak good English when he was in the service, he knew from experience the feeling of loneliness.

Mom Baker helped at the canteen with the cooking and guiding the young ladies with the duties of being a hostess. She also played the piano for the sing-a-longs the servicemen liked to take part in, a place away from home that would be like home to them. No one was turned a way, all servicemen and women were welcomed. A place they could spend a few hours to forget all the fighting and heartbreak that war brought to everyone. The hours slipped by so fast and the fun and excitement would come to an end, each one would go their separate way back to the realities of life and their duty as servicemen.

The American Legion sponsored the canteen and so there was plenty of help when needed. On holidays they would have special parties planned for that occasion. There was a special celebration for the upcoming Valentine's Day, lots of hustle and bustle with cooking, decorating, and planning for this big event for the well-deserved men and women in the service. The food was extra special that evening and Mom Baker and Father had worked very hard to make it special so the memories would stay with these service people. They all danced, sang along, and just talked until late in the evening when Father (Pops) decided to go home and go to bed because he was so tired, but in good spirits. He was a father who had known the wages of the World War I and the results; understood the needs of his children more then they would realize, a firm hand and a loving heart, with faith in an eternal God. He had experience in his life none of the family knew about until years after his death. Secrets he held within him, not daring to disclose to anyone, not even his wife; secrets which Maxine, to her astonishment, learned many decades later of his behind-enemy-lines activities in WWI in Germany, the country he had left the security of his family business to journey to the freedom of America as an eighteen year old, eldest of four brothers.

The next morning was Valentine's Day 1944 and as the morning broke and the family back home in Jackson was finishing breakfast, the neighbor from up the street came down to tell Mother there was a long-distance phone call for her, and Mother said, "I know what it is," and went to answer the phone. When she came back she told them, "Your dad passed away in his sleep during the night. He is gone, and I knew it because I dreamed it last night." This ability to dream prophecy ran throughout the family and was an ability that Maxine discovered she also had inherited as she got older and experienced times when she, too, was blessed with this gift.

It was a sad day for all; arrangements had to be made to make the trip to Dearborn for the funeral. Dad had requested to be cremated and his ashes blown over the Detroit River. Mother didn't really like the idea, but she had to go along with it because if she didn't, the American Legion wouldn't pay for his funeral, and they wanted to abide by his request. Dad died just ten days after Carol Jean had died and appar-

22

ently, the trip to see her was too much for him, plus all the preparations that went along with the great Valentine's Day celebration the night before.

The day of the funeral arrived and Aunt Millie, Mother's sister, and Uncle Paul came and picked up the family to go to Dearborn. It was a sad day. Maxine hardly spoke a word but thought, "Why did this happen, first to Carol Jean and now Father?" She didn't know much about death and couldn't understand why. These thoughts kept going through her mind as they drove. It seemed like a long way to the funeral home but finally they arrived and parked the car and were escorted inside the funeral parlor up to the casket. Many people stood around looking at the family as they passed by to see him for the last time.

There he was, so still, yet looking so peaceful. It was so hard for Maxine; she had loved her Father so much. Mother stood strong, motionless and tearless. Maxine admired her strength and tried so hard to hold back her tears also, which was difficult for a fifteen-year-old girl. She didn't realize she was allowed to cry, but her Mother set the model for the family, and this suppression of emotions would haunt her for the rest of her adult life. Her daddy was gone; she loved and idolized him, and it really was heartbreaking for her to look at him, knowing he would never put his arms around her and give her a big hug and kiss, as he always did when he came home to see them. Even though it wasn't very often, at least she would look forward to his coming. So many flowers surrounded his casket, such beautiful bouquets and plants. The chapel was crowded and there was hardly any place to sit, servicemen stood at attention at the head and foot of the casket. The song "My Buddy," one of the most popular tunes of World War I, was played on the organ and "Taps" was played on a trumpet. What a sad time for the family.

After the Chaplain said the eulogy, everyone was escorted out to their cars and the funeral possession began and there were so many cars you couldn't see the end of them. The family didn't realize he had so many friends and fellow veteran soldiers. They arrived at the cemetery and the crematorium and were seated. The casket was draped with the American flag and the servicemen removed it and presented it to Herman who was home from the Navy, otherwise Snookie (Henry

Jr.) would have received it, he being the eldest son, but he was in Europe at the war front. The trumpet played "My Buddy," Father's favorite song. It was so sad, then they played "Taps" again, the casket was lowered and there was a twenty-one-gun salute – the final sound. It was over, but they knew his spirit lives on and he knew it too. Mother refused to take any part of the ashes, and at Father's request they were all strewn on the Detroit River.

The trip back home seemed even longer; it was snowing hard and it was hard to see where they were going. Uncle Paul was a good driver and it was so quiet, no one said much so he could concentrate on driving. It was good to be back home safe and sound. So many things had taken place and clouds of the unknown had gathered in Maxine's mind, so much she couldn't understand. She was only fifteen years old and had attended two funerals in two weeks and was just heartsick. It seemed like she had no one to talk to who would understand how she felt, her emotions were suppressed once again, trying to please others by not asking any questions, having been taught not to speak unless you are spoken to. Soon the routine was back to normal with everyone going about their duties at work, school and play, but Maxine still didn't get her questions answered, leaving a cloudy haze of uncertainty in her mind.

Harold's wife, Jeanne, was not well and the doctors did not know what was wrong with her. They told Harold to take her out dancing for some entertainment to get her mind off of the baby's death. Harold did and she felt worse and complained that he was killing her, so he decided to take her back to the doctor to do more tests. So he did and they found she had tuberculosis and would have to go into a sanitarium. They could go and visit her only by talking through the door window because tuberculosis was so very serious and contagious. She was always so glad to see them come. She said she got lonely sometimes to see her family and her friends, and her grief for the baby was hard for her to bear.

Maxine met another girl who lived only two blocks from her house, and they became friends. Jody was from the West Intermediate School and had moved into the neighborhood and was happy to have a friend, too. She was invited to a party and asked Maxine to go with her on Friday night, so Maxine got permission from her mother and went. The party was just two doors from Aunt Millie and Uncle Paul's home on Lincoln Street.

At the party Maxine met a young man named Jerry Miller. He paid attention to her and asked if he could come over to her house and see her and she said yes because she seemed to like him, and come to find out he had been going with one of her best friends, Arahbelle, but then decided to date Maxine. He came over to the house a couple times a week and they would go to the movies once in a while and go roller-skating too. Then Jerry started going with another one of Maxine's girl friends, Dorene Donnelly, the friend who she went to church with. What a disappointment this was for her, this was the first boy she had begun to care for.

Springtime 1944 had come by now and the trees were budding, the grass was getting greener, the flowers were beginning to bloom and things were looking much brighter. Each day the neighbor children would go to the next corner to catch the city bus to ride to the high school, the earlier you got to the bus stop the better seat you would get, or else you might have to stand. The high school was a big one compared to the intermediate schools and this was the first semester for Maxine to attend the high school. She had missed time in the first half of fifth grade and was held back a half a semester so she had to start high school in the spring instead of the fall. When the days were warm and they were ready to go home it was nice to walk and enjoy the warm sunny days, laughing and joking along the way. Also some of the students would walk downtown everyday at lunchtime, when it didn't rain of course; this was good exercise and they would go to the bakery and get glazed donuts, which were a treat, they were so good.

One day as they were walking downtown, they were strolling down Michigan Avenue when Maxine and Jody went past a group of boys from the west end of town who knew Jody and spoke to her. She stopped and said hello to them. Maxine didn't know any of them, but one boy in the group stood out in her mind above all the others. There was something about him that she couldn't forget.

Mother had been talking with Aunt Millie about Maxine's new friend Jody, and she found out that Jody used to live by Aunt Millie who said Jody had a bad reputation and that Maxine shouldn't run around with her because she would be judged the same as Jody was being judged. But Maxine couldn't see anything wrong with her and continued to be her friend. Maxine didn't realize that people thought "birds of a feather flock together," and that people would judge her by her friends.

Maxine couldn't get this boy off of her mind; he had made quite an impression on her and his image stayed with her all that day. The days seemed to go by fast and the weekend came and Maxine and her neighbor friend, Jenny, had planned to go to the teenage dance at the Jackson County Building. Maxine loved to dance, she would dance around the house when she was doing her housework, one of her favorite pastimes was dancing, that's why she liked to ice skate and roller skate so much because of the rhythm and the joy she felt as she danced, her heart bubbling over with joy, she loved life.

Mother had given Maxine permission to go, but one of the rules was she couldn't go anywhere until all of her work was done, no matter how long it took, it had to be done. So whenever she was going someplace she completed the work in a hurry and made sure it was done well or it would have to be done all over again. Maxine had accepted her responsibilities because of the respect she had for her mother and the fact that her mother was always there for her. She was there early in the morning to fire up the furnace with coal in the winter to make sure it was warm in the house when the children woke up, and to make sure the meals were always on time. Mother was so reliable it gave them all a sense of security and a faith in her because of her love for them.

Getting ready for the dance on Saturday, Maxine and Jenny exchanged clothes. Maxine wore Jenny's blouse and Jenny wore Maxine's skirt, it seemed like she had more clothes this way. Bobbie socks and saddle shoes were popular at that time and so were loafers. Their mothers would just shake their heads and smile at them and remember when they too were teenagers, and the fun they had whenever they got to go somewhere.

The crowd was large and many friends were present; there were many more girls than boys because of the war, so the girls had to dance with each other, which was very common then, keeping time with the music and walking arm-in-arm or doing the fox trot. As they were step-

26

ping around the dance floor, a young fellow spoke out and motioned for Maxine to come over and talk to him. She recognized him as the young man she had seen the week before on Michigan Avenue and her heart began to beat faster and faster because she hadn't forgotten him all week. Maxine was very shy and so the girls walked around the dance floor a few times and each time they went by, he motioned for her to come and talk, so finally Jenny said, "Go and see what he wants." Maxine had told her about him, so they wandered over and Maxine said, "What do you want?" He mentioned that he remembered her, too, and wanted her to show him where the drinking fountain was. She said, "Follow me," and he did, along with Jenny and his friends. When they arrived at the drinking fountain he took a drink and said, "Ha! Ha! I knew where it was all the time, but I wanted to talk to you." His name was Jack. She and Jack talked in the hall for some time and then she and Jenny decided to leave for home because it was getting late and they didn't want to miss the bus. By then the dance ended and the teens began to scatter in all directions to go home.

They decided to walk home because the boys were walking north toward Ganson Street and they were going that way too. The boys followed behind them laughing and talking and when they reached Ganson Street they stood and talked some more, getting acquainted with each other. Jack asked Maxine to go to the movies with him the next Saturday night and Roger, his friend, asked Jenny to go with him too. Maxine said, "I will have to get permission from my mother first and will let you know, you can call me at Jenny's house because I don't have a phone." Jenny gave him her phone number.

The boys went west and the girls went east to their homes. The girls were so excited about meeting the boys and looking forward to next Saturday that they were home before they realized it. The walk seemed so short, but was at least two miles. Arriving home Maxine couldn't wait to ask Mother if she could go to the movies next Saturday. So she asked, "Mom may I go to the show with this boy I met tonight at the dance? Jenny will be going with his friend, Roger, too."

Mother replied, "Yes, if you get home by ten o'clock." Oh, what joy filled Maxine's heart!

All during school the next week she couldn't think of anything but meeting Jack and going to the show; she couldn't concentrate on her schoolwork or pay attention to anything that was going on around her. Jack called her to find out what the answer was and said they would be over to get them about seven on Saturday night. Jenny and Maxine were trying to make up their minds what to wear and tried on so many different things they thought would look good on them and would feel comfortable. Saturday came and she had to do her weekly chores, which she really didn't mind doing today, so she danced around and sang while she dusted, mopped, and cleaned. She was as happy as a lark.

As soon as supper was over, the dishes were done in a flash, no song sheet tonight to sing and ponder over. She could really move fast when she wanted to go somewhere or do something she wanted to do. Of course, that's human nature. She hurried up the stairs to the bathroom to get ready for her date and as she was climbing the stairs she looked at her mother and thought to herself, "Gee, I hope I will never be alone like Mom." Mother very seldom went anywhere or did anything because she couldn't afford to. Her first responsibility was her family and home, and she would try to give the children money once in a while for helping out so much. She was very contented being a mother, and it was a fine example, which Maxine remembered in her adult years.

Jenny came over as soon as she was ready and they waited for the boys to arrive. When they arrived and knocked on the door, Maxine answered and invited them in and introduced them to Mother, who asked them to make sure they came home on the last bus, and the boys politely answered, "Oh yes, we certainly will." They all left to catch the bus for town. It was so exciting for Maxine; she had never felt this way before. It was a brand new experience, her heart was beating fast and she tried so hard to look calm as they walked to the bus stop. They tried to get more acquainted with each other by laughing and joking with one another.

They arrived at the movies and the boys bought the tickets and wanted to sit in the balcony. So up the stairs they all went, clear up to the last row of seats where it was high and dark. The movie began with a very serious love scene with the leading man giving the leading lady a

28

long loving kiss, and while this was going on Jack reached over and kissed Maxine on the cheek and made a real loud noise with his lips. It could be heard all over the theater and everyone laughed, then Maxine hauled off and gave him a big slap on his cheek and it could be heard all over the theater also, and a big roar of laughter from the audience rang out. Jack got up and seated himself about four rows from where they were. After about thirty minutes he came back and apologized to Maxine and all was forgotten. The rest of the evening went pretty smooth. Jack even asked Maxine to go out with him again the next Saturday and she said she would if she got permission from her mother. The boys saw the girls home on the bus and they all sat on the front porch talking and laughing until Roger took Jenny home so they could be alone, and Jack and Maxine could be alone too. Mother called out and said, "It is time to come in now," because it was late. The boys had to walk home because they missed the last bus and it was a long way to walk, especially that late. They walked about five miles across town to their homes. Jack's parents were rather upset with him for staying out so long, but he explained about missing the bus.

CHAPTER FIVE

A NEW LOVE FOR LIFE

On Sunday morning, Jack called Maxine at Jenny's house and wanted to see her again before Saturday; he wanted to come over and get her so she could meet his folks, so she ran home to get permission from her mother. It was just fine with her, so Maxine ran back to let Jack know it was alright and to find out what time he would be there. That afternoon he arrived with his cousin Harold in a Model T Ford with a rumble seat and they tooted the horn. "Well," Mother said, "Don't you dare go out there. If he doesn't have any more manners than that and can't come to the door after you, you're not going with him." Maxine was so excited she could hardly wait, so a few more toots, then silence. Finally, a knock on the door was heard and Maxine answered it with a big smile and said, "Hi, come in." She told him her mother didn't think it was very polite for him to honk for her to come out and that he should be a gentleman and come to the door and he agreed with her.

The ride was fun. She had never ridden in a rumble seat like that before, and Harold went over the West Avenue Bridge, which was quite a thrill. It took your breath away because it was so steep. After the joy ride they went to Jack's home and Maxine was so nervous, she had never been invited to a boy's home before. Walking up the driveway, they approached Jack's little brother Donnie who said, "How come you don't get a girl with long hair?" Maxine didn't know what to think of that remark, then the front door opened and his stepmother came out and Jack introduced them. Her name was Vera, and she was so nice and sweet and she made Maxine feel at home. Maxine finally relaxed and joined in the conversation after all the children were introduced. Vera's children by a previous marriage were Sharon, John and Rosie. They all crowded around Maxine as she sat on the couch; they all laughed and talked and got acquainted with each other. Maxine liked children and felt comfortable around them.

It was such a nice day, so much love and happy spirit among the family, but it was getting time to go back home, and they had to catch a bus because Harold had left. They all said "Goodbye and come again," and Maxine said she would. As they walked to the bus stop they talked about Jack's family and about his mother and father's divorce and how much he was hurt by it all. He also explained he had a sister named Marilyn and that she lived with her mother most of the time, but would visit on holidays so Maxine would probably get to meet her later. By this time the bus was getting close to Maxine's house and she thought of how much fun she had that day and how much she had learned about Jack and his family. She had also told him about her sister and brothers and that her father had passed away earlier that year and how much she had loved her father and missed him.

When they arrived at the house they let her mother know they were on the front porch and wanted to talk awhile. Then it was time to go in and Jack kissed her goodbye and asked to see her again and she said that she would like that.

During school hours Maxine could hardly keep her mind on her schoolwork because she had met someone who really made her heart go flip-flop and all she could think about was Jack. Almost every evening he would call her at Jenny's and they'd talk for hours; Jenny's mom was so sweet, she never complained about her being on the phone for so long. Rosie was Jenny's mom's name and she sure could play the piano and the girls would sing tunes along with her like, "There is a shanty in ole shanty town." They would sing to their hearts' content. Jenny's dad was Homer; he never said much, just sat there and read or just sat quietly. Every once in a while he would go somewhere in his old car, called "Old Bessie," usually to go get his beer; Old' Bessie would spit and sputter along, jerking down the street. Jenny and Maxine would sit in it while it was parked in the driveway and just talk, Jenny knew how to drive but her dad wouldn't let her take the car because it was so old and gas was rationed and they used it just for their needs.

School was out for the summer now and it seemed like the weeks went by so slowly waiting for Saturdays to come, knowing that they would be going out with the guys again, yet not knowing just where they would be going. It was one of those Saturdays that the guys showed up: Jack, Roger, and Harold and his girl friend. They went for a ride out in the country and then decided to go stealing watermelons. So they found a good patch of melons and cut open a few, and boy, they were good.

The evening was so warm, they just sat there talking and joking. One of the guys told a joke and they all laughed so hard, but Maxine didn't understand it at all. They decided it was time to leave before someone discovered them in the watermelon patch where they didn't belong, let alone taking the melons and eating them.

Sunday was a beautiful day and Mom and the girls fixed a lovely dinner as usual. During dinner Maxine said, "You know they were telling jokes last night and I couldn't understand what they were talking about," and Corkie looked at Clara and she said, "Well, tell us and maybe we can explain it to you."

So Maxine went on to say, "A boy and a girl was dancing and the boy said to the girl 'You have Evening in Paris on' and the girl said, 'And you have a hard on.'" Mother was shocked, Corkie and Clara laughed and Mother said, "Clara you take her upstairs and explain to her."

My, how naive Maxine was, but how could she have known? Mother never told her the facts of life, so now it was up to her sister to explain to her these facts. She felt so humiliated; now she had to go back downstairs and face her mother again. "How dumb could one be," she thought. There was silence for the rest of the dinner. She was fifteen years old when this happened to her.

That evening when Jack called her, she told him about the incident, and he laughed; again she felt so dumb. It was hard for her to understand about things like that because she had never been taught or told about sex and things like that. She had to learn from others about her periods; she was past fourteen years old when that first appeared and Clara told her how to care for herself.

The neighbor lady, Fran, talked to her some about her periods and told her what to look for and not to be afraid, so that helped her to understand her more. She spent a lot of time over to Fran's house because she was so sweet and understanding and would talk to Maxine about things her mother wouldn't talk about. But, Maxine was so ashamed she didn't even tell Fran about the joke.

This was the age of innocence for Maxine, and now came a life-changing incident for Maxine. Later in life, she wondered why she never asserted herself to find out about sex. Even though in those days

32

talk of sex was suppressed, family members usually filled in the gaps so that teenagers would be prepared. She vowed that when she had kids of her own, she would tell them about the facts of life just when they reached puberty, and would advise other mothers to do the same to avoid embarrassments like this.

The summer wore on and it was about time for school to start again, so there was shopping for clothes and shoes to be done. This was the first time Maxine had gone out shopping with Mother for school clothes. Always before, Mother had picked them out and put them on layaway. This time Maxine went to try them on before they were purchased. She knew what she was getting and that made her so happy and so grown up. She sure liked shopping, and they went out for lunch that day also. It was fun to spend time with Mother and learn about buying clothes and shoes.

School started and the days were busy with homework, household chores and errands that had to be run, so during the week Maxine tried to keep her mind on these things, but Jack was uppermost in her mind. Jack had a job working the afternoon shift at the Way Baking Company. A couple of times a week he would meet Maxine out in front of the high school at lunch time and they would walk downtown together and walk back so she wouldn't miss school; it was a time to be together during the week. Jack had dropped out of school and was taking welding courses at a technical school downtown during the morning hours. Maxine's classes were English, Latin, geometry, home economics, art and gymnastics. Latin and geometry were both hard for her to understand, although she tried very hard. She really liked her modern dance class and they had an exhibition one evening. Jack and Roger attended it and it was such a thrill for her because she loved to dance and was so graceful. The boys said they enjoyed it and didn't realize Maxine could do those kinds of dances.

Also, the school had talent shows during assembly and Maxine and Jackie Boss, her neighbor and friend worked up a tap and tumbling routine and entered into the talent show. Maxine and Jackie were so active and so high-spirited , they just loved doing this type activity together.

Maxine had learned Jack's previous girl friend's name was Molly

33

and she was in Maxine's home economics class that year, so she finally got to meet Molly. Vera had always teased Jack about Molly, she told Maxine she didn't care for Molly because she was so snobbish and stuck up. There seemed to be a little jealousy in Maxine's heart about Molly because Molly had been the first girl Jack had liked. Also, one time he took Maxine to a place where he had taken Molly and told Maxine he tried to get fresh with Molly and she rejected him and told him she didn't ever want to go with him again. He tried many times to see her again and she just ignored him and wouldn't answer his phone calls. This confession hurt Maxine because she felt he shouldn't have brought her there, let alone tell her about Molly. Was Maxine someone he was seeing because he had been rejected by Molly? She had to get this thought out of her mind and think only about being happy and thankful that he wanted to be with her. Later in life, Maxine would question why she was not more assertive early on, like when Jack told her about this incident with Molly. Maxine was such a passive, compliant person; taught never to ask questions, just to accept whatever happens.

October was here and Maxine turned sixteen years old and Jack brought a birthday gift for her: a beautiful perfume and powder set. She had never received anything like it before, and she was delighted and thanked him for it. She was so happy. Mother bought her a birthstone ring that she had wanted for a long time – what a wonderful birthday, sweet sixteen. This day was such a special day; a day she would never forget and her love for Jack grew deeper than ever.

Fall was such a beautiful time of the year in Michigan, all the leaves turning color and falling, and the crisp air was invigorating and fresh. The month of November was well on its way and Thanksgiving was just around the corner. Jack had invited Maxine to go with him to his mother's for dinner. She had never met his biological mother before and was excited to meet her and her husband, Whitey, and his two girls, Arleen and Vivian. The day finally arrived and Jack and his mother, Helen, came to pick Maxine up to drive out to Leoni, the small town where they lived out in the country on a little farm. Grandma Gracie Ort, Helen's mother, was there, also Donnie, his brother, and Marilyn, Jack's sister. So this was the other side of the family all together, and Maxine was so scared she would mess up, all eyes would be on her for their examination, and she wanted their approval.

This was the first time she had been exposed to divorced people like those in Jack's family. Divorce was something Maxine hadn't heard much about and it was hard for her to understand, and questions kept coming into her mind. Why? Whose fault? Finally she had to put it all back in the recesses of her mind to think about later, and just enjoy the day. It was such a good dinner with all the trimmings and a beautifully set table, with elegant china and silverware on a snowy white table-cloth. She had never seen such elegance, and the dinner was so good with many different things she had never tasted before. Her mother couldn't afford all these luxuries and special foods to enhance a dinner. After dinner, they sat around the table talking and getting acquainted with Maxine, although she was shy and it was hard for her to carry on a conversation. She tried to be a lady as her mother had instructed her many times and to conduct herself in a ladylike manner at all times. After some time had passed, they all decided it was time to do the dishes, so the women went to the kitchen and the men went to the living room for their smoke and conversation.

Jack had brought his gun along and wanted to go rabbit hunting in the cornfield so his mother suggested that Maxine go along with him and said she didn't have to help with the dishes. It delighted her to be with Jack alone, and besides, she had never walked in a cornfield be-fore, let alone gone rabbit hunting, so this was another new experience for her. It was so much fun walking between corn rows and seeing how high the corn stalks had grown, way above their heads; you couldn't see anything but corn stalks and the path between them. Maxine's brother Snookie used to go rabbit hunting and bring the rabbits home and Mother would cook them. They were good to eat and that's all she knew about hunting. Up jumped a rabbit, BANG, the gun went off, the rabbit turned flip-flop several times before it lay still. "I got him!" Jack yelled, and Maxine's stomach quivered; she had never seen anything killed before. They went over and picked the rabbit up and Jack took his knife out and slit the rabbit's stomach and cleaned the inwards out, then wiped his hands off and they headed back to the house to show off the rabbit

It had been a good day for Maxine and she hoped that everyone liked her because she liked them. In her mind's eye she accepted them as part of Jack's family and tried to understand his feelings of initial response toward Vera and about the situation of the stepfamilies. Maxine thought, "Divorce affects the lives of all the children in each one of the families and must be heartbreaking for them all. I hope and pray I would do everything I could to prevent my children from experiencing divorce."

Jack had called Maxine later on that week and told her that his mother really liked her and approved of her very much and she was so delighted to hear that because it meant a lot to her, to meet their approval. This was one of Maxine's greatest weaknesses later in life, but in this case early in her teen years, it was important to be accepted by others. Her family never showed their emotions toward one another by embracing one another with a hug except when Father was living and came home. Maxine would go to him and he would give her a big bear hug and a kiss and she knew he was happy to see her as she was to see him. Now he wouldn't be coming home anymore, her source of unconditional love was gone. He was a source of approval that she needed.

Christmas season was coming and the stores were all decorated with lights, nativity scenes, toys, and beautiful gifts and decorated trees. What a sight! Christmas songs were being played in the stores as people shopped, with the spirit of Christmas on their minds. It was such a joyful time of the year and a busy one with all the preparations. Many boxes were sent to the servicemen for their Christmas Day celebration, filled with homemade cookies, fruit cakes, candies and special presents they were allowed to have. Of course, those boxes sent overseas during the war were all checked before they could receive them but it was still fun to pack them and visualize how surprised they would be when they opened them. Mother always decorated the cookies and candies, and they were, oh so good. She did such a good job and took such time and pleasure doing it for her two boys in the service, Snookie and Herman.

The Christmas tree was pretty, although it was a small one this year. Snookie was the one that always got the tree, and it usually was a large one that went to the ceiling after it was cut to fit. The family tried hard to keep the Christmas spirit, although the boys weren't there to celebrate with them physically. But they were there in spirit and on everyone's mind and in their prayers. Mother was such a quiet and reserved person, she didn't show her emotions, but they all knew she must be going through a lot of trials and tribulations with the boys gone and being responsible for the children at home with such limited resources. Snookie always sent part of his pay home to help out with expenses, and he also bought war bonds with his pay so that when he came back home he would have something to fall back on.

Clara was working at Western Stamping Company, and she helped out also by giving the younger siblings some spending money once in a while. Clara liked to go places with all of her friends and to have a good time. She had a boyfriend, and if he was not on time to pick her up she wouldn't wait for him. She would say, "He isn't the only fish in the sea," and would go out by herself to be with other friends. Clara ran with a different crowd of people who smoked and drank a lot. She was just the opposite of Maxine who was so sensitive about others' feelings and Maxine's feelings got hurt easily about what others thought about her, especially, when they judged her because of her family. Maxine was to come true to this character trait later in life, for it was the cause of much of her troubles. Looking back she saw that part of her adopting that attitude was to differentiate herself from Clara because she couldn't understand how Clara could be so fickle.

Maxine had been invited to go to Jack's dad's for Christmas dinner and was anxiously waiting for that day to come. Finally, Christmas arrived and she awoke in the morning with such high spirits and high hopes, she bounded out of bed and ran downstairs to open the gifts under the tree. No one else was up yet except Mother who, as usual, got the coal shoveled in the furnace so it would be warm for the family when they got up. She always saw to this even though her legs were bad with a large open sore on her ankle that she had to keep cleansed and bandaged, caused by large varicose veins that had broken many years ago; the doctors could not find any medication that would heal it. She very seldom complained about anything, she was such a good mother and Maxine vowed to follow her example as she got older and had a family of her own.

Soon everyone came downstairs and the Christmas wrappings began to fly all over. What joy, a new blouse and skirt, and then she opened the present from Jack. Oh how pretty! A dresser set with a comb, mirror and brush. She just loved it and was so delighted with everything she received, but forgot to pay attention to what the others received with her mind on spending the evening with Jack.

The time came for Jack to pick up Maxine, and she was ready to go in plenty of time because she didn't want him to wait for her; she liked to be punctual, especially for him. When he arrived, she opened the door and motioned for him to come in. She thanked him for the dresser set and told him how thoughtful he was. She showed him the other gifts she had received from her family, she was so elated and happy. After visiting a while, he said, "Let's leave now because dinner will be ready when we arrive home." They said goodbye to everyone and left in his father's car, that he let Jack use once in a while.

They arrived at Jack's home and she thought, "My, so many cars, how many people are here?" She began to be frightened as she thought, "What will I do? What will I say? Don't eat too much and watch your manners," these thoughts ran around in her mind. As they reached the door the little sisters came running to meet them and were bubbling over with joy to show Maxine their new Christmas gifts. They hung up their coats and Jack began introducing her to everyone: aunts, uncles, and cousins. His grandma & grandpa on his father's side of the family were there also. "Oh my, I will never remember all of these names," she thought. Uncle Harvey waited until Maxine got under the mistletoe and then gave her a big kiss, her face turned red and laughter rang out from everyone because they knew she was so shy.

Sharon and Rosie grabbed her hand and wanted her to sit between them on the couch, so she went along with them and was happy to do so. This was good for her because she forgot all about her fears for a while. They told her all about their new toys and showed her some of them they had received and their stocking they had hung up with so many little items also. They looked so pretty in their new dresses and were so sweet to Maxine, who didn't move from the couch until they announced that dinner was ready. "Oh my gracious, so many people and what a beautiful table setting and so much food," she thought and her fears started once again with thoughts such as, "Don't take too much food, be careful and mind your manners, sit up straight, don't spill any food on yourself." All of these things had been drilled into her all her life and she couldn't relax, but everyone tried so hard to make her feel at home. They all laughed and joked during dinner and talked about their work, catching up on all the news of the family. This isn't the way her family did things, everything at home being so formal and routine, but she enjoyed this new way, it was different and relaxing.

The afternoon wore on and the men left the table and decided to start a card game, so the ladies cleared the table and went to the kitchen to do the dishes, talking and laughing. Maxine joined in to help take care of things and do the dishes while getting better acquainted with everyone. These were all of Vera's family, her sisters and their husbands and families. They were all so nice, even Harvey who continued to tease Maxine because he liked to make her blush. Jack's father's mother, his paternal grandmother, and her husband were there. Her name was Anna and his was Orf Williams. She had divorced her husband, Ira Derr, and married Orf and they had a daughter Helen, who would be Jack's dad's (Don) half-sister. " My, such a mixed up family," she thought and was wondering about the intricacy of divorce and the impact on family relationships, would she be able to fit all the pieces of this family puzzle together?

After the kitchen was all cleaned up, the ladies went into the living room to converse and relax.

Maxine was afraid to get up even to go to the bathroom because the guys all teased her about kissing her under the mistletoe but eventually she had to get up. Up jumped Chet, Evelyn's husband, to catch her; again her face turned beet red and they all laughed. They all enjoyed teasing, and Maxine was somewhat used to her brothers teasing her at times. By this time Jack had decided to take her down to his other grandmother's house, which was at the end of the same street about two blocks away and his mother and all her side of the family were there, so they went there for the rest of the day.

When Maxine arrived back home, Mother was sitting in her chair, home alone, as usual, and she asked her if she had a good time and she answered, "Oh yes, Mama, you can't believe how many people I met today, and how much food they had," and she went on and on. After she had run down with nothing more to say she went to the refrigerator to look for something to eat.

Mother said "I thought they had so much to eat, why are you so hungry?"

"Oh, Mama, I didn't want them to think I was a pig and I was afraid to eat too much."

Mother said, "They probably wouldn't even notice how much you ate."

This had been a wonderful Christmas with so many memories to keep stored in her mind; she had never experienced anything like it before because her family was not close like Jack's family. Only Aunt Millie came over once in a while to visit Mama. Mama would take the bus over to see Grandma and Grandpa Wheeler once in a while, and Maxine would stay with them overnight once in a while and go down the street to visit her cousins, but otherwise they didn't have big meals together or celebrate holidays together. Most of them were very poor and didn't have cars to get around so that must have been one of the reasons why. Grandpa Wheeler was such a kind man, he loved everyone; he had been treated badly by a cruel farmer he had worked for when he was a teenager and would never treat anyone badly. One time when Maxine stayed with Grandma and Grandpa Wheeler, she did something she wasn't supposed to and Grandma told Grandpa, "Frank, you take her in the other room and spank her!" So he took her in the front bedroom and told her, "Now when I clap my hands together, you yell out 'OUCH!'" So she did. Grandma never knew that Grandpa didn't spank Maxine, it was their secret. Grandma was a little feisty woman only four foot eleven inches and Grandpa was six foot four inches but as gentle as a lamb.

Mother had two brothers: Roy, who was married to Bertha and Bill who was married to Kate. They lived on the same street as Grandpa and Grandma, Avery Street. Other relatives lived on that street too, both Grandpa and Grandmas Wheeler's relations. That street had many Wheelers and Bennetts living there, so whenever Mama went to visit, she spent most of the day so she could visit them all, whoever was home at the time.

Maxine learned later in life that Grandma had been married once before she married Frank and she had Bill by her first marriage; then she had Mama, then Uncle Roy, and then Aunt Millie. Grandpa adopted Bill and gave him the name of Wheeler. Uncle Bill and Kate had one daughter named Leona. Uncle Roy and Bertha had a son named Frank and a daughter named Delores. Grandma's maiden name was Lucretia Bennett. Aunt Millie and Uncle Paul had seven children: Pauline, Robert, James, William, Donna, Alice and Butch. The family never talked about serious matters whenever children were around, so with all her mother's brothers' and sisters' marriages that were successful through all those years, she didn't know about Grandma and Grandpa until her mother told her one day when Maxine told her about so many divorces in Jack's family.

CHAPTER SIX
ENGAGEMENT PROMISES

New Year's Eve came and Maxine, Roger and Jennie had been invited to go to Jack's home to a card party with his folks and some friends. Maxine had never played cards before and she had to learn how to play, everyone was so kind and patient teaching her. She enjoyed herself very much, there was laughing and joking among all the players at several tables. Each time the game was done, the losers would go to another table, keeping a card punched with the games they had won or lost, and this way they got to play with different partners. They had a lot of fun trying to get their cards punched for winning the games and teasing the losers, playing the card game with enthusiasm and sportsmanship. After the games were over, refreshments were served and they visited until the clock struck midnight and everyone kissed each other and yelled, "Happy New Year." Maxine had never known that people celebrated like that, it was another new experience for her, her life had been so sheltered she never knew how other people lived, let alone how they celebrated.

On New Year's Day Maxine went over to visit with Jenny about how much fun they had and how everyone was so friendly. Jenny knew all about celebrations and card parties, because her family used to have them until the war came and they moved from Horton, a little town southwest of Jackson. They talked about the boys, Roger and Jack, and hoped they would continue dating because they were having so much fun going places with the boys. Jack called Maxine while she was there and talked about the night before and he was happy she enjoyed herself. They talked and talked as usual.

After lunch Maxine went over to Fran's house to tell her all about her New Year's Eve date, because she always took time to listen and was interested in what was going on in Maxine's life. She was such a good friend. She laughed and joked with her because she knew Maxine's mother was so serious most of the time, especially about dating.

It wasn't long after New Year's Day, on a Saturday, that Jack called and wanted to see Maxine, so he came over and they went by bus out to the country. They walked to a wooded area that had a natural spring of fresh water and Jack said, "I have something for you." He pulled out an engagement ring and asked, "Will you marry me? I love you and want you to be mine."

She was so happy and excited, she answered, "Yes, I will," and she gave him a big hug and kissed him and said, "I love you so much." So he put the ring on her finger and kissed her again. Jack had put the ring on layaway and had been paying on it for six months and kept it a secret from her. He was so happy that she accepted his proposal. Oh, what a beautiful experience for both of them there in such a beautiful setting of God's nature and beauty. They lingered for awhile until it was almost time for him to go to work; it was hard to separate and go after such a wonderful experience of joy, love and communion they both felt.

Maxine went home and just couldn't wait to show her ring and tell her mother and everyone else that Jack had asked her to marry him. She was engaged, and she felt like she was on cloud nine.

She ran into the house calling "Mama, Mama" and checked everywhere downstairs, then opened the cellar door and called out again, but there was no answer. Then she ran upstairs and her mother said, "Here I am, in the bathroom hanging up my wet nylons."

Maxine stuck her hand out and showed her mother her engagement ring and said, "Mama, Jack asked me to marry him and I said yes!"

Mother looked puzzled and said, "Oh, no Maxine, he drinks and you don't believe in drinking. He will give you nothing but a life of hell."

"Oh, no Mama, he loves me and he will quit drinking," Maxine replied. Mother just shook her head and sighed a deep sigh. Mother knew that leopards don't change their spots, as Maxine was to find out in the years ahead. She would later realize just how wise her Mother really was.

At this time nothing could stop the happiness Maxine felt as she ran over to see Jenny to show her the ring and to tell her the good news. Maybe she would have something good to say and would be happy along with Maxine. She needed to have someone's approval and to share the happiness she was feeling. This just had to be the happiest day in her life and she wanted to let others know about it. Jenny was sure surprised and happy for Maxine and told her, "This is serious; engagement means marriage in the future and you are still pretty young."

Maxine said, "I realize this, but I am so happy to know he loves me so much that he wants to marry me, isn't that wonderful?" After talking for a while she decided to run over to Fran's house to tell her the good news

Fran and her husband Hank were home and she opened the door and ran in and with her hand stretched out in front of her. She showed Fran her ring and told her that Jack had asked her to marry him and how excited she was that he loved her so much to ask her to marry him. Fran was overjoyed for her, and said, "Congratulations, Maxine. I know how much you love him and I give you both my blessings." Oh, it was good to hear those words of encouragement and positive thinking from someone. Her friend Fran's opinion meant a lot to her and it gave her a feeling of peace and contentment. Maxine couldn't tell the difference between a compliment from a friend and wisdom that was coming to her from other directions, and would learn the difference the hard way.

The next day Jack called and asked Maxine and Jenny to meet him and Roger downtown to go to the movies, so they took the bus and when they got off Roger said, "I thought you would have your hand stuck way out in front of you to show off your new ring," he laughed. Jack must have told him how excited she was to receive it and he liked to tease, like all guys do. Maxine could not hold her feelings inside, her happiness glowed and her smile was a dead giveaway of the joy she felt, a joy only given by God and His love, a love so deep it flowed throughout her being. The movie they went to see was not given much attention by Maxine and Jack; they were just happy to be together and hold each other close, as close as they could in the theater.

Attending school every day was getting to be routine and Maxine looked forward to seeing Jack whenever he could come over or to see her at noon in front of the high school, after he had finished his welding class at trade school. On one such day in February, Jack announced to her that he was going to join the Merchant Marines if his folks would sign for him after his seventeenth birthday. He had quite a time convincing them to sign because of the war and he was too young to go, but when his birthday came he had his mother sign the papers. She signed reluctantly, and with apprehension his father also signed. The Merchant Marine was not a part of the government armed services, although they did go into the battle zones carrying supplies and transporting servicemen.

The day came for Jack to leave; Maxine was so sad she didn't know what she was going to do without him, he had become such a special part of her life. His father and Vera came over to pick her up to go with them to the train station to see him off. It was so quiet in the car, no one said much. Jack held her hand and squeezed it tight; tears came to her eyes and she knew she loved him, more than she had ever loved anyone else before in her whole life. They arrived at the train station and there were many people waiting for the trains: several servicemen waiting to go back to their base, their loved ones seeing them off and wiping their tears not knowing if they will ever see them again. Families being separated for the first time, mothers and fathers with only one son to give, brothers and sisters being separated who would be grown up when they returned; so many walks of life represented here at this place of departure with the future unknown.

They waited until the train came, Vera checking with Jack to see if he had everything. Then it was time for him to depart. Dad and Vera kissed and hugged him and said good bye, Jack took Maxine's hand and drew her near, looked into her eyes, which were full of tears, and said, "Write to me often, I love you and I want to hear what is going on in your life and I will write as often as I can."

"I love you too," She answered.

He hugged her tight and kissed her many times and they both said, "Goodbye." They didn't want to let go of each other's hand, but finally did and off he went to get on the train, on his way to boot camp in New Jersey for the Merchant Marine. He promised his folks also that he would write as much as he could and let them know where he was, if he could. The train left the station and the building was empty, everyone going in different directions back to their individual lives and routines with hope in their hearts of seeing their loved ones once again. Hope is something not seen but faith in believing it will take place. Looking forward to that day is what most of the families kept uppermost in their

45

hearts and minds, it motivated them to keep the home front burning with enthusiasm to do whatever it took to help with the war effort to bring their loved ones back home again.

Every day Maxine checked the mail to see if any letters had arrived for her, waiting in anticipation for word from Jack. Finally a letter came and joy filled her heart. He said he missed her very much and kept her picture in his locker and another in his wallet. She answered the letter right away reassuring him of her love for him and that she missed him. She kept his letters, each and every one. She read and reread them many times, also sharing them with Jenny.

Spring had come and the daylight hours were getting longer, the trees were budding and the grass seemed much greener as the songs being sung were "Over There, Over There," "I'll Be Seeing You," "This Is The Army Mr. Jones," "When The Lights Go On Again All Over The World," and so many more. The movies were nearly all war-related and news was always seen at the theater to keep everyone informed of what was happening on the war fronts. Besides newspapers, the radio news broadcasting the news, newsreels shown at the movie theatres were a major source of war imagery. (This was before television.) With so many ways of communication, most everyone kept up with what was going on and talked about it.

On one of those spring days Jenny came over and told Maxine, "Jack is on the phone from New Jersey and wants to talk to you."

Oh how happy she was. She ran over to Jenny's to talk to him, "Hello, oh it is so good to hear your voice."

"It is good to hear yours too," he answered, "I called to see if you can come to New York City because I have a weekend pass and would like to see you."

She answered, "I don't think my mother can afford a train ticket but I will go and ask her, will you call me back later?" He said he would.

Maxine ran home to ask her mother and she of course said, "No, Maxine, in no way can I afford to give you money to go to New York."

Clara was there and she said, "I have always wanted to go to New York and I will pay Maxine's way, if it is okay with you Mom."

Mother answered and said that was all right with her. Maxine jumped up and down with joy and went out the door running to wait for

Jack's call. She called Jack's parents and told them she was going and they were happy for her.

The day had arrived for them to leave for New York. Maxine and Clara were so excited about going. They took the bus to the train station and waited patiently for the train. The trip to New York seemed to take so long; it was the farthest either one of them had ever been away from home. Two teenage girls, one looking forward to seeing the city and the other looking forward to seeing her fiancé after being away from him for over three months. Jack had told them to meet him at Grand Central Station, and not knowing just how big the station was, they were astonished at the size and the different levels there were in the building. They stood in awe just looking and wondering how they would ever find Jack. Finally, they went to the information booth and had him paged to meet them where they were, and he finally came and apologized for not telling them exactly where to meet him, then he hugged and kissed Maxine and said how happy he was she came and thanked Clara for paying for the trip. They found their way out to the street and decided to find the hotel where they were going to stay, which was across from Grand Central Park not too far from the station. Walking to the hotel, they window-shopped and took in the sights all along the streets. My, what a big city with so many people coming and going, Maxine felt so small in such a big place, yet so excited about being there with Jack.

The hotel clerk took the information from them for their room, Clara paid for the room and said that Jack was their stepbrother so they didn't have to get an extra room and since he was willing to sleep on the couch. Jack had told her to do this because he didn't have the money for a room. "Oh my, is this right?" thought Maxine, but just being there with him was all that mattered at this moment and the thought left her mind. They took their bags to their room and settled down to talk a bit and freshen up because they were going out to eat. The view was just beautiful from the window of the fifth floor. They could see the park, the station, and all the big signs on the buildings advertising all kinds of things. It was time to go find a place to eat so they asked the hotel clerk where a good place was to eat and he suggested a place directly across from Grand Central Station. They went there and found out that it was a very exclusive high-priced place and realized it was too expensive for them, so they left and found a place they could afford. After dinner they took a stroll in Central Park and a horse and buggy ride, which was so much fun, there were people sitting on the grass and on the benches just taking it easy. It was such a big place and so many people.

They returned to the hotel and Jack whispered to Maxine not to go to sleep. It was quite late, but finally Clara went to sleep, so Maxine tiptoed over to Jack and very quietly sat down beside him waiting to see what he wanted.

"Maxine, I don't want to be engaged any longer because I want to see other girls," he told her.

What a shock! She thought, "Did I come all the way to New York to hear this?" Tears filled her eyes and she began to sob and he whispered, "Please don't cry, I wanted to tell you this in person and not in a letter."

This sure didn't help the hurt she was feeling or the pain in her heart. Maxine went back to bed with Clara and just covered her head and sobbed most of the night. What little sleep she did get wasn't much and she awoke with this bad news still on her mind. She didn't even want to look at Jack it hurt so much.

Clara had no idea what had taken place and woke up and said, "Let's go get some breakfast and go sight-seeing. We can go to the Statue of Liberty today and maybe Coney Island, okay?"

They all agreed that this plan for the day would suit them just fine. Maxine's emotions of disappointment ran deep and she wasn't able to express how she felt. Keeping this very private and not on display was a living testimony to the way her family hid their emotions. Clara didn't even sense that anything was wrong with her sister throughout the whole day they spent together. Maxine thought about returning the ring, but waited until Jack asked for it; he never did so she wore it until she got back home and put it away.

After breakfast they took the subway to where they could go see the Statue of Liberty and when they got there they went on a boat that went out into the harbor, but couldn't go on the statue itself because of the war, as it was too risky because of sabotage. It was a disappointment to them but they could see it from the boat and besides it was still an experience for them to see it up close. They got directions to Coney Island and caught the subway. The day wasn't that exciting for Maxine because, naturally, she couldn't get over what Jack had said to her last night. What a mess! She thought, "I am crying on the inside and laughing on the outside trying to make Jack think this breakup isn't bothering me, but it hurts."

The subway started above ground and then went underground for some ways, it came back out and went way above the roads on bridges. They could see peoples' laundry hanging on lines stretched from building to building, something they had never seen before, it was quite a sight for them to see. They finally arrived on Coney Island. It was a huge place with the boardwalk, a huge roller coaster and other rides they had never seen before. Jack and Maxine rode the roller coaster and it was such a thrill, it took their breath away. They could see so far away when they reached the top, then it went back down, what fun. They looked at each other as if to say, "Are you okay? Wasn't that fun?" Maxine was laughing on the outside and crying on the inside.

They strolled along the boardwalk for quite awhile, enjoying the waves splashing against the pilings; it was windy and not too hot that day. Jack wanted to go to one of the little bars on the midway because he had a uniform on and they wouldn't ask him for identification there and that made him feel grown up. Clara and Maxine had some good Coney Island hot dogs and root beer to drink as they rested and decided what to do next. Maxine knew she should use this private time to confide in her sister about the news Jack laid on her about breaking the engagement, but once again, Maxine couldn't break the barrier of silence that she kept around her nearly all her life.

They had seen some sideshows along the boardwalk and thought it would be fun to go see one of them. So they went to one that had Siamese twins, an elephant man, a real fat lady, a two-headed cow, and a sword man who swallowed swords. Most of the show was real but the elephant man had a piece of skin from his forehead hanging down to his lips and the holes for his nose were visible and he just flipped the skin up and down. It was supposed to look like and elephant trunk, but they could see no resemblance at all. There was also a man with scales on his skin like a fish, which look very deceitful.

It was getting late so they all decided to go back to the hotel because they had to get up very early in the morning to go back home. Morning arrived and they took a cab to the train station. It was a long walk through the station to their gate, each step got harder and harder because it meant Maxine wouldn't be seeing Jack for a long time, maybe never again if he had his way. The closer they got to the gate they could hear. "The train leaving for Detroit and Chicago is ready for departure in ten minutes." She knew this was it. She sadly looked into Jack's eyes and the tears began to flow, she couldn't hold them back any longer. "Oh God, I love him so much I hope and pray he will come back to me," she thought. She hugged and kissed him tenderly and he returned the kiss and he had the nerve to say to her. "Please don't worry and write to me faithfully." Ever compliant, Maxine agreed she would, then hurried through the turnstile for the train.

The train was crowded, with not even enough seats for everyone; soldiers and sailors were sleeping in the aisles resting their heads on their duffle bags. Clara and Maxine shared a seat with a sailor who was going to the Naval Station in Chicago; he was from New Jersey and had been home on leave to visit his folks. His name was Bill and he was very friendly. This trip had started out so wonderful going to New York and ended in discouragement and heartbreak, so Maxine didn't say much. She finally told Clara what Jack had said to her and Clara said, "What a jerk. You shouldn't stand for that, Maxine, I never get serious over any guy just because of that reason. I am not about to let anyone break my heart." Nineteen-year-old Clara was smart for her years, but Maxine didn't listen to her because of the way she went about her life.

There were many servicemen on the train and some of them came over and talked to the girls and wanted to get acquainted. Clara was very friendly with them but Maxine still had Jack on her mind and wasn't very friendly. The sailor sitting beside them asked Maxine, "What's the matter?" and with tears in her eyes, she explained why she was so sad.

"I sure would like to have a girl like you that would wait for me to come home to after the war," he said, and then they talked and talked. Clara had already fallen asleep and Maxine was getting so tired she kept nodding her head and he then told her to lay her head on his shoulder and she did and she fell asleep. When she woke up she apologized to him and told him, "You are very kind," and he said, "It was my pleasure." He was such a gentleman, he kissed her on the check, she blushed and smiled, thinking, "He was so nice and it was good to have someone to talk to and get things off of my mind."

Later on Clara said to Maxine, "You see, there are many fish in the sea and you don't have to hang on to just one, because if you do the good one may get away."

Maxine stuck to her stubborn guns and thought, "That is well and good for you to say but that is not how I feel." Clankity, clank clank, mile after mile the train wheels kept repeating the sounds as she looked out the window at the scenery. As the telephone poles went by she stared and just wondered, "What had come over Jack in such a short time they had been away from each other. Did he find another girl? If he did why does he want me to keep writing to him? What kind of man will he turn out to be? Maybe Mother was right when she said he would give me nothing but a life of hell."

The conductor announced, "Jackson, Michigan the next stop," and the girls gathered their things to be ready to get off the train. They said goodbye to the servicemen that had been so friendly toward them and wished them a safe journey.

They were happy to be back in their hometown once again and to see the familiar places they grew up around. They took the bus and were greeted at the front door by Mother. "Home at last," Maxine thought, "there is no place like home. It was a long trip back and I will be happy to get back to school and the routine I am accustomed to."

Mother was happy to see them and asked if they had a good trip and they both said, "Yes, we saw such beautiful sights, we got lost in the train station, we saw the Statue of Liberty, and went to Coney Island. Oh, Mama, we had such a wonderful time."

Mother never asked about Jack and Maxine didn't bring it up yet, she wanted to get settled before she told her mother about the breakup and had asked Clara not to say anything to her yet because she would say, "I told you so." Maxine vowed to never be so distant from her children and that she would be involved closely with their lives and emotions.

CHAPTER SEVEN
QUESTIONING THE DECISION

Clara met a young sailor named Lenny Wilson shortly after she and Maxine returned from New York; they courted for a short time and he asked her to marry him. This sure was a whirlwind courtship. His aunt and uncle lived in Jackson on the west side of town and they said the couple could live in a little apartment in the back of their home until his leave was up, if they would like to. So they decided to live there after they were married. It was very small and was convenient to the factory where Clara was working. After Lenny left to go back to base she decided to stay there until he came home again and his Aunt Mary and Uncle Gene Wilson agreed that it would be all right for her to stay there.

In the spring and summer of 1945, the war in Europe was over and the troops were coming home. Jack was on one of the Merchant Marine ships that was transporting servicemen from Europe; they were wall to wall, sleeping on the decks, but so happy to be returning back to the United States of America. There was a gigantic celebration in every town in America when the war was declared over, no one went to work that day, the streets were filled shoulder to shoulder with people celebrating, so elated their loved ones would be coming home. Confetti was thrown from the buildings in masses, horns blowing, church bells ringing and this went on most of the day. Maxine and Jenny were there also. Maxine was again hiding her feelings, crying on the inside and laughing on the outside knowing Jack would be home soon. "Would they get back together again?" she wondered as she observed everyone's happiness and jubilation. After they went home Maxine went to her room and cried her heart out and prayed, this was the only way she could relieve herself of the sadness she felt not knowing what would happen when Jack arrived home. He had been writing to her and even sent a little souvenir hankie from England telling her he loved her, but didn't know what their future together would be until he came back home.

The day Henry (Snookie) returned home from the Army he looked at Maxine and put her over his knee and spanked her. She yelled out,

"Why are you spanking me?"

"That is for dying your hair," he replied.

She and Mother both spoke at the same time and said, "She didn't dye her hair, it turned dark naturally."

Then he apologized to Maxine and gave her a big hug and said, "It is so good to be home, it has been over three years since I have been here. I can see how there was time for her hair to grow darker." Henry felt so responsible for the younger children since Father died, he sent money home to Mother faithfully every month to help. After a week or so of rest and visiting Grandma and Grandpa he went to work at Western Stamping Company, the same place Clara was working. He had been in Africa, Italy, France, and Germany and was gone for thirty-six months without leave and was so happy to be home. His fiancé, Doris Meyers, had waited for him faithfully all those years and they decided to get married in August 1945. Herman and his girlfriend Gale were married in August, and Clara and Lenny Wilson were married in August, too, and moved to the Wilson's apartment. Mother had just lost three children from her household in one month. Henry's wedding and Clara's wedding were small and quiet. Herman and Gale had a big wedding and the reception was in one of the Hayes Hotel's banquet rooms. Many people were celebrating by drinking and dancing. Maxine and Jenny attended for a while but Mother sent them home early because she caught them drinking some of the spiked punch and they were acting very silly. They giggled all they way home on the bus and everyone just stared at them, looking very disgusted.

It was the latter part of August and school would be starting soon and the thoughts of getting ready for another year of studying and school activities were on Maxine's mind, along with thinking about Jack and what he might be doing after he arrived back in the USA. They were serious thoughts about him because of his decision he had told her in New York. She wondered if he would have told her that if she hadn't gone to New York to see him. Had she done the right thing? So many questions arose in her mind and she prayed about it and asked God to help her to understand why this had happened. Maxine still hung on with such hope in her heart things would work out. Maybe it was false hope, but she wanted him to love her as much as she loved him and it took many years after to learn love has to be a shared relationship.

Her junior year of high school started the day after Labor Day, 1945. New teachers and classes were assigned so there would be much to think about and to learn this year. There were a lot of new faces and the joy of learning was replacing some of the sadness and heartache she was feeling. Her classes were English, Latin, algebra, biology, home economics and physical education, a busy schedule to keep her mind occupied along with a lot of homework to do, plus her chores would help ease her heartache.

Jenny came over one evening to let her know that Jack was on the phone; he was home for a short leave before he got shipped out to help transport the thousands of soldiers home from Europe after the war. What a surprise! She literally flew over to Jenny's to talk to him, all the heartache was gone, and he called her— wow! It was so good to hear his voice, my how she loved him, and words could not describe it. Jack wanted to see her! He said, "I want to see you and I am sorry I disappointed you in New York for what I said." She was ready to forgive him right away and told him so, and, said she would see him if he came over. He said, "I will be right over as soon as possible," and she was so excited, she told Jenny, "He is coming over to see me," then ran home to get ready.

He borrowed his father's car to pick her up so they could talk and spend some time alone. They drove out in the country to a lonely spot and parked. Jack took her in his arms and kissed her and said, "I really do love you very much and I realized how much after you left New York and I had some time to think about what I had said and done."

Maxine said, "I have thought about it a lot and it did hurt me very much, but I forgive you. When Jenny said you were on the phone I knew then all was forgiven and hoped we could go on."

He was relieved and happy to hear that from her; he took her hand and held it, then they embraced each other very close and were embraced with the spirit of love about them as if there were no other human beings on this earth but them, a love that only God could create for His creation.

It was getting late, they had been parked for quite a while talking about the future and Jack's going away on a ship to wherever they would send him, as of this time he didn't know where. Jack began to feel the natural instincts of a man and asked Maxine for her permission to fulfill those sexual urges, and she at first refused, as she had many times before this night. He promised her, "If anything happens that you would get pregnant, I will marry you for sure." So, believing his promise (she was so trusting of people, especially him, she believed anything he told her), she gave in and agreed to his advances. She was not a person with these kinds of sexual feelings; her love was a spiritual love for him, an unselfish love. Foremost in her mind was not what she wanted, but what he wanted. After the loving act was over and after a few more hugs and kisses, he said, "Now remember, if anything happens and you are pregnant we will get married," and she said, "Alright." They decided they better head back home so he could get his father's car back. So they drove to Maxine's with her sitting as close to him as she could possibly get, with his arm around her, "Oh, what a wonderful evening this had been," she thought and was so happy to be in his arms, believing he had come back to her for good now.

She said goodnight and went into the house just bubbling all over and greeted mother with a cheery hello and mother asked, "Do you feel better now that Jack is back?" And Maxine answered with a positive yes. It was time to go to bed so she went upstairs, and all the time meditating over the things that went on that evening, recalling that Jack had promised to marry her if she was pregnant. She got on her knees and prayed: "Please God, let me be pregnant so we can be married, I love him with all of my heart." (She learned later that this was not the wise thing to do, to pray for her own desires.) Of course, God knew this all the time. He knows our hearts before we do, plus He knows what we need way before we do, and a small voice inside her said, "This may not be what you want, but what you need." Maxine climbed into bed thinking about what had come to her mind, "What did it mean?" Her emotions overcame her budding talents of personal prophecy that ran in the family. Why didn't she see the warning of things to come?

The time came for Jack to go back to base and they said their goodbyes reluctantly. After arriving at the base he was assigned to a troop transport going to Belgium to pick up soldiers on their way home after being in battle in Europe. He worked in the kitchen helping out with the cooking on the way over there.

The ship was docked in Belgium for a few days to get supplies loaded before the soldiers came aboard. Jack wrote to Maxine while he was there and sent her a souvenir, which she cherished and kept: a small beautiful silk hankie with flowers and "Belgium" and "I love you" embroidered on it. He wrote that the ship was loaded with so many men, they were bunked down on the decks like sardines. Some were badly wounded, some had spent a long time on the front and were ready to go home because their time was up and they were tired and homesick. When off-duty Jack would go up on deck and talk to some of the men and listen to their stories, play cards or shoot dice, anything to pass the time quickly so they would not be bored. These men had nothing on their minds except to get home to the good and beloved United States of America and freedom from war.

Maxine continued to write as often as she could and let Jack know how everything was going and that she loved him so much and couldn't wait to see him once again, and Jack wrote to let her know about his travels and how soon he would be able to get back home. In the Merchant Marine, they could go home after each trip they had made if they wanted to, so he said he would be home soon in between trips. By this time it was Maxine's seventeenth birthday, October 8, 1945. It was a nice birthday, Mother made a banana whipped-cream cake for her. She had requested it because that was her favorite, oh it was so good, and she had invited Jenny over to share it with her.

October was going by pretty fast and Maxine hadn't had any signs of her period that month and she was very worried; she didn't know whether to tell anyone or not so she kept silent and waited. Jack finally called and said he was back home and wanted to see her, so they made a date for him to come over. It was Saturday night and they went to the movies with Roger and Jenny because he couldn't get his father's car to be alone. They had a good time at the movies and it was so hard for Maxine to keep quiet, but she wanted to be alone with Jack when she told him; this was something very serious and she was really afraid to say anything to anyone. After they returned back to Maxine's, Roger and Jenny went over to Jenny's, and Maxine and Jack sat on the front porch for a while and Maxine whispered to Jack, "I believe I am pregnant, I haven't had a period this month."

He was sure surprised and said, "Are you sure?"

"It will soon be time for another period and maybe I will have it then," she answered.

Jack didn't know what to say, only, "Don't worry, I told you I would marry you, didn't I?"

"Yes, you did." It was very quiet and he didn't stay long after that, he went over to get Roger so they could go home.

The next week Jack only called twice and talked about the situation and was wondering just what to do if she was in the family way. He didn't say anything about going out on Saturday and Maxine wondered, "Why didn't he want to see me this weekend?" She found out when Jack's cousin Bud Ellis came over to see her on Sunday afternoon to talk to her. He said, "Do you know why Jack didn't come to see you last night?"

"No, why?"

"Because he went with a bunch of guys out to Pulaski to a dance. He got drunk and asked a girl to go to Akron, Ohio to marry him, because they wouldn't have to wait for a blood test there, but she told him no."

Maxine thought, "Oh my goodness, why is he doing this to me?" and she began to cry.

"He isn't worth it, Maxine," Bud said.

Then she told Bud that she was pregnant with Jack's baby. Bud was so upset with Jack for doing such a cruel thing to her, he said if there was anything he could do to let him know.

She went in the house and went upstairs and cried her eyes out and thought, "Dear God, what have I gotten myself into?" As the days went by, this betrayal was eating her heart out. She wouldn't talk to Jack when he called and it was so hard to concentrate on her schoolwork, she went about in a daze.

Mother finally asked her, "What is the matter with you, Maxine?" She answered and told her what Jack had done on Saturday night out at the dance, and Mother said, "Maxine you don't have to take that kind of treatment from any guy. He is not worth it."

Maxine was in the dining room standing by the heat register to keep warm, then she went in the living room and stood on that register by Mother's chair for a while, then she went into the dining room again and was thinking, "I have to tell Mother I am pregnant, how am I going to do that?"

Then back to the living room again, and finally Mother asked, "Maxine, do you have something you want to tell me?"

Maxine began to cry and said, "I am pregnant."

"Maxine! I would have thought it of your sister, but I would have never thought it of you!"

Oh, what a terrible weight of guilt came over Maxine, it was like hitting her over the head with a hammer. She thought, "She trusted me and I betrayed her trust."

Mother said, "I have been checking in the loads of laundry on your monthly periods and wondered when you were going to come to me about this. We better go see Jack's parents to find out what is going to be done about this. He is not going to get away with it if I have anything to say about it. This is such a disappointment to me. I want you to go with me over to Grandma and Grandpa's house today, I need to talk to them."

They walked to the bus stop and waited. It was hard for Maxine to even face her mother because she felt so guilty and so full of shame. They arrived at Grandma's but Grandpa wasn't there and Maxine was disappointed because she loved her Grandpa very much and wanted to share this news with him too. Mother told Grandma, "I am so upset with Maxine, she is pregnant and I really don't know what to do."

Grandma said "First, you realize she isn't the only one that has ever done anything wrong, so don't act as if she was, and second you need to go see Jack's parents about it because she didn't do this all by herself. It took both of them."

Mother agreed with her and they continued to talk about other things that were going on in the family. Maxine was so relieved that Grandma was so forgiving and so wise.

The next day Mother and Maxine took a bus over to Jack's parent's home and went to the door and knocked. His father answered the door and invited them in the house. Mother said, "Your son got my daughter pregnant and he is going to marry her or I am going to know the reason why. Then he had the nerve to go to a dance and get drunk and try to take another girl to Ohio to marry him. Just what do you have to say about that?" she said in her angriest voice.

Don, Jack's father, looked so surprised. He said, "No one told me about this, and I agree with you he does need to marry her. I will confront him as soon as he gets home from work, and I am so sorry you had to be the one to tell me this. We like Maxine and we want to do what is right for her."

All the while this was going on Maxine was heartbroken and so hurt to think of the promises Jack had made to her and she believed he would be willing to marry her. She didn't want it to turn out this way. She so much wanted Jack to do this on his own, without being forced into it, believing he did love her enough to do what was right. Maxine didn't realize the consequences of her wishful thinking – that forcing it this way sets up patterns that grow into problems in later life.

The bus ride back home was silent. After they returned home Maxine went up to her room and prayed to God, crying and realizing what she had done and wondering what she was going to do, just how would this turn out? (She remembered that little intuitive nudge she received after her first prayer to God about getting what she needed, was this her payback?) These and more questions filled her mind until she finally fell asleep for a little while. She woke up with this still on her mind, plus thinking, "I have to go to school and tell the principal about this, they won't let me stay in school. Oh my! This is the worst yet." She began to cry again, weeping so hard because she thought, "I know I have sinned against God and will go to hell for sure now." The guilt was so strong within her she could hardly think - what a burden to be carrying.

She went downstairs and Mother knew she had been crying and said, "You made your bed, young lady, now you have to lay in it, I sure hope we hear from Jack about what he plans on doing before long."

Maxine didn't need to hear this, she thought, "I am already carrying such a burden and I know I am the one who will suffer the consequences for what I have done, I love him and believe what he told me."

Monday morning came and Maxine knew what she had to do that day at school. She still hadn't told Jenny yet and decided to tell her on the way to school so Jenny would know why she wouldn't be going back home on the bus with her that afternoon. Jenny was so surprised. She just stared at her and asked, "What are you going to do?" Maxine told her she had to see the principal today.

The bus was so crowded that morning they had to stand up all the way downtown until they transferred to the next bus. When they arrived at school, Maxine said to Jenny, "I have to go into the principal's office and let him know my condition so I will see you back home later."

The walk down the hall seemed so long and so sad, and the tears began to flow. She had to keep wiping them off of her cheeks, as she thought, "I love school and now I won't be graduating, and I'll have to live with the shame I have brought to myself and my family." By this time she had entered the principal's office and requested to see him.

The young lady showed her in to see Mr. Howe, the principal, and he asked, "Just what can I do for you today, Maxine?"

"Mr. Howe, I have to quit school." By this time she was crying again as well as sobbing.

"I don't understand," he said, "why would you have to quit school now? You have only a year and a half to go before you graduate and your grades are good."

"I am pregnant," Maxine said.

He replied, "Oh, Maxine, I am so sorry to hear that. You know we can't allow anyone to continue school if they are pregnant, don't you? It would be a bad example for the other students and it would be hard on you also because of the shame you have caused for yourself."

"Yes, I know. It hurts me to think I will not be able to finish school and graduate."

"I am so sorry, Maxine, but that is our rule and it does help to deter other students from getting in this situation."

After going to her locker and removing all of her belongings, she headed for the door. All the way to the door she cried and thought, "I am so sorry, I love school, what have I done?" This question kept going over and over in her mind and she thought, "This must be my punishment for what I have done." The guilt was getting worse then ever and she felt trapped. All the way home she realized this would be her last trip to and from school, just what would she do now? It was the first of November and it was getting colder and she realized she wouldn't be able to ice skate this winter or go roller skating either. It seemed like her thoughts were all so negative. She had always been so happy and positive about everything, but things just hadn't gone like she thought they would. Maxine wanted to marry Jack so much she realized how selfish she had been by only thinking of what she wanted and what she had done. She thought, "Oh, your sins will find you out. Is this the way God works?" Each step she took was one of uncertainty, "What am I going to do?" she thought as she boarded the bus to go back home.

That evening Jenny came over and said Jack was on the phone and wanted to talk to her. Maxine said, "I wonder what he wants, he didn't have much to say to me the other night." Jenny was a good friend and she knew what he had done to Maxine and Jenny didn't hide her feelings about how she felt about Jack. They went into the house and Maxine said hello to Rosie and picked up the phone and said, "Hello, how are you?"

"Oh I'm okay, I guess." Then Jack asked, "Can I come over to see you? I have something to ask you."

"Are you sure you want to?"

"Yes, I am sure."

"Alright, what time will you be here?" She hung up the phone and looked at Jenny and said, "He wants to come over and ask me something." Lots of doubts and concerns began to fill her mind. She couldn't let herself get excited about his coming because he didn't say what it was all about. She would just have to wait and see, he had disappointed her so many times before she kept a tight hold on her emotions.

Mother was very concerned also. She didn't want him to hurt Maxine any more than he already had, so she told Maxine, "Don't get your hopes up, you know how much he has hurt you already."

Maxine went upstairs to get cleaned up so she would be ready when he came for her. She thought, "Mother is right, first was what he did in New York and now this, can I trust him? But I do love him so much, isn't that enough to make this thing work out?" The doubts began to leave and the joy returned as she thought about seeing him once again. He was at the door when she came down the stairs and she let him in.

He said hello to Mother and Maxine, and asked, "Will you go for a ride with me? We need to talk." She asked her mother if it was okay, and Mother said yes, with a wary look in her eye.

They went to a place east of town to park and talk. Jack said, "My folks told me you and your mother were over the other day and told them about us and they wanted to know what I was going to do about it. Well, I have been avoiding this too long and my parents said the right thing to do is to marry you. I am so sorry for the way I have treated you, and I do want to marry you like I told you I would, but I didn't realize this would happen so soon and it was a shock to me."

She answered, "You know, I believed you but when Bud came over and told me about you wanting to take another girl to Ohio to get married, it was like sticking a knife into my heart. Do you realize how much it hurt?"

He apologized and apologized some more, asking her, "Please forgive me. I don't know what I was thinking about, I know I promised you I would marry you if you got pregnant, but I never thought it would be so soon."

Suddenly she realized he was just as scared as her, both of them seventeen years old and being faced with such an abrupt change in their young lives. It was silent for some time, neither one spoke, only looking at one another until Jack eventually came around to asking the question.

"Will you marry me? We can get our blood tested this week and get married on Friday. My Grandma said we could live down there with her and pay her room and board; she will only charge us five dollars a week."

Maxine didn't know what to say, she was so surprised to hear all this. She thought, "He must have been doing a lot of planning before he came over to ask me." She answered, "Are you sure you want to do this or is it because your parents are forcing you into it?"

He replied, very seriously, "Yes. I do. I heard you had to quit school and how hard it was for you to do that. We will have to get our parent's permission in order to get married because we are both under eighteen but my father said he would sign the papers. Do you have a

62

doctor we can go to for the blood tests?"

"Yes, we can go to Doctor Meads, he has been our family doctor for years."

The doctor's office was downtown in the City Bank building on the fourteenth floor. They waited in the waiting room for about an hour, then the nurse called them in and the doctor talked to them for a short time and told them the process they had to go through to get their license and told Maxine to come in as soon as possible to get an examination and prenatal care for her and the baby. The nurse took blood from Maxine first and when it was time for her to take Jack's blood, he fainted. They revived him and asked if he was going to be all right and he replied he would be okay. The nurse took his blood and he was so embarrassed. The doctor said some men are weak when it comes to taking blood from them, especially when they watch their girlfriend give blood first. They were told that they had to wait for two days for the results so they could get the license to be married.

By now, Maxine was so happy to think they were really going through with it and that they even had a place to stay. She thought, "How could have I doubted?" Jack took her home because he had to go to work. He was working at the railroad yard in the round house; his father was a switchman for the railroad and helped him get work there. Jack was earning sixty-six and two-thirds cents an hour.

It was Friday, November 2, 1945, when Jack arrived to pick up Maxine and her mother to get the blood test results and to go the courthouse where they were going to be married by the judge, because they were both underage. When they got there they found out that Jack's mother had to sign the papers also; they needed both his mother and father's signature because he was under eighteen, and Maxine's mother didn't have to sign because a girl's age can be sixteen years old in order to get married in Michigan. So they took her mother home then drove out to Leoni to get his mother's signature, but did not make it back in time before the courthouse closed. This was a disappointment to them, because now they would have to wait until Monday. So, they decided to go to a movie with Bud and his girlfriend Marjorie that evening. "It was so good to be with him and to be so happy again," Maxine thought as they watched the movie. Jack seemed to be happy too, because he kept his arm around her and kissed her a lot that night. On the way home Jack asked, "Bud and Marjorie, would you like to stand up with us on Monday when we get married?"

They both replied, "Yes, we would like that."

Neither of their parents wanted to be there at the judge's chambers during the ceremony and they needed two witnesses. The marriage file would be recorded and kept unpublished and no one was able to get the information but Jack and Maxine.

On Saturday Maxine did her chores with vim and vigor, happy knowing that on Monday she would be married. Mother had told her when she finished her work she would take her downtown to buy a new dress to be married in. Maxine was so surprised, she answered, "Oh Mama, thank you so much."

Mother explained that her brother Henry helped with the money because he thought it would be nice for her to have a special dress for that day. He had always been so thoughtful and such a good brother to all of them. When the work was done, Mother took her shopping and they found a light blue princess-style dress with a white collar and cuffs. It looked so nice on Maxine, and she was happy to think that on Monday she would be a married woman and would be leaving home to live with Jack at his grandmother's home on the other side of town. Just think, this was the fourth child to leave Mother and to get married this year, four out of seven in one year. Harold was already married to Jeanne, so the only ones left were Fritz (Ernest), who was in the state home and Corky, the youngest.

CHAPTER EIGHT
MANY MOVES IN DIFFERENT DIRECTIONS

With anticipation and joy that Monday morning, Maxine proceeded to repack her clothes because she knew she would not be coming home once she was married that day. While she was packing, her sister Clara came in the room and said, "At least I didn't have to get married!"

Maxine looked at her and said, "No, you didn't. You were one of the lucky ones who didn't get caught." Maxine thought, "This was not a very nice thing to say to a sister who had been so kind to her all these years," but Maxine didn't realize that once words were said they cannot be taken back and shouldn't have been said in the first place. Even though Clara had judged her first, it was not for Maxine to judge anyone. It was time to go and Jack, Bud and Marjorie were there to pick her up. She said ,"Bye, Mom."

Mother never showed her emotions and just said, "Goodbye and I hope things turn out alright for you. You made your bed now you have to lay in it."

Maxine took her clothes and left; this was November 5, 1945. It was a very cold day, Bud was driving his car and they arrived at the courthouse and went to the fourth floor to City Clerk's Office. They told the clerk what they were there for and she went to get the judge; he escorted them into a small room and asked who was to be married and if they had the parent's signed permission.

After everything was verified, he read the marriage vows to Jack: "Do you, Jack, take this woman, Maxine, to be your lawful wedded wife to have and to hold through sickness and health, though richer or poorer till death do you part?" and Jack answered, "I do."

Then he asked Maxine: "Do you, Maxine, take this man, Jack, to be your lawful wedded husband to have and to hold through sickness and health, though richer or poorer till death do you part?" And she answered, "I do" at the same time vowing within her heart of hearts, "I'll make a go of this marriage if it kills me!" She was strong willed and trying to prove to her mother that this was not a mistake. After they were pronounced husband and wife, they kissed each other and said, "I love you." They left and went to see Jack's Grandma Derr who had told them she wanted to take their pictures and give them a gift.

Vera had a wedding shower for Maxine and many relatives and friends came; it was so much fun and she received so many nice things. She had never received so many things in her life: there were baskets of groceries and paper items, even a pancake turner, and a can opener (a hand-held one). Dad and Vera gave them a large set of dishes that was a service for twelve, oh how pretty. Maxine asked Don if she could call him "Dad" and he said, "Sure." From then on he was Dad to her. The family was so friendly, they seemed to have so much fun and enjoyed each other whenever they all got together. They accepted Maxine with open arms and treated her as one of their own.

Jack's grandmother Grace Ort was a widow and they rented one of her bedrooms for five dollars a week for room and board, plus Maxine helped with the household chores. Jack would go hunting for rabbits, pheasants and squirrels to help with the food cost, although Grandma Ort never complained, she was so happy to have company there with her. Grandpa Floyd Ort had passed away just a few years before this; he and Jack were very close and they would go hunting together and sometimes he would take Jack to the bar with him. Grandpa Ort was a heavy drinker. Grandma said she didn't know how he got home because he would be so drunk that he would drive the car home and pass out in the driveway. Jack really missed his Grandpa Ort and talked about him a lot, how they were such good buddies. (This could have been an influence on Jack to develop his drinking habits that caused so many problems later in life.) Jack spent a lot of his time at their house because they let him get away with things his father wouldn't. Jack's mother Helen was their only child and Grandma loved children very much and was happy to share her home with Jack and Maxine.

Maxine was happy and contented to be with Jack and couldn't wait until he came home from work every day. He had to catch the bus to go to work early in the morning so he and Grandma would walk to work together. She worked at a garment factory downtown and had been there for many years. Jack didn't like working at the roundhouse and was getting discontented because he only earned sixty-six and two-thirds cents an hour.

Only a few months after they were married Jack came home and said to Maxine, "I want to go back to work on another ship because we need more money for our expenses." He had decided to go back into the Merchant Marine for another trip. This paid much more money and soon they would have the expense of the baby.

Maxine was a little upset because she would miss him, but agreed with him and said, "Okay, then I will go back to my mother's and live while you are gone, is that alright with you?" Jack agreed with her, so they moved her things back to her mother's.

While at her mother's home she received a letter from her brother Harold who had moved to Pittsburgh, Pennsylvania, and he asked Maxine if she would come there and help his wife, who was expecting a baby in February, as they needed help with her other little girl. This was Harold's second wife, Sunny. He had divorced Jeanne because he didn't know when she would ever get out of the TB sanitarium. Maxine thought it was a good idea to go help. Harold said he would call and tell Maxine the details about the train ticket and schedule. He sent the ticket and gave instructions about meeting her. This was another new experience for Maxine, a trip to Pittsburgh all by herself. Here she was, seventeen years old, married, expecting a baby and going on this trip to help her brother and sister-in-law, so young yet so grown up.

Harold met her at the station and they took a cab to the apartment. They walked up to the third floor to a two-room apartment. Maxine had to sleep on the couch but she didn't mind it, it was kind of fun being there with them. Sunny and Maxine went shopping and bought some material to make baby clothes, this helped pass the time while it was too cold to do much of anything else, until it was time for Sunny's baby to be born. Finally, the day came and they had a good and healthy baby boy, Harold Louis Bohl, Jr. Maxine stayed there and helped for three more months, getting used to handling a newborn, from the first of February until the first of May when Jack showed up unexpectedly after his trip. He had been writing to Maxine and knew where she was and decided to stop in Pittsburgh and travel back to Michigan with her. By this time Sunny had recovered and was able to care for the children with Harold's help.

Jack had been to Tam Pico, Mexico, on an oil tanker and was happy to be back. He had enjoyed being in Mexico but said it was too hot for him. He couldn't get over how the children there were begging for money whenever they saw sailors or servicemen, and wanted them to go see their sisters who were prostitutes. He brought back photos and some beautiful souvenir pictures of real feathered beautiful tropical birds, in glass covered, wood carved frames.

It was so good to see Jack, and now they were on their way back home to Michigan. Not knowing where they would live from here on, they went to Dad and Vera's and they said it was okay for them to stay there until they found a place. Vera had a baby shower for Maxine and she received so many nice things for the baby, it was so much fun to open all these things, from cloth diapers, baby oil, sweater sets, undershirts; so many things that a baby needs. She looked them over and over and tried to imagine how they would look on the baby. This family was so generous and sharing, Maxine had never had so much given to her as a child and was thankful for everything. She helped Vera do the housework and get the meals. There were four children under their roof, three of Vera's and one of Don's: Rosie, Sharon, John and Donny. It was fun to be with them.

Jack wanted to move so they could be by themselves, so he bought a small travel trailer, eight feet by fourteen feet, from one of his friends, Don Furlong, for one hundred and twenty-five dollars that he had earned on the boat trip to Mexico. They pulled the trailer down to Grandma Ort's yard and parked it there. She had an acre and a half and had told Jack it was just fine to put it there. They could get water from her house when they needed it and could use her washing machine. There was an outside toilet and Jack connected an extension cord for the electricity. By this time the weather was beginning to get warmer, and they could get outside and enjoy the sunshine. It was the middle of May and getting close for their baby to be born.

Jack had found some duck eggs one day when he was hunting and put them under a laying hen and she sat on them until they hatched; they were so cute and it looked so funny seeing those ducks follow a chicken. When they got a little bigger, Jack took a big box his grandpa used to mix cement in and filled it with water and those little ducks swam and dove under water, it was so much fun to watch and Jack enjoyed being outside relaxing. Maxine was getting bigger and bigger with child and Jack would tease her about it. She had always lived in the city and this was a new way of life for her. Jack had quit the round-house and had gotten a job as a welder, a skill he had learned in technical school. He rode his sister's bike back and forth to work where he was welding.

One day he came home and said a man had accused him of shooting some windows out of his greenhouse. He didn't see Jack do it but that day Jack had been hunting and was carrying a gun, so he called the police and reported Jack. The police came and picked Jack up and took him to jail. Maxine got so upset she started to have contractions and called Vera and told her. The contractions were getting closer, so Vera took Maxine to the hospital, but then the contractions stopped, so the doctor told Maxine to go home until they were much closer. Jack's dad got him out of jail and proved to the police that it wasn't Jack who shot the windows out, but the damage was done and it made Jack very angry with the law. His attitude was very negative and he couldn't seem to get over being accused of doing something he didn't do. The next day, after Jack had gone to work, Maxine started to have contractions again and made up her mind she was not going to the hospital until it was time, because she said it was too embarrassing walking out of the hospital still pregnant. The contractions were getting closer, and by the time Jack came home from work they were getting closer and sharper. She felt like she had to go to the bathroom and so she went to the outhouse and sat there. Jack called Vera and she came running down there and said "Maxine get off of that toilet. You'll have that baby in there if you don't!"

Maxine explained she felt like she had to go to the bathroom, and Vera said, "You come home with me, right now." So she did and walked around and around the dining room table for hours until it was time to go to the hospital.

Great-Grandma Tatman, Grandma Gracie Ort's mother, had come over to the house and talked to Maxine and comforted her. She explained so many of the things that Maxine would be going through and it helped to calm Maxine. This lady had many children and helped them when they gave birth, like a midwife, so she was very experienced and knew just what Maxine was going through. In her years, many children were born at home.

Finally, it was time to go to the hospital because the contractions were very close and the water had broken, so off they went. Jack was there this time and that helped also. He held her hand and comforted her as the nurse got her prepared for the delivery room. Then they rolled her down to the delivery room on a gurney and gave her ether, saying, "Count to one hundred."

When Maxine woke up she was in her room and the nurse announced, "You have a seven pound fourteen ounce baby boy." This was June 6, 1946 (Maxine's father was born on June 6, 1889). Many family members were there: Jack, Maxine's mother, her brother Herman and Gale, his wife, Dad and Vera and they all said, "Congratulations, he is such a nice baby."

Jack got sick from the smell of the ether and had to leave the room for a while. It was a four-bed ward and the other beds were all filled with new mothers and they were all very friendly and talkative with the family until they all had to leave to go home and to their jobs. The family had brought Maxine some presents: flowers, candy and some new nightgowns. She thanked them all for being so kind to her. Finally, the nurse brought the baby in for Maxine to see. Maxine undressed him from head to toe to be sure he was all right and there were no parts missing or no birth marks on him. "Oh, thank God!" she thought and bundled him back up again. She was so delighted and happy. She hugged the baby and said, "Jack." Maxine and Jack had planned on naming him Jack Donald. Jack's name was Jack Dean, and they didn't want him to be called "Junior." She decided to call him "Jackie" so that he had his own unique name and wouldn't be confused when anybody called for Jack, his father.

Nursing the baby was a priority; the nurse brought Jackie in to be nursed and showed Maxine how to handle this plus how to care for herself. He was very hungry and took to the nipple and wouldn't let go until he was full, then he fell asleep. "Oh how beautiful he is," Maxine said to the other ladies, one of whom would not nurse her baby because she said, "It was too much bother." This lady spent more time reading than she did paying attention to her baby and Maxine couldn't understand how anyone could feel that way.

The lady directly across the room introduced herself as Virginia Rainey. She was such a friendly person and would joke and have fun, they laughed a lot, and they got to be good friends. The doctor made Maxine stay in bed for fourteen days before she could go home. (This is the same doctor that brought Maxine into the world feet first, seventeen years ago. He had been trained in this unorthodox way of bringing the baby from the mother because she wouldn't have to dilate as far and it would be easier on her.) He said, "A woman takes nine months to carry a baby and at least eighteen years to raise the child and she deserves to stay in bed fourteen days." And he really meant it, because he caught Maxine on the third day sitting up and combing her hair and said, "You lay down there, young lady!" Much later in life Maxine would reflect on how hospital policy has surely changed when they presently keep birthing mothers in the hospital for only a few days. What a luxury fourteen days of rest was for women in those days plus the babies being cared for in the nursery was an added reward.

Fourteen days had passed and it was time to go home. The baby had been circumcised on the eighth day, he was eating well, and had gained the weight back he had lost, as they usually do. Maxine had been up that day getting used to walking a bit and was ready to go home. With the nurse's help, she dressed Jackie in his new clothes and covered him with a small flannel blanket; he was so sweet and cuddly, Maxine thought, "Oh, what a gift from God."

The day was beautiful and they drove to Dad and Vera's because Vera wanted to help Maxine get used to bathing the baby and to teach her many things about newborn babies she never knew. Besides, Vera loved children so much she couldn't resist doing this for Maxine. Sharon, Rosie, John, and Donny were waiting at the door to see the baby; they were too young to go to the hospital to visit and were thrilled to see him and to be able to hold him, he was like a little doll to them. Maxine, Jack, and Jackie stayed there for a week, and by that time Maxine was confident to take care of Jackie without any help. The new family went back to their little trailer to live. Vera had set up a small crib and stored all the necessities for them. It was good to be back home, even if it was this little trailer, it was home. Grandma Ort came out to see them that evening and said, "I have dinner ready for you." This was a nice surprise for them.

Little Jackie was such a good baby, so contented and sweet. Maxine loved him so much and was thankful God had given him to her, he belonged to her, oh what a gift. Even though the trailer was so small she made do with a card table that was folded up after every meal, a couch that made into a bed, the water bucket that had to be filled so often now with fresh water, and then the outside toilet didn't seem to be that inconvenient for her because she was so happy. One evening Jack wanted to have an intimate moment with Maxine and was about to when Jackie woke up and cried. It was time for him to nurse, but Jack said, "Leave him alone," but the baby continued to cry and Jack got mad and spanked him.

Maxine had a flashback in her mind – she remembered when she was standing in her crib as a child and saw her father spank her brother with a stove poker and how afraid she was of her father - and a wall went up in her mind between her and Jack. From then on things were not the same between them because she didn't like him being mean to Jackie. The baby was innocent and didn't deserve spanking, he was hungry. Jack was getting discontented and was staying away from home until late at night; he was out drinking with some of his single friends. Maxine didn't say anything because she didn't want him to get mad at her until she found out he was going out with other women and confronted him about it. He did not deny it and said "I want to move out for a while until I decide what I want to do. It is not right for me to be living with you while I go with other women."

So, just four months after little Jackie was born, his father moved out so he could be with other women. Another betrayal, another piercing of the heart for her, and an act which showed just how fleeting was Jack's commitment to Maxine and little Jackie. "Could the pressure of his responsibility toward a family have been too much for him? Or was it his sex drive to have what he wanted when he wanted it without interference of the baby's need to nurse?" Maxine pondered this in her heart.

Fall days are beautiful in Michigan, the trees so beautiful with so many fall colors, and Maxine would put little Jackie in a stroller and take a walk to go see Dad, Vera and the children whenever she was lonely and wanted to talk to someone. Dad was very disappointed in the way Jack was treating Maxine and tried very hard to do whatever he could for her and little Jackie. He told her, "I believe he has too many of his mother's ways. She was a woman who would see other men whenever I was out of town on a trip, when I drove big semi trucks. I took it until I finally had to put her out of the house because of her unfaithfulness. Then later I met Vera who also had a bad marriage and an unfaithful husband and we courted for some time and decided to marry, she with three children and I with my three." Maxine hadn't heard the full story from Jack and now realized the reason for his parent's divorce.

Grandma Ort was usually busy whenever she wasn't working but would stop once in a while to see if Maxine needed anything and would hold Jackie for a while and keep her company and tell about some of the family Maxine hadn't met yet, cousins, aunts and uncles on her side of the family.

It was getting close to Halloween and Jack was still gone. The children were getting excited about what to wear so Maxine helped Vera design an old fashioned hoop-skirted dress with a bustle in the back for the girls. They used hangers for the hoops and filled the bustle with a pillow, the sleeves were full and puffy, with lace sewed on them and the neckline. Rosie and Sharon looked so sweet in the dresses and they won first place at the school Halloween party in both their classes. They were so elated and thankful for Maxine's design and all her help making them.

On Halloween the roller-skating rink had a party and Maxine thought. "I would like to go, Jack's not around anymore and I'm free to go if I can find a baby-sitter." She went into Grandma's attic and found some pretty material to make herself a dress just like she had designed for Rosie and Sharon. Grandma had so much stuff stored in her attic: sugar, flour, canned food, linens, lots of material, and anything that was hard to get at that time. So Maxine thought, "Grandma won't miss it anyway." She cut and sewed the material on Grandma's sewing machine during the day while Grandma was at work and did the hand stitching in the evening out in the trailer until it was done. It was so pretty and looked so nice on her, she wanted to win the first prize, which was a pair of roller skates.

Preparations had been made for Jackie to stay with Dad and Vera the night Maxine was going roller skating. They thought it would be good for her to get out and enjoy herself as long as Jack wasn't living with her anymore. Vera took her to the rink and said, "We hope you have a good time and you win first prize."

Maxine thanked her and went in to see if Jenny was there too, since they had talked about it earlier that day. She put on her mask, bought her ticket, and put on her skates, which were about worn out from so much use before she was married. Jack didn't like to roller skate so they never went. He couldn't do the dances and didn't like Maxine dancing with other guys. He just liked to skate fast around and around the rink. Excitement of just being back on roller skates filled her mind along with the joy of seeing her friends that came up to her and said how happy they were to see her after all the time that had passed. Goldie was still playing the organ and was also dressed up in a costume and was as friendly as ever. She announced the all skate, the waltzes, the tangos and that the judging would be at intermission time.

Skating in this long hooped-skirted dress wasn't the easiest thing to do, but "This is so much fun and it is so good to be here," Maxine thought as she glided over the hardwood floor, keeping in time to the music and she enjoyed every minute of it as she went around and around the rink. When the music stopped they all knew it was time for those wearing costumes to be judged. They would be listening for instructions to follow so they all vacated the skating area and waited.

"Please file one by one starting in front of the stage until all those in costumes are in line. Then, when Goldie starts the music, skate slowly around the rink until you are eliminated from the line. Those left skating will be the winners."

There were so many unusual costumes, it would be hard to pick a winner, but one by one they were eliminated until only three were left. Maxine was one of the three and she was so excited and prayerfully thinking, "Oh God, could I possibly get a prize?" The music stopped and the judges asked the three to step over to the table where they were. The third prize was presented, then the second prize and then they announced, "The first prize will go to Maxine because her costume is

74

so unique and so well made, especially to be able to roller skate in."

"My goodness!" she said.

The rest of the evening was so much fun, she had forgotten how much she loved to skate. The owners of the rink awarded her first prize and told her they would get the right size skates for her before the night was over so she could take them home with her. They sold skates and equipment in a little shop in front of the rink. Jenny and her friend were so happy for her; they congratulated her and told her they would take her home when she was ready to go.

Maxine didn't dare to stay too late because her breasts were filling up with milk and they would be leaking all over her dress. She had pumped some out before she left so Jackie would have some while she was gone. Arriving back at Dad and Vera's, she thanked Jenny's friend for the ride home and told Jenny to keep in touch with her, then she ran into the house showing off the roller skates she had won and telling them how much fun she had that evening. Vera was happy for her and said, "Maxine do you realize three of you won prizes with those costumes you designed?"

She answered, "That is right, and it was so much fun too."

Henry and Doris were expecting and they had a baby girl, Linda Sue. Doris had a hard time delivering her, and Henry asked Maxine if she would come over one day and help Doris, because her sister couldn't be there, and she said she would. Maxine bathed Linda and did some other chores around the house for Doris and they visited. When she had finished helping out that day, Henry took her and Jackie back home and thanked her for the help and for staying with Doris for the day.

November had come and it was about time for Maxine and Jack's first anniversary and here they were separated once again. "Will he decide to come back or not?" she wondered; it was hard to tell just what he would do. Late one evening he came over to the trailer and was very upset with Maxine. He had heard about the Halloween party at the roller rink and how she had won first prize. He said, "Grandma told me you went up in her attic and took that material without asking, is that right?"

She hung her head down and, with guilt and tears in her eyes, she confessed, "Yes, I did. You do what you want to do all the time why can't I? I am sorry, I know I shouldn't have taken it without asking."

Jack turned away and left without saying any more. Maxine sat down and cried and asked herself, "What have I done now? It seems like a roller coaster ride – happy for a while, then sad again, is this what marriage is all about?" She cried herself to sleep.

By this time Jackie was five months old and was sleeping all night without nursing and she rested well. Later in life, Maxine would wonder why she was so timid to Jack. After all, he had left her and she was nurturing his child and all he could be concerned about was his grandmother's material? He was probably just jealous that she acted independent of him and had won special recognition. Obviously, he wanted to control her from a distance. He wanted his cake and to eat it too. She learned later in life to never stand for that behavior from anybody and always advised people she saw acting timid like that to break the mold before it's too late. Jack always seemed to turn the blame on her instead of where it belonged, leaving her timid and constantly feeling guilty about how this whole thing happened.

Almost a week later Jack came over again and wanted to talk to her about coming back there to live if she would have him back. He said, "I don't want any other woman but you. I didn't know how much I would miss you and Jackie. Will you take me back?"

She answered (wise beyond her years), "We can't go on doing this to each other, so you will have to make up your mind what you want and stick to it. I need a few days to think it over."

He was surprised she didn't say yes right away and so told her over and over how much she meant to him. She let him know, "It has been lonely here without you, but leaving every time you have an urge for other women isn't worth having you back and not knowing when it will happen again."

She finally had the gumption to stand up to Jack and he gained a measure of respect for her, at least for the moment. What she didn't realize was how expertly Jack would play on her emotions and manipulate things to get what he wanted to satisfy his immediate needs.

Jack played with Jackie for a while and they talked about Thanksgiving coming up soon, wondering where they would each go to spend the day. He decided to leave and asked her, "I will call at Grandma's in

76

a couple of days to see whether or not you want me to come back, okay?" She agreed it would be all right, and they said goodnight.

"Decisions, decisions. I have to make this one again. Will he do it to me again?" she pondered over and over in her mind. Then as she was nursing Jackie, she looked at him and thought, "He needs a daddy and I need to forgive him. Maybe he will be contented and stay with us now." She had made up her mind by the time Jack had called. She told him, "It is alright for you to come back."

He appeared to be so happy. "I have my clothes packed and will be right over. I love you very much." It sure didn't take long for him to get there. This first year hadn't been easy for them, being so young and all, but now maybe they had learned more about each other's likes and dislikes, as well as being able to cope with them. Grandma was happy they were back together again and invited them in for dinner on Sunday to let them know she approved and it was for the best. Grandma Ort was a good Christian woman and she lived her faith.

As usual, there were many Thanksgiving dinners to attend: Dad and Vera's, Helen and Whitey's, and Maxine's mother's, so they had to start with one and end up in the evening with the last one, so full of turkey and dressing, plus all the trimmings. Vera even gave Jackie some mashed potatoes and gravy, and boy, did he like that. It was good to be with them once again and to catch up on all the news in the family. Of course, Jackie got full attention from everyone, being the first grandson, and loved every minute of it.

Spending winter in the little trailer wasn't too bad, with the radio programs to listen to like *Arthur Godfrey, The Breakfast Club, The Hit Parade* and country music. Also working on puzzles helped the time go by. Once a month on a Saturday night they went up to Dad and Vera's to play cards with Chet and Evelyn and Harvey and Ethel. It was fun and they all had a good sense of humor. Rosie and Sharon would watch Jackie and play with him; they were so good to him and he would let them do anything, like change his clothes, play peek-a-boo and teach how to crawl and pull himself up to the furniture. Coffee and dessert were served after the games and a lot of conversation between all of them, with jokes and laughter ringing throughout the house, until it was time for everyone to depart.

Kelsey Hayes Brake Plant was hiring, so Jack put in his application and was hired right away and it was within walking distance. He would be earning more money now and he was on the second shift from 3:00 p.m. until 11:30 p.m. Maxine spent a lot of time with Jackie playing with him and teaching him little things like getting up on the couch by himself and how to get back down without falling. She liked to make special things to eat and try new recipes. Sometimes they were flops; she cooked on a hot plate and used Grandma's oven for cakes and cookies. It seemed so good for Jack to get a good-sized paycheck and they could start saving for a car now that the doctor and hospital bill was finally paid. Hunting season was a good time for Jack to shoot some game to help keep the grocery cost down. Besides, the wild game was so good and healthy for them. Sometimes during the day Jack would watch out the window and wait for rats to run in and out of the chicken house, then he would slowly open the window and shoot them with his .22 rifle. This was good target practice for him.

Snuggled in their blankets and listening to the radio, Jack and Maxine talked about Christmas coming soon and how much they loved one another and wondering what the future would be for them. Jack would tell Maxine all about his hunting trips and how he saw the game and just how he shot. She loved listening to his stories. Jackie was a little over six months old by now and so much fun and still a happy little fellow. They would let him crawl in bed with them and play. Maxine would let him nurse in bed with her, but was always careful not to fall asleep and roll on him and she didn't think it was wise for him to sleep with them anyway. "Oh, how happy I am now and contented to be together," she said to herself, over and over.

Christmas Day was here and they had made arrangements to ride to church with Dad and Vera and the family, so they were ready when Dad picked them up. Everyone was dressed so nice and was full of holiday spirit. The little church was almost full of worshippers and the pastor greeted them all with a "Merry Christmas." His sermon was about God's gift to everyone, Jesus Christ His Son, and if they received Him into their hearts, He would wash away all their sins and they would have life everlasting. Jackie was restless and Maxine put her finger in his ear and rubbed it lightly for a while until he fell asleep. This was a way Maxine found to help calm and comfort him, especially when they were in public places. The lady sitting beside her looked amazed. When the service was over and after they talked to friends from around the neighborhood, they all went to Dad and Vera's.

Magnificent is a word that would explain the table setting and decorations that Vera had already arranged that morning. It looked like a picture in *House Beautiful* magazine. The ladies pitched in to finish preparing the food as the men sat around and talked while children played with their new toys. Such a happy day for all. Jackie was so surprised with all his toys, and he had mashed potatoes and gravy again for his dinner, Vera saw to that. It was such a joy to sit and relax after dinner with a cup of coffee and dessert, so many different kinds and so delicious. By this time Maxine was not as nervous being there and they kidded her about the first holiday she came to dinner with them and wouldn't even get up to go to the bathroom she was so shy. But now she was part of the family and blended in quite well.

Later, Maxine and Jack wanted to go down to Grandma Ort's house because Helen and Whitey were there for dinner and they would have Christmas gifts to exchange. Grandma Ort had been dating a man named Charlie Hicks and he also was there. This was the first chance they all had to meet him and get acquainted. It was hard for Jack to accept this, because he thought no one could take his Grandpa Ort's place and things would not be the same if Grandma married this man, which she announced they would be doing soon. Jack wouldn't have the freedom he had always been given at Grandma's home. It was getting late and they wanted to leave in order to put Jackie to bed as it had been a long day for all of them. They thanked everyone and bid everyone, "Happy Holidays." Of course, they didn't have far to go, just across the driveway to their little trailer.

New Year's Eve was a fun time at Dad and Vera's; they had a party for the card club members and a few of the neighbors to celebrate the coming of the New Year. They played cards plus other games throughout the evening with much joy and happiness amongst them all; young and old were there enjoying this evening just being together and fellowshiping. Maxine had never known or experienced anything like this and was so overwhelmed with the fun she was having, plus getting to know more of the friends of the family and neighbors. Many were drinking moderately and could handle themselves with dignity and respect to the others who chose not to drink alcohol. The evening went along with harmony and joy. When the clock struck twelve they kissed their partners and yelled "Happy New Year." It was now 1947, a new year for all to carry on with their lives and take steps in the right direction for their families, their jobs and for the country's future after the depression and the war years. It was a time of renewal and a new focus for the future.

CHAPTER NINE

ABANDONMENT

The winter of 1947 was really cold, but Maxine and Jack kept pretty warm and comfortable in the trailer. By February Jack was able to buy a car. It was a 1936 Ford, and boy that seemed so good to have their own transportation. To be able to go and come whenever they needed or wanted to was wonderful. One evening Jackie was very sick and he cried and cried and they were not able to calm him down, no matter what they did, so they took him up to see if Vera would know what to do. She walked and walked with him, then she rocked and rocked him but he wouldn't quit crying; they were up all night with him and Maxine decided she and Vera should take him to the doctor's in the morning as soon as he was in his office. Jack slept in because he stayed up late after work with them until he decided, "I better get some sleep and there isn't much I can do anyway."

The time arrived and they went in and waited in the waiting room, with Jackie still crying, then the nurse came out and asked Maxine to come in. She was surprised and said, "But it is Jackie that is sick, not me!" The nurse just said, "The doctor wants to see you."

Astonished, she went in and when the doctor said he wanted to examine her, she asked, "Why me?"

"You may be pregnant again and are poisoning Jackie's system with your milk and I want to find out."

She was surprised because she had been told she couldn't get pregnant while she was nursing. But, she learned that is just an old wives tale. This was another consequence of the lack of sexual education that Maxine experienced while she was growing up. She was sure to advise her own family and friends differently.

Doctor Meads explained "I believe you are pregnant, but I am going to fit you for a diaphragm anyway so after the birth of this new child you can start taking precautions to prevent any more children. These two will be very close in age. As for Jackie, you better put him on a bottle. As soon as he gets some nourishment he will be just fine. The nurse will come in and explain to you how to use the diaphragm and how to care for yourself, and I want to see you in another month from now." So, bewildered and scared, she said. "Okay."

Leaving the doctor's office Maxine explained to Vera what had gone on and what he had said to her. Vera, too, was surprised and said, "That makes sense, so we had better get this baby something to eat so he can get some rest along with the rest of us."

This, of course, was not good news for Jack. When he heard the news, he was very upset and asked, "What are we going to do with two children. We don't have room for one let alone two!"

Maxine replied, "Maybe I am not pregnant, we will have to wait and see, okay?"

Then, to make things worse, Jack was laid off at work and they wondered just what they would do. Maxine said, "What about me going to work? I heard Gilbert's Chocolate Factory is hiring help and I can work until you get called back."

"That is a good idea. I'll take you over there to put in your application."

It wasn't long before Maxine was called to go to work, and so she did. It was a job dipping chocolates. She took different kinds of fillings one at a time between her fingers, and she dipped them into a pan of melted chocolate. This seemed like fun to her. Day after day she went to work not knowing what kind of chocolates she would be dipping and it was another new experience for her. But, after she had been working for two or three weeks, she would get sick a couple of hours after she had arrived. She would have to go to the restroom because smelling the chocolate made her sick, she knew it was because of her pregnancy, but couldn't help it.

One morning she found a note on her time sheet that said, "Due to your condition, your employment is now terminated." In those days pregnant women were not allowed to work in factories, no law against it, just the custom of the time. She thought, "Oh my goodness what are we going to do now? Jack will be so upset, I have to call and tell Vera to go tell him to come and get me."

Sure enough he was upset and asked the same thing she had asked herself, "What in the world are we going to do now?"

The next day he called his mother and told her about the situation and he certainly didn't want another baby and she told him, "Go buy some quinine and give it to Maxine and maybe she will abort the baby." He did just as his mother had told him, then he told Maxine what to do because he didn't want any more children right now. Maxine, being gullible, and wanting to please him, took what he told her to take and her head started ringing and she felt very faint and would not take anymore. She thought, "Why am I doing this? This is not right, oh God help me." She was so scared and sorry for what she had done, thinking, "Why can't I be stronger and tell him no when he wants me to do dangerous things like this." This also caused her to have second thoughts about advice from Jack's mother, who would put her in such jeopardy, just to please Jack and his intentions.

The days went by, then the weeks and no sign of a menstrual period so they knew she was still pregnant in spite of the quinine. By this time Jack was called back to work at Kelsey Hayes and things seemed to be going okay until he started going out nights on the weekends drinking again and coming in late. This made Maxine very angry and one night after he had been gone for some time, she went into the garage where he kept his beer and took one, then grabbed a couple of empty bottles. She went into the trailer and took a couple of sips of beer so the smell would be on her breath, then poured the rest of it out and laid the empty bottles and caps she had found in the waste basket on the floor so when he came home he would think she had been drinking. Well, it worked, when he arrived home he was very upset and went out and got another bottle of beer and said, "Here, have some more!" Of course she refused and said, "No thank you, I have had enough." He never knew the truth of this until fifteen years later when she told him one day. He got a taste of his own medicine, which set him back on his heels, and showed him that Maxine had some backbone in her.

It wasn't very long after that he came home and said, "I want to leave again, so I can date other women, and I won't live with you while I do."

Maxine was shocked. It was hard to believe what he just said. She thought, "After all I have forgiven him for so many times, how can he betray me again?"

She answered him by saying, "Okay, but I want you to move this trailer over to my mother's house."

Jack agreed and made preparations to move the trailer, first checking with Maxine's mother to see if it was alright, and Mother said, "Yes, it will be alright with me if it is legal to move it here under city regulations," and it was.

This all happened the first part of June 1947. The sixth of June was Jackie's first birthday and so Maxine made plans to celebrate his birthday at Grandma Bohl's house and invite the neighbor, Fran Cooper's little girl, to come over and have cake and ice cream. It seemed so different being at her mother's. It didn't seem the same as it did when Maxine lived there, and it really wasn't because her mother had a boyfriend living with her. It made Maxine feel ashamed; she never thought her mother would live like that and not be married. Whenever he was there after work, Maxine wouldn't go in the house much. About the only time she did go in the house was when Jack would come over to visit Jackie, then she would leave them alone in the trailer because she didn't want to be around Jack. One time he said "You never used to be like this," and Maxine answered angrily, "You made me like this!" and she went into her mother's house. When he was ready to leave he let her know, so she could go back in the trailer to be with Jackie. Then she and Jackie would either go for a walk, with Maxine pushing Jackie in the stroller to get exercise and fresh air, or go over to Fran's house to visit because it was too nice to stay indoors.

Maxine's mother knew how unhappy she was and told her she should go and file for a divorce. So Maxine called a lawyer and made an appointment and went to see him. The day came to go see the lawyer; she put Jackie in his stroller and took the bus downtown. She thought, "Here I am pushing one child in a stroller and pregnant with another one, almost ready to be born, and I am only eighteen years old!" Arriving at the office, the secretary told Maxine the lawyer would be with her in just a few minutes. When she was told she could see the lawyer, she carefully got up (with a big tummy it wasn't easy to get up and down from a low couch) and pushed the stroller into the office. The lawyer asked, "What can I do for you?"

With tears falling down her cheeks she answered, "I want a divorce from my husband," And proceeded to tell him why.

He looked at her and said, "You have a child in a stroller and one almost ready to be born and from what you say, I believe you still love your husband. I don't think you really want a divorce, do you?"

Maxine answered tearfully, "No, I don't." He got up from his chair and put his arms around her and said, "Try to work it out if you can."

Then Maxine asked him, "How much do I owe you?"

"There will be no charge for this appointment," he answered. Maxine felt good to know that someone really knew how she was feeling and cared.

Jenny and Maxine were still close friends and they spent some time together going shopping, taking walks or just having girl talks. One day Jenny said, "I am going over to see a fortune teller, do you want to go with me? It isn't far from here and we can walk."

Maxine said, "Yes, I will go with you, I have never been to a fortune teller."

So Maxine asked her mother if she would baby-sit for Jackie while she went with Jennie, and Mother said she would. They walked four or five blocks and came to a large dark brown house on Pleasant Street and Jenny said, "This is it, let's go in."

Jenny had her fortune told and then the fortune teller asked Maxine, "Do you want your fortune told?" and Maxine answered, "Yes."

The fortune teller looked at Maxine's hand and said, "Your life line says you are going to have a little girl."

Maxine was so surprised to think she could tell her what her baby would be, and believed her, she then told her, "My husband left me, and I want to know if he will ever come back, I told the lawyer I don't believe in divorce and really didn't want one, because I do love him."

She answered, "He will be coming back to you soon."

On the way home Maxine told Jenny what she had said and asked Jenny "Do you believe what she tells you?"

"Yes, that is why I go to see her."

Eventually, a couple of months later, Jack begged Maxine to let him come back and live with her again and she kept saying "No" because of his past deeds and she didn't want to be hurt again. Every time he came over to see Jackie, at least once a week, he would beg and then go home unhappy because she turned him down. He would tell his parents, "I am really sorry for what I have done and I really do love Maxine and I want to make a go of our marriage, what shall I do?"

Dad and Vera talked it over and Dad told Jack, "If you can find a place to live I will help you get it by mortgaging our house."

So Jack looked in the classified ads for houses for sale and couldn't find anything that was in the price range that they could afford. Dad and Vera went over to see Maxine and talked to her about going back with Jack because they thought he was ready to settle down now and they would be willing to help get a home for her and the children. Maxine said she would try again if they thought he really meant it.

Then one day they found an ad in the paper about prefabricated homes and Jack called Maxine and asked, "Will you go with my folks and me to look at some homes? I want to provide a home for you and the children and I am ready to settle down with you." When they got there, Jack came in the trailer and told Maxine, "I am very sorry, will you forgive me?"

She answered in a stern voice "Yes, but don't you ever do it to me again!" Afterwards she was thinking, "If he is trying so hard to get a place for us, I should forgive him, I am sure that is what God would have me to do, He teaches to forgive seventy time seven." She was forgiving, but not forgetting.

The four of them went to see the prefabricated homes out on Lansing Avenue. They were very nice homes but a little too expensive. They did have a demo home already set up but it had to be moved. The businessman said he would sell it for one thousand dollars if they paid to have it moved, which he said would cost approximately two hundred dollars. It was twenty foot by twenty foot framed house with windows and a roof and could be moved with a permit. This was a good price so they decided to buy it and have it moved. Jack had already bought three acres of land about ten miles from Jackson on the Reynolds Road. The purchase price of the land was one thousand dollars with three hundred thirty-three dollars down so he could acquire a deed and abstract to a half an acre on the property to put the house on. The remaining payments were twenty-five dollars a month to be paid to the former owners, Mr. and Mrs. Dryer, who lived close by, so they didn't have far to go to pay every month.

After the arrangements for the purchase of the house and the movers to move it, Jack took Maxine out to see the property he had bought. It seemed like it was so far away, and she thought "My goodness, where is he taking me?" Maxine was a city girl and it was so different to be moving out in the country so far away from town, but she felt she was doing the right thing because they would be together as a family once again. They arrived and got out of the car and Jack explained to her where the house would be and they walked to the back of the property so he could show her how much land three acres included. Their house would sit right on the front half of the middle acre. There were only three or four houses scattered along the road near their land and a few others farther down the road toward the main highway, which was approximately two miles. On the way back home Maxine asked Jack, "How long before we will be able to move in the house?"

"I hope it will be ready by the time you get out of the hospital with the new baby in September."

Jack and his father began putting in the foundation for the house and had cleared some of the trees for a driveway. They worked hard and long hours, and it wasn't easy because they both had jobs besides. There was no water on the property yet and it was very hot. They dug a hole for the outside toilet and built one with two places to sit on, which came in handy many times later on.

Jack had moved back in the trailer with Maxine by now and they had made arrangements with Herman and Gale to take Jackie while Maxine was in the hospital. He was fifteen months old by this time, and Gale loved children. She never had any and was so happy they had asked her to take him.

On Labor Day weekend, Dad and Vera went on a camping trip with friends and asked Maxine and Jack to stay with their children. Before Vera left she kidded Maxine, "Now don't you to go to the hospital before I get back."

"Oh no, the baby isn't due for another week, there is plenty of time," Maxine said. Everything was going well until Sunday evening when Maxine's water broke and she told Jack "We better go home."

They found someone to stay with the children and left with Jackie to go back to the trailer. Jack went to bed but Maxine couldn't sleep because the contractions were getting closer. She had to wake him up to tell him it was time to go to the hospital, it was 11:00 p.m. and he said, "Is it time to go to work already?"

"No, I need to go to the hospital now!" Maxine went into her mother's house for her to take Jackie so Herman and Gale could pick him up in the morning after Mother called them. It was a good thing the hospital was close because a baby boy was born at 12:01 a.m. Monday, September 1, Labor Day 1947. He was ready to come into this world, now! Maxine's brother Harold's birthday was September 1, also.

The first thing Maxine said to Jack after she was clearheaded and the ether had worn off was, "Now I can really get close to you," because he didn't like her to lay against him with the big belly, feeling the baby bothered him. Maxine told Jack it was his turn to name the baby and he said, "We will name him Leroy."

"Well," Jack's dad said, "I do not like that name," and frankly Maxine didn't like it either.

So, Jack told his dad, "Well, you name him then!"

And Dad said, "I will, it will be Daniel Darwin."

Maxine agreed that would be just fine. She stayed in the hospital for ten days and promised the doctor she would go to Vera's and stay another four days in bed, this was also a wish that Vera had so she could help take care of her and Danny.

Herman and Gale brought Jackie to see Maxine; he was now potty trained at fifteen months old because she didn't want two children in diapers at the same time. His vocabulary was so good for his age and he asked Vera, "Where is my mommy?"

"She's in Grandma's bedroom."

He went running into Vera's bedroom and saw Maxine in bed and stopped, put his hands on his hips and asked her, "What are you doing in bed, Mommy?" then he jumped up on the bed and hugged her and said, "I miss you Mommy."

"I miss you too, Jackie, but we will be together again now. You have a new baby brother."

Herman and Gale came in to see Maxine and the baby and she

thanked them for all they had done for her and Jack, and Gale said "I had so much fun with him it will be hard to leave him because I will miss him so much."

Jackie had a wonderful time with all his aunts and uncles. He was a very obedient child and very easy to get along with. They treated him like a little prince while Maxine was fulfilling her stay in bed as she had promised the doctor. Vera was like an angel, she helped in so many ways and was so supportive just like a second mom. Caring for Maxine and Danny was right up her alley, her love overflowed toward everyone. Daniel was doing well; he was nursing well and was gaining weight like he should. Rosie and Sharon were interested in watching Danny get his bath and after that they would put him in the buggy and push him around the house until he fell asleep.

Jack had sold the trailer for seventy-five dollars and had moved their belongings out to the new residence. When Danny was two weeks old, Jack wanted to go out to the house on Reynolds Road to live. There was no water, no electricity, no phone, and no inside plumbing. There was an old icebox to keep the food cold and just a shell of a house with sub-flooring and studs and no ceiling, either. But they moved anyway. Eventually Dad came out and helped put sheetrock up on the ceiling with insulation above and on the sidewalls to help keep some of the cold out. Kerosene lanterns were the source of light and a three-burner pressure camp stove was used for cooking with a small separate oven Vera had given them to bake in that fit on top of the stove. Jack would stop daily at the schoolhouse on the corner of Reynolds Road and M-60 to pump fresh water for drinking. He used an old water heater he filled at his dad's for laundry, dishes and baths. Every few days, he would take the back seat out of the car and lay the water heater down and fill it, then bring it home and back the car up to the back door and slide it in the kitchen and put it on cement blocks so they had "running" water. Maxine would heat the wash water on the stove and fill a number three tub to wash in, scrubbing on a wash board, wringing the clothes out by hand, rinsing them and wringing them out once again and then hanging them on the outside clotheslines to dry. In the winter the clothes would freeze and she would bring them in the house and put them on a wooden clothes rack to finish drying. Oh, how clean and fresh they smelled from the fresh winter air!

Whenever Maxine would begin to think negative thoughts or start feeling sorry for herself, she would think, "My mother had seven children and I have only two." So she would work that much harder because she loved her family so much and it didn't seem like a chore but rather something she was doing for her family's welfare. Even mopping the living room floor was a challenge. There were cracks between the boards and the water would drain down too fast. She used many pails of water before she was done. They had put blankets up on the studs that divided the bedroom from the rest of the house for privacy. Maxine told their friends, kidding them, "We have three rooms and a path," which they did. "And we live between the Gilberts and the Ryersons," both of which were millionaires: Ryersons a mile and a half north of them and the Gilberts a mile and a half south of them

The first Christmas in their new home was an unforgettable one. Maxine had been making some pretty aprons for the female relatives because they couldn't afford to buy gifts. Jack had been laid off again and money was tight. One evening Jack came home with a beautiful Christmas tree and didn't tell Maxine where he got it and they decorated it with ornaments that were given to them, plus they made and strung some popcorn also. When they finished and went to bed, Jack couldn't sleep. He tossed and turned and finally got up and started to take the tree down and Maxine asked, "What in the world are you doing?"

He answered, "I couldn't sleep thinking what I have done, I stole this tree, I cut it down from Ryersons property, that is stealing and we are supposed to be celebrating Jesus' Birthday, He is the Way, the Light and the Truth and I can't keep this tree knowing that this is wrong."

The next morning he took the tree in town and told his dad what he had done and Dad said, "There is no use of it going to waste I will take it, we haven't bought our tree yet." And he gave Jack the money to buy a tree so he could have one to put up in their house. Maxine was very happy when Jack came home with another tree and told her what his dad had done for them. Seriously thinking it over in her mind, she thought, "What a surprise! With the seriousness of Jack's sins in leaving me and lying with other women, and here he is losing sleep over a tree taken off private property that the Ryerson's will never discover having been cut. Jack's moral compass sure has a funny tilt and his dad's attitude, too, about this whole thing."

She was making Jackie a new coat from material she had cut out of an old coat someone had given her. She realized how much she had learned in her sewing classes at school and how handy it was to know how to make things and be creative.

During hunting season Jack would go hunting so they could have meat to eat: rabbits, pheasants and squirrels, which they were so thankful for. Maxine learned how to help Jack clean the game and she learned how to cook the game several different ways so they wouldn't get tired of it. Sometimes he would invite his friends out to go hunting with him and they would bring their wives along to visit with Maxine and she usually asked them to stay for a meal. The guys would talk about the day's hunting experiences while the ladies cooked and did the dishes. Maxine would stir up a cake from scratch and bake it in the camp stove oven, so after they played cards that evening she could serve coffee and cake before the company went home. Other times, Maxine's sister Clara and her husband Jim would come out and Jim and Jack would go cut wood all day for the stove and then in the evening eat dinner and play cards to pass the time away.

Maxine was still nursing Danny and this game was good nourishment for him as well as for her, and she always had plenty of milk to keep him satisfied. He was a good baby, too. Jackie wanted to help, so he would go get diapers for her and would talk to Danny when he was in his crib, keeping him company. During the day, the house was plenty warm and at bedtime they would put lots of coal in the stove and the stove pipe would turn red hot, but by morning there was usually ice in the water bucket. But it didn't take long to warm up once they started the fire. Jack tried to save money, so he took a trailer in town about every other week to get a trailer load of coal. He saved a five-dollar delivery fee by getting it himself; that was a lot of money in those days. One day he was bringing some coal home and the tongue of the trailer broke and the trailer went flying down a hill and coal went all over and he had to go back and pick it all up. From then on he had it delivered.

One day in the spring they smelled a skunk and Jack drove down the road until he found it. It was road kill and he put it in a gunny bag, tied it to the bumper of the car and they took it into town to sell the hide. It was so funny to see the look on the people's faces when they drove by. Jack received ten dollars for the hide but the smell stayed on the car until they washed it at Dad's house, and he wasn't too happy with that.

One time on the way back home from the folks, Maxine started to nurse Danny and Jackie was standing in the seat between Jack and her (this was a long time before they ever had car seats for children) and Jackie leaned over Maxine's shoulder and said, "Me want a bite too, Mommy."

They just chuckled as she told Jackie, "You are a big boy now and Danny is a little baby, you used to have some when you were a baby."

"Okay, Mommy," Jackie said.

The old Ford wouldn't start very good during the winter and Maxine would help Jack push the car in order for it to start. It was standard shift and was easy to push. Then when the winter months had gone by and the springtime thaw brought muddy roads and the cars couldn't get through the mud, Jack would have to leave the car on a solid place and walk home with the water pail and whatever groceries he could carry. Eventually the road was passable and things went back to normal. Jack was thankful for that because he worked the second shift and had to walk home about a mile in the dark. As soon as the road was dried out and the cars could drive on it, they decided to have the electricity hooked up and Jack built a back room on for some storage, coats and boots. Dad said they had better put up the rest of the sheetrock on the sidewalls and partitions before next winter. So when they finally got that all done, Jack and Maxine painted it and then put down some linoleum on the floors. It looked so nice and was so much easier to keep clean, and they had electric lights, besides. And how happy and thankful Maxine was that she had decided to take Jack back and try to make a go of it once again. Because now she and the children were living in better conditions than she was in that little trailer outside her mother's house.

May was about over and Danny was nine months old and still nursing, when one day Maxine didn't think he had eaten enough and tried to give him more and he opened his little mouth and shut it quickly

92

and bit her, and she reacted so fast by slapping him and thought, "Oh my goodness, I had better put him on a cup." He had been drinking water and juice from a cup anyway and he was too old to be put on a bottle now. It was a good thing this happened because Jack got laid off from work from Kelsey Hayes and they decided that Maxine would go in to get a job until he got called back to work, because they had a mortgage to pay. She answered an ad for a waitress job at a restaurant downtown in Jackson and they hired her; she worked the second shift and Jack had to drive her back and forth to work because she didn't know how to drive. Jack did the laundry, helped out with the chores and watched the children while Maxine worked until he got called back to his job, approximately three months, then she quit her job and stayed home.

Grandma Ort decided to cash in a paid-up insurance policy for two hundred dollars she had on Jack. With that and a hundred and fifty dollars more, they could get a well dug and at least have water there at the house. This they did that summer and, boy, it was great even if they had to hand-pump all of the water they used. It was fresh water from one hundred thirty-five feet deep. Maxine would pump the water for washing at night and get up early in the morning to put it on an electric heater, and then she would go back to bed until the water was warm enough to do the laundry. In the summer Jack bought a fifty-pound chunk of ice for the icebox and put it on bumper of the car, but by the time he arrived home it had melted almost in half.

CHAPTER TEN
YEARS OF ENDEARMENT

With each of the challenges that came, it seemed like this family was taking them one at a time as they could afford them, such as the electricity, the water, the wood and coal for the stove, the insulation and sheetrock, then the linoleum for the floors – each one a step forward to make their home more comfortable to live in. So now it was time to buy a new stove to cook on, she was still using the three-burner camp stove all these months. So Jack ordered one from the Spiegel Catalog Company and when it arrived they were so happy. It was a bottle-gas stove and it was so nice to just turn on the burner without pumping up the gas tank, like Maxine had to do on the old camp stove. When this was paid for, they went to Sears and Roebuck and bought a new refrigerator. It had ice cubes, modern food-saver and vegetable drawers and was easy to keep clean. Maxine kept these appliances clean and shiny because she was so grateful for them and had gone without for so long. Another giant step was when Jack decided to do away with the coal stove and get a fuel-oil stove to heat the house with; it was much cleaner and there were no ashes to clean up, thank goodness.

Sharon Kay was born to Clara and Jim on January 22, 1949, and Clara wanted to go back to work in Jackson. They had moved to Lansing and she didn't want to drive back and forth every day so she decided to live with their mother, Hazel Bohl, and have Maxine baby-sit for Sharon Kay from Sunday night until Friday night. Clara would then pick Sharon Kay up from Maxine and drive back to Lansing for the weekend. This went on for two years and Maxine became so attached to her. Sharon had asthma bad in the winter and Maxine would sit up with her all night so she could sleep on her shoulder. Maxine called her 'Wiffett' because she was so small and petite. Jack realized how much Maxine was getting attached to Sharon and he asked Clara and Jim if he and Maxine could adopt Sharon and, of course, they said no. So Jack told them they would have to find someone else to care for her because Maxine was getting to love her too much. Maxine was very upset and cried; she knew she would miss Sharon. Again she was too submissive to Jack's unreasonable demands and had to be the one who gave up something she enjoyed doing. It wasn't that far over to Lansing to go see them, only about forty miles, so whenever the weather was good, Maxine, Jack and the family would drive over to visit. During the deer-hunting season Clara and Jim would let Jack and Danny stay with them so Maxine could go deer hunting with Jack. One hunting season, Jack was laid off so he decided to go deer hunting up to Gladwin, but he had to go back to Jackson to sign up for his unemployment check. They planned on getting up early in the morning in order to make it back on time. They were sleeping in a tent on the car seats he had taken out of the car and when the alarm went off, they got up and lit the Coleman lantern and looked at each other and about died laughing. The kerosene stove had smoked all night and they were all black except the white of their eyes showing through. It was a good thing they had set the alarm or otherwise they may have never awakened. They cleaned up the best they could and gathered up all their clothes and blankets so they could wash them while they were in Jackson. Oh, what a mess, but thank God for Vera's washing machine and the bathtub. They went back up north for a few days to hunt some more, but didn't get any deer. Maxine liked to go out in the woods with Jack to walk and just sit and wait to see if they could spot any deer for Jack to shoot.

So many things could be done to help with the grocery bill and Jack was good at finding ways to help, especially during the seasons when he couldn't go hunting and shoot rabbits, squirrel and pheasants to eat. So he built a shed so he could raise rabbits to sell and for them to eat also. Then the next year he would raise chickens to eat; he would wring their necks and Maxine helped pluck the feathers off. They dipped the chickens in scalding hot water and that would help loosen the feathers. This city gal was becoming quite a country gal by now, and was learning so many new ways she had never known before. They plowed some ground for a garden and raised corn, potatoes, peas, green beans, squash, tomatoes, cucumbers, onions and radishes. These were so good to eat and Maxine froze some of the vegetables for further use and cut down on the cost of groceries.

Their dogs loved to run around the yard and play; Blackie was a cocker spaniel given to Jack by his dad, because they lived in the city and didn't want to tie him up all the time. He adjusted very well because he liked to hunt pheasants with Jack. Rusty was a basset hound given to Maxine by Jenny's brother Billy one day while she was in town to see her mother. He brought it over to show Maxine and said he was giving it away and Maxine said, "I will take him, my husband wanted a hound dog to hunt rabbits. He had one when we lived at Grandma Ort's and he died, his name was Tequila." Jack was so happy to see the dog and so were the boys. He named him Rusty, and as he grew he became a good rabbit dog. Both dogs were the happiest whenever Jack would take them hunting. The family enjoyed many rabbit and pheasant meals because of those faithful dogs.

Early one spring Rusty came up missing for a couple of days and they couldn't figure where he was. Then one morning Maxine looked out the front window and saw Rusty inching his way across the yard on his stomach. She ran outside and looked at him and saw he had been shot with shotgun pellets all up and down his side. Jack called the veterinarian who told Jack to wash the wounds with Epsom salts and keep him quiet. So Maxine cleansed him well and sat up with him all night watching and waiting patiently. He just lay there hardly moving or opening his eyes for about a week, it was so sad. Maxine got an idea to lay him on the table beside the window so he could look outdoors, and she did. Eventually he raised his head up, then he sat up and showed some life and it wasn't long before he was up and back to normal. Later they found out that one of the neighbors down the road had chickens and a dog had been getting in the chicken coop and killing some of their chickens. When they saw Rusty out by the chicken coop they shot him. From then on Rusty was tied up most of the time except when he was hunting or in the house at night.

Dad and Vera bought a new washing machine and gave their old one to Maxine. It was a wringer washer, and that was great because she didn't have to wring all those clothes out by hand anymore and it was electric too, plus they bought double rinse tubs for rinsing.

Maxine was happy with her life and family to take care of, things were going really well. Jack would come home after work and they would sit and have coffee and dessert, whatever she had baked that week, cookies, pie or cake, then he would get his gun and go hunting. Whenever he clicked the shell up into the magazine of the gun Rusty would hear it and start to bark, getting so excited about going hunting. Jack loved to tease him.

Jackie liked to play outside, but he wouldn't stay out of the road. He was about three and half years old by this time and Maxine tried every kind of punishment for a little boy, her hand on the bottom, a little stick on the legs, a pancake turner on the bottom, but he still insisted on going to the road. The cars would go by so fast and they would never see a little boy, let alone have time to stop before they hit him. Maxine surely didn't want anything to happen to him so she thought and thought, "What am I going to do? I know he wants to play outside. Oh, I know, I will buy a harness and hook him up on the clothesline." The next time she went shopping she bought a harness and a leash and when he wanted to go outside she put it on him and took his toys and him out to the clothesline and hooked him up. He sure didn't like it very much, but she explained to him why he had to be there. "Jackie you keep going in the road and Mamma don't want you to get run over by the cars, because I love you," she said.

Well, on the third day she took him and his toys out to the line to tie him up and he looked up at her with tears in his eyes and said, "Me no go in the road no more, Mamma," and he never did. Thank God for giving her the wisdom to know what to do to teach him. The neighbors thought she was cruel, but Maxine loved her son enough to prevent anything from happening to him and he did learn a lesson.

Jack had been trying to teach Maxine how to drive their 1936 Ford, but she honestly didn't want to learn to drive because she wanted to depend on him. This was her natural tendency to yield to his leading the family, which had its drawbacks as time went on. He insisted, though, and she in time was thankful he did. She wasn't very coordinated at first until she got the hang of it. The car was a stick shift and the brakes weren't very good either. Whenever they would go up north hunting, Jack would let Maxine drive so she could get some practice. After a time, she decided that she did like to drive. When Jack got laid off and Maxine had to go back to work, she was able to drive to and from work. She went back to work for Art Dolan at the Burger King, located in the Greyhound Bus Station, in Jackson. She met Martha Ruggles, another waitress, and a few years later Martha and her husband became some of Jack and Maxine's best friends. Mr. Dolan had three restaurants in town and Maxine would work wherever he wanted her to, he was a very kind and a good man, and understood whenever Jack wanted her to stay home.

Once in a while Jack would go into town and get Maxine's Grandpa Wheeler to go hunting with him because he knew how much Grandpa liked to hunt. He was eighty-five years old but was in good health. He told Jack he used to walk from Jackson along the railroad tracks to Reynolds Road to go hunting many times when he was younger. Grandpa was such a gentle man; he was six feet three inches tall, a big man, yet so kind. Grandma Wheeler was only four feet eleven inches tall, but she was the spitfire in the family.

Realizing Maxine had been driving for quite some time without a driver's license, Jack told Maxine they should go into Jackson and get one before she was stopped and found without a license. So they drove up to the sheriff's office, beside Field's Department Store on Jackson Street, and went in. The sheriff was sitting behind the desk asked, "May I help you?"

"I am here to get a driver's license."

The sheriff looked at Maxine and asked, "How long have you been driving?"

"For about two years, off and on, going up north on camping and hunting trips."

The sheriff looked at Jack and asked him, "Is she a good driver?"

Jack replied, "She sure is, a very good driver."

The sheriff said "Okay," and issued her a driver's license. Maxine was shocked, she didn't even have to take the sheriff on a road test because he believed if a husband says his wife can drive that is all the proof he needs. That was the custom in those days, husband authority. The wife submitted herself to her husband's wishes and followed his lead. As they left the building Maxine thanked Jack for telling the sheriff she was a good driver and said, "I was so scared to take him for a driver's test, thanks so much."

Jackie was going to school now and he walked to the little red schoolhouse up on Reynolds Road and Horton Road. It was about a mile or so from home. The teacher taught kindergarten through the sixth grades, she fixed the wood stove in the mornings to keep it warm, shoveled the snow off the sidewalks, did the janitorial work and all that was required of a teacher at that time. Some of the parents got together and formed a parent's club to raise money for things the school needed, like bookshelves and playground equipment. They had special dinners and garage-type sales. At one of the dinners a lady came up to Maxine and asked "Do you remember me?"

Maxine said "You look familiar, but I can't remember."

"I am Virginia Rainey, I was in the hospital for my son the same time you were there with your son Jack."

Maxine was so surprised, she said, "Oh my goodness! I am so glad you recognized me and spoke. I remember how much fun we had in the hospital and could never understand why that other woman would never make over her baby. Do you live around here?"

Virginia answered, "Yes, just across Horton Road up Reynolds Road one block. Isn't it ironic, our boys are going to school together?" Maxine and Virginia continued to be good friends from then on.

The teacher had scheduled a Christmas program for the parents to attend in the evening and so the Mother's Club planned a party afterwards. The children had sung their last Christmas song and the front door opened and there was a loud, "HO! HO! HO! MERRY CHRISTMAS" and Santa came walking down the aisle and Jackie said out loud, "That is my Uncle Herman!" Everyone just laughed, he wasn't fooled one bit. It was a good party and everyone had such a good time and a happy spirit. On the way home Jackie said, "Mamma I knew who that was, didn't I?" Uncle Herman was impressed that he couldn't get away with it with Jackie.

Jack had been saving U.S. Saving Bonds and decided there was enough money in them to add on to the house so they would have more room. He called Tom Robinson & Sons to dig a basement with a backhoe and then ordered cement blocks for the walls. As Jack laid the blocks, Maxine mixed the mortar to go in between; she mixed this in the same square box that they watched the baby ducks swim in at Grandma Ort's.

When the walls were done they got an electric cement mixer and poured the floor in the basement. They mixed the cement with sand that they had delivered and they pumped the water to mix it with. It was not an easy job but they were young and needed to keep costs down. This was about 1950 or 1951. Jack purchased some used lumber to help cut the cost and Maxine removed the nails during the day so he would have it to work with in the evening after work. Maxine helped as much as she could and Jack worked hard to get it done, some of their friends came over and helped with the rafters. Dad came out on weekends and helped, also, until it was finally done so they could sheetrock the inside and put down the hardwood flooring. Jack showed Maxine how to lay the flooring and she did it during the day when he was at work. She did hit her thumb many times with the hammer, but realized it was worth it to have such a beautiful floor. It was so nice to have so much more room and a basement with an oil furnace heating the whole house.

The daily routine was one Maxine tried to keep so she could spend the weekends with her family without doing housework. One spring day she was doing the washing and Jackie came home with some pennies and she asked him, "Where did you get these pennies?" and he said, "I found them." Maxine didn't believe him; she had seen a man drop him off in the driveway that day and thought he had probably given them to him and wondered why. She kept asking him and he answered the same every time. So she dropped it, but still the question filled her thoughts. On Fridays, Maxine would go pick Jackie up at school and go in town to get Jack's check to pay the bills and get groceries, so she was in town this Friday and she heard Jackie say to Danny, "If I tell you where I got the pennies, don't tell Mamma, okay?" Danny replied, "I won't."

Maxine was surprised and stopped the car and pulled over to the curb and turned around and said to Jackie, "You tell me right now where you got those pennies or you will get spanked!"

So he lowered his head and said, "That man who brought me home the other day gave them to me and told me not to tell anybody."

Maxine said "Why did he give them to you?"

Jackie said, "I was in the back seat and Patty Hemminger was in front with the man and he told me not to look, but I did and he did something bad to her, and I am afraid he will hurt me."

Maxine was totally shocked and decided to go back out to see Patty's parents and tell them. She was so upset all the way back out there. Thank God they were home.

Maxine told Mrs. Hemminger she had better have Patty examined because of what had happened and they should report it to the police. They did report it and the police did not have anything to go on except what the children had said, so it was in limbo so to speak, until one day when Maxine was doing the laundry. She was pumping water when Jackie came running in the yard and yelled out, "Mamma there goes that man, he tried to pick me and Suzie Miller up and I ran into the cornfield like you told me to and I told Suzie to come too."

The neighbors were in their yard and Maxine yelled, "Go after that man and get his license number NOW!" and Pete Lawrence took off in a hurry without any questions why. He returned with the license plate number a few minutes later, and Maxine explained the situation and he said he was happy to help. Now Maxine had something to go to the police with so she went to the neighbor's and called the police and gave them the license number.

The next day a detective came out and asked Maxine to gather up Patty, Suzie and Jackie to look at a mug book of sexual offenders. When he laid the book on the table, with the three children standing around him, he turned the pages one by one until all at once they pointed to the same man and said, "That's him!" The detective read the caption under the man's name and said, "He has been charged with this same crime before and he lives on Reynolds Road about three miles up from here. Now we have something to go by when we take him to court. We will notify you all when there is a hearing." They did notify the families of the children involved and the date for them to appear in court.

They had picked the man up and arrested him. He was out on bond, and he appeared in court. After the formal beginnings, his lawyer called Jackie to the witness stand and began to question him about what had happened and what day it was, and so on. He tried to confuse him about what day Thanksgiving fell on, as if a five year old would know. The lawyer kept questioning about the day, why he didn't know what day it was, then the prosecutor questioned Jackie with simpler questions he could answer. Then Maxine was called to the witness stand to testify and the lawyer asked her which day it was when Jackie came home with the pennies, and she said, "Either on Monday or Tuesday, if it rained on Monday I washed on Tuesday." He kept asking over and over the same question and by now she was getting pretty upset, thinking, "You may confuse my little son, but you are not going to pin me down on a certain day." He knew this man had an excuse for one of those days because he had attended a funeral, but the lawyer was trying to get a definite answer out of Maxine, and she wouldn't commit to a certain day. He hammered more questions about the day she had Pete follow the suspect and get his license number, was that a Monday or a Tuesday? Maxine looked at him and asked with a stern voice, "Do you remember which day you took your bath that week?" and the whole courtroom laughed, even the judge.

In the closing arguments the prosecutor said, "Like Mrs. Derr said, do you remember which day you took your bath that week." The sex pervert was found guilty.

Summer was here and Jack had dug a hole for a septic tank and drain field so they could have indoor plumbing, running water, an inside toilet and a bathtub. No more pumping wash water and dumping it out by buckets every washday. What an improvement when it was done. They were now living a modern lifestyle. It was so much easier for Maxine to keep the house clean and enjoy doing it. They had bought their first television set and enjoyed watching the shows in the evenings together, then when they could afford more materials, they put knotty-pine wood paneling on the living room walls and ceiling and in the entranceway, plus white and blue tiling on the kitchen and bathroom floors which made it so much easier to mop and keep clean. The kitchen cupboards were nice to keep the dishes and pans in, although they did not have doors on yet. Winter had passed by quickly and it was now spring of 1953.

Kelsey Hayes was finally hiring the wives of those who already had worked there and Jack had told Maxine about it and she asked him, "Can I go to work there? We need shingles on the roof, some siding and the cupboards finished and my working will help so you don't have to work so hard and long to get them finished."

"Okay, go in and put your application in," he answered.

Maxine was hired and was put on the second shift to work, which made it nice because Jack worked the morning shift and that way they didn't have to hire a baby-sitter for the boys. She started to work at the shop on April 7, on an assembly line putting brake cylinders on wheels. It was hard at first until she was finally able to keep up with the line. On the third day she was working, the foreman came to her and said someone wanted to see her at the front office; she was startled and worried, "Has something happened to one of my children?" All the way there she just couldn't imagine what it was or who wanted her. When she arrived at the office, she saw her brother Harold and his wife Jeanne and they said, "Corky is dead. He was killed by a train in Leoni." Maxine was so shocked, he would have been twenty-one years old in May and he had just been married on News Year's Eve. Harold explained, "On his way home from work, Corky was delivering some dry cleaning and he stopped at the railroad crossing, the train was coming around the bend and didn't blow the whistle. By that time Corky, had already started across the tracks and the train hit his car and pushed it about a quarter of a mile down the tracks."

Maxine went back in and told the foreman and he said, "You can leave now if you want to, I will explain to the boss." She went over to her mother's to see her and Mother was crushed. He was her youngest child and he looked after Mother and did so much for her. Even after he was married, he stopped every night after work to see if she needed anything before he went home. Henry, Herman, Harold and Clara were there and the guys decided to go see the car at the service station that had picked up his car off the tracks. When they got there, they found his wife searching through the wrecked car looking for his bankbook. When she found it, she saw that Corky had not put the account in her name yet and she got very upset.

After everyone left Mom's house, Maxine stayed with her for a couple of days to comfort her. After the funeral, Mother said, "I will be alright now, you need to go home to your family and go back to work." After some time had passed, the railroad company offered Corkey's wife some money for a settlement and she took it and the family never heard from her again. It was told to Herman that she married her first husband again.

The enjoyment of working, meeting new people, and knowing they would have the money to finish their home was a spiritual uplift to Maxine. She was able to be at home to send the boys off to school in the morning and get her household chores done in time before she had to go to work. One of the neighbors, Chuck Essex, worked the second shift. He and his wife, Marquitta, and their children lived in a basement house. They were also trying to do the best they could to build and provide for their family. Maxine rode back and forth to work with Chuck until she was able to bid on the first shift and get that position. They hired a high-school girl to come in the morning to help the boys get ready for school and see that they got on the bus. Jack and Maxine rode back and forth to work together now and arrived home just before the school bus brought the boys home from school. This worked out very well because the family was all together in the evenings and a routine was established with meals, doing homework, watching television and bedtime.

Chapter Eleven
Enjoying Life Fully

Summers were hot and humid in Michigan and Jack decided to buy a speed boat and motor, one he could pull water skis with so when they went camping they could learn how to water-ski as well as go fishing. Jack taught Maxine how to run the boat so she could pull him on the skis. The boys liked the boat and they wanted to learn how to water-ski, too. It was easy pulling them up, they learned how to come up out of the water in a hurry. Jack told Maxine, "It is time for you to learn how to ski." So she put on the life jacket, got in the water, and put on the skis. Holding the rope attached to the boat, she leaned back with the skis pointed out of the water and motioned Jack to go. Well, she didn't get up, but hung on to the rope and was dragged around by the boat. This happened several times; she tried and tried and could not get up. The problem was she wouldn't let go of the rope, so it dragged her as she went blumpty-blump up and down in the water. She tried hard and finally she gave up.

A week or so later they went on a camping trip up north to Lake Mitchell campgrounds with friends, the Millers and Fran and Kay Robinson. Arriving at the campgrounds, they all set up their tents and fixed a lunch and talked about taking the boat across the lake to the town of Cadillac to do some looking around. Jack said he wanted to stay there at the campground. Maxine knew why he didn't want to go; he wanted to be intimate with her without so many others around. The others left in the boat and Jack and Maxine went into the pitch-black tent. Maxine found her suitcase so she could get the gel for her diaphragm and instead of the gel, she grabbed the toothpaste and squeezed the tube. She smelled it and told Jack what she had done. He just roared with laughter and Maxine said, "Please don't tell the others what I did." Well, he couldn't wait until the others got back to the campground to tell them. They sure got a big laugh out of that one, and from then on every once in a while Mike Miller would remind Maxine of it by saying, "Oh, the toothpaste." It seemed like things like this embarrassed Maxine so much, especially when they made fun of her. Other than that she had such a good time on that trip because she finally learned how to ski on the first try the next day. That made her feel like she had accomplished something she had tried so hard to do and failed before.

Many times after work they would go home and pack a picnic lunch and go to the lake. It was a family activity and they all liked to ski. By this time they could all ski on one ski and jump the wakes; Maxine could ski on one ski, put her other foot out in front of her and hold the toe rope on her foot, holding her hands up in the air. Also, while on one ski, she put her other leg out in back of her raised up as she bent forward holding the rope with one hand, like a swan-dive position. For someone who took so long to learn how to get up on skis, she became quite a skier. Jack was very good also, he liked to go fast and jump the waves as high as he could, swaying back and forth across them. Other times, they both would ski at the same time whenever they could get someone else to run the boat for them.

Life seemed to be such a joy doing family things together and being able to have enough money to do it. It had been many years of hard work and sacrifice for this family and now some pleasure had come into their lives that they all could enjoy together.

Cold weather began to set in, so boating and picnics were now out of the question. Besides, the boys were back in school with homework to do and early bed times. On Saturday nights Maxine and Jack would hire a baby-sitter and would go out dancing alone or with Mike and Lillian Miller. They all loved to dance and listen to the music and spend time with adults sharing conversation and ideas. Jack had been working with Jim Linsday at the shop and invited him out to the house to go hunting with him. Maxine recognized him as a neighbor she had known when she was a kid on Bates Street before she was married. "It is a small world," she thought when they both recognized each other. A couple of weeks later when he brought his wife out to visit, it was Martha Ruggles, who Maxine had worked with at the Burger King a few years before. Martha said she also had lived on Bates Street as a child and she had gone to school with Maxine's sister Clara. Jim and Martha would also go dancing with them once in a while on Saturday nights. They became good friends from then on and visited each other to play cards and socialize.

Maxine and Jack decided to have a costume Halloween party and to invite their friends, so she sent out invitations, bought supplies and made up games to play. "Scavenger hunt would be fun," she thought, so she made a list of ten different items that would be hard to get, especially out in the country where the homes were so far apart. The night arrived and so did the guests in their unusual costumes, in which some were hard to identify. When they had all arrived they were instructed about the scavenger hunt and they were to go out in carloads of four, still with their costumes on and whoever got back with the most completed list would be the winners. Some of the items on the list were: a horse blanket pin, an old calendar (the oldest one won), an empty thread spool, a paper clip, a used flypaper hanger, a burnt-out light bulb, a large rubber band, and a woman's hairpin. Not all of the groups found their ten items, although it took a while to find the things they did. One carload was invited into a house where a lady had just baked fresh bread and shared it with them while she looked for some of the items on the list. Those country folks who were approached by the participants were so good about trying to find whatever they could on the list. Mike Miller went in the Horton Tavern and took a flypaper hanger off the ceiling and told them he needed it for the scavenger hunt, and that was the only one of those that was found that night.

After they had all returned back at the house, Maxine asked them to tie balloons on their back side and instructed each couple to keep bumping into each other until the balloon broke, they all agreed to do it. They laughed and had such fun. It was especially fun to watch Jackie and Tom Johnson, because he was so tall and she was so short and one can imagine how well the balloons lined up, well they really didn't. It was time for refreshments to be served and later on they all danced and had such a good time. Friendships meant a lot to Jack and Maxine and they loved having these parties for the fellowship with acquaintances they had made through the years.

It was deer hunting season in November and Jack and Maxine had made plans to go hunting with Jim and Martha up north to the upper peninsula near Iron Mountain. They made arrangements for the boys to stay with Clara and Jim in Lansing while they were gone. They drove south to Chicago and it was the busy time of the day with lots of traffic going through the city. Then they drove into Wisconsin and then up into northern Michigan to where they had rented a cabin near Iron Mountain. They had gone that route because the wait for the ferry that crossed the Great Lakes was long and tedious and they thought it would be faster going the way they did. Besides, they would get to see some new scenery they had never saw before. They hunted and enjoyed their stay in the cabin until Jack got a little touchy with Maxine because she had asked Jim if he wanted some leftover fried potatoes and gave them all to him and didn't ask Jack if he wanted some first. She apologized, but it was too late—the damage had been done and Maxine wondered what Jack had in store to pay her back for that little mistake. The only one to get a deer was Jim and that sure made him happy and he did share the meat when they arrived back home.

Maxine had been dieting for quite some time and she felt good about herself and the way she looked and was beginning to have more self-confidence in things she tried to do. Work was fun. Maxine worked on a line assembling master cylinders for brakes. The line was enclosed in a separate room because of the large tubs of fluid used. The workers usually got their work done in record time and had some free time by the end of the shift. They could relax and talk before it was time to punch out on the time clock. Several times Jack would walk by on his way to the tool room and look in the window and see Maxine and others laughing and having so much fun. He was setup man and job leader on the welders. He had put in many good suggestions on how to increase production, how to make things work better and many more that would make more money for the company. He received awards and certificates for those suggestions.

Winter was a beautiful time in the country and the children loved to make snowmen and play out in the snow. Once when it was real slippery on the road, the Millers came around with a toboggan attached to their car and asked if the family wanted to go with them. They did and had so much fun. Then when Mike was driving and Jack, Maxine, Jackie and two of the Miller children, Barbara and Suzie, were on the toboggan, Mike was going too fast and Jack kept yelling, "Slow down." But he ignored the warning and when he turned the corner the toboggan slid into the ditch and turned over. Jack was very upset with Mike, but realized this was not the time or place to let him know it. Barbara broke her leg and the other children had minor bruises and were very scared. Jack and Maxine got up and tried to help the others, not realizing that Maxine had been hurt, also. When she arrived home and removed her ski pants, she had a bad bruise on the front of one of her legs, it had swollen and formed a large blood clot, and the doctor cut the skin and removed most of the clot and told her to stay off of it for a while so the blood flow would be normal. After notifying her employer she stayed home from work for a couple of days and rested as the doctor prescribed.

This year, on Christmas Day, Henry had all the Bohl family over to his house for a big dinner. It was good to be with them all, even Grandpa Wheeler was there. Grandma was too sick to come so she stayed home and had dinner with Uncle Bill and Aunt Kate. The children, Jackie and Danny (Maxine's sons), Linda, Peggy, Lexie (Henry's children), and Sharon (Clara's daughter) had lots of fun playing together.

This was just one of the Christmas dinners. They usually had two more, one with Jack's dad and Vera, and another with his mother and Whitey. The children got so many gifts that Maxine would put about half of them in the attic and then give them to the boys a few months later when they would appreciate them more. On their way home from the Christmas dinners, Jackie asked, "How come we have so many Grandmas and Grandpas? And why doesn't Grandpa Derr and Daddy's mother live together?"

Jack looked at Maxine, then said, "You explain it to him."

Maxine explained, "Jackie, they couldn't get along very well so they decided to get a divorce and marry someone else."

Jackie said "Oh!" This explanation seemed to satisfy his innocent mind and nothing more was said. Maxine was thankful because of the questions children naturally ask about divorce and how hard it is to explain it to them. -+Jack didn't want to talk about his parent's divorce and this reinforced Maxine's reluctance to divorce.

New Year's Eve had come and gone and all the celebration of the holidays had died down and all was back to the normal routine. Clara and Jim came to visit with Sharon Kay about once a month. Clara was pregnant with another child and late in January she had a little boy they named him Richard. Jim's middle name was Richard and at that time there was a television show called *I Love Lucy*, with Lucille Ball and Desi Arnez, her husband. Their screen name was Lucy and Ricky Ricardo. So Clara and Jim nicknamed their baby, 'Ricky.' Maxine's cousin Pauline and her husband Norman would come out with their little son James and daughter Patricia to visit once in a while. Jack really liked those little girls and held them and talked to them and he would say, "I wish I had a little girl like you, all I have is boys."

Saturday, January 28, 1954. What a night to remember. Jack and Maxine hired a baby-sitter and went dancing at the Rainbow Inn; it had been a romantic evening for them being alone and enjoying one another's company after working so hard at the factory every day and doing all of the chores that had to be done around the house daily. They drove home feeling so good about the evening and after arriving home Jack took the baby-sitter home. Once in bed Jack was ready to be intimate and whispered in Maxine's ear "Leave out your diaphragm and let's try for a little girl."

Maxine was so surprised and thought, "He does want something I want." She thought this because after Danny was born he told her, "I don't want any more kids because when you have kids you can't have anything else." Well, Maxine was so responsive, she knew she had conceived. The next day Jack said to Maxine "I thought I had a different woman in bed with me."

Maxine was so happy, all she could think about was, "I just know I am pregnant and I am going to have a little girl." Her spirits were high all day Sunday and couldn't wait to get to work on Monday to tell her friends. When she told them they asked, "How far along are you?" and she answered, "I just got that way Saturday night." They sure looked puzzled when she said that but that was okay. She thought, "I know I am and that is all that counts." On her way home from work that night she stopped at Dad and Vera's to tell them about the good news and Vera was so excited when Maxine explained, "I just know I am pregnant with a little girl, and Jack really wanted this one."

Some more good news came when Maxine learned that Harold and Jeanne had adopted a little girl and they named her Pamela Jean. She was born on February 4, 1954, and they took custody of her the day after she was born. The excitement was overwhelming for the Bohl family: first Ricky, now Pamela and soon Maxine's child. Grandma Bohl was sure pleased about all of these new grandchildren and the fact that Harold and Jeanne had remarried just a few years before. They had their name in the adoption agency for quite some time because they wanted children and thought a child would fill their hearts with joy, and would help fill the empty void of Carol Jean. Pammy was a little curly redhead and so petite, she could steal anyone's heart when she looked at you.

The days that followed were happy ones for Maxine and her spirits were high; she felt so good with lots of energy and there was no morning sickness so she continued to go to work every day. Then one day Maxine went to the nurse's station at work with her friend Doris to get weighed so she could see how much she had gained, and she said to Doris, "Gee, I haven't gained much since I got this way." The nurse must have heard her since it wasn't long before she received a notice that said, "You can no longer work while you are pregnant and you will have to go on a leave of absence." This didn't bother Maxine that much because she was happy to stay home with the boys and looked forward to having the baby. The neighbors had a baby shower for Maxine and almost everything was pink for a little girl, or neutral colors in case of a boy. There were many nice gifts for the baby and also a beautiful nightgown and negligeé for Maxine to wear after the baby was born. She thanked them many times for everything. As she looked them over she thought, "How nice it is to have such wonderful neighbors who have blessed me with so much for our baby." It wasn't long after this shower that Vera insisted on having another shower and invited about all their relatives and friends. Maxine said, "Good gracious, so many more nice things for this baby, she will be the best dressed child in the county," because Maxine was still sure it would be a girl.

Grandma Lucretia Wheeler was very ill and had been in the hospital with cancer of the stomach. She had been in the hospital for two weeks in the spring of 1953, the year before, and was sent home to convalesce. Through the year her health failed; she was admitted in the hospital again and was diagnosed with cancer, after spending a week in the hospital she went home. Jack and Maxine went to visit her, and

111

when she heard Maxine's voice she sat right up and looked at her and smiled. Grandpa said, "That is the first sign of life she has shown since she came home from the hospital." It wasn't too long after that she died, and from then on Grandpa was so sad because he had loved her for so many years and missed her so much. It was hard for Grandpa to live alone in his little apartment so Aunt Millie, his daughter, took him to live with her and care for him. It was so hard to see Grandpa grieving for Grandma; he had always been such a joy to be around and such a gentle loving man.

Jack and Mike Miller had planned a fishing trip up north to Bear Lake, a good fishing spot. After all arrangements for the children had been made and Friday night arrived, they packed their gear and headed up north. It was always fun to go with the Millers; they had such a good sense of humor and were easy to get along with. After they had arrived the guys went out fishing, Lillian and Maxine went to town grocery shopping, and Lillian asked, "Do you think we should get some meat for dinner or do you think they will catch a bunch of fish?"

Maxine replied, "Oh, I think we had better at least get some hamburger just in case they don't catch any fish."

Well, when the ladies arrived back at the campsite, there the guys were with a large bunch of fish they had caught, and ready to be cleaned. Dinner was soon ready, the teakettle had boiled and the water had been poured for Lillian and Maxine's tea. In the meantime, Jack was teasing Maxine about being fat. She asked him not to be saying such things, but he continued to tease her, and she said, "Please stop, Jack!" but he had to say it one more time. She had lifted the tea cup to her lips and in just one second flipped the cup in his direction and poured hot tea all over him, thinking, "It is just as much your fault I am fat as it is mine, you wanted this baby as well as I did, I warned you to stop teasing me." Jack knew he had it coming, so he got up and went into the tent and stayed there until he thought Maxine had cooled down. It took awhile, but as usual she forgave him for his childish behavior.

The summer was going fast and they had purchased a used bright yellow 1952 Lincoln, with a black hard top. It was a beautiful car, just like new. They still had the Mercury they had been driving for some time when Bill Reed wanted to trade Jack a motorcycle for the Mercury, so Jack decided to do it. Maxine didn't like that idea very much because she was afraid Jack would get hurt on it. But that didn't matter to him he said, he would be very careful driving it. It wasn't long before Bill wanted to trade back and get his motorcycle, which Jack agreed to do.

Only a few weeks after Bill got the bike back, he was killed in an accident with it, this was such a shock to everyone. Bill Reed was the young man who gave Rusty, their hound dog, to Maxine when she was pregnant with Danny back in 1947, and he was one of Jenny's brothers. Her other brother Bob and his wife lived down the road from Jack and Maxine and they liked to go to the lake and water ski. This was good because Maxine couldn't ski or run the boat that year because she was quite far along with the baby. She would go along and enjoy the picnic and talk with other friends they had made at the lake. By this time she had been asked many times what she was going to name the baby and she would answer, "Jack wants to name her Raynetta Kay, and I said it was okay because it was his turn to name one of the children." And they had agreed that if it were a boy they would name him Mark. Jim and Martha were expecting a baby, also, and she had told Maxine she was going to name her baby Mark, and Maxine liked that name. She asked Martha, "Do you mind if we use that name too if we have a boy?" And Martha said, "I don't mind at all." The two families were expecting the babies about the same time in November and thought the timing was quite a blessing.

The boys were asking questions about the baby. Danny asked, "How did the baby get in your belly, Momma?"

And Maxine told him, "God planted a seed in Mommy's tummy."

Jackie was eight and Danny was seven years old and very inquisitive and needed an answer they could understand. But this answer still left questions in Danny's mind, because one day when they were at Dad and Vera's home, Danny asked Vera, "If God planted the seed in Mommy's tummy, where did it come from? The coffee pot?" He knew his mama drank a lot of coffee and that was the only way he could figure out how the seed got there.

Dad and Vera sure got a big laugh at that and thought Danny sure was a serious thinker. Danny thought if anyone knew the answer

113

Grandma Derr would. This was like a second home for the boys and they loved being there with their grandma and grandpa.

Some Friday nights, Jack wouldn't get home until early morning hours and Maxine wouldn't get upset because she was so happy to see him home safe, and besides she had the boys and she was going to have a baby girl soon and nothing could bother her. She lived in a dream world, it seemed. The time was getting closer and closer and on one of those November nights he was out somewhere drinking, and Maxine started her contractions and began to worry. It was real early in the morning and Maxine sent Jackie down to get Lillian Miller to take her to the hospital. Lillian took the boys down to her house to stay while they were gone. She agreed to keep them for a couple of days so they could go to school while Maxine was in the hospital.

The doctor, Dr. Meads, came in to examine Maxine and asked, "Where is your husband?"

She had to tell him she didn't know. Dr. Meads stayed at the hospital for a long time before he finally decided she was ready and it was time to go into the delivery room to prepare for the baby's birth. He used a procedure that turned the baby and brought it out feet first because he said the babies come out much easier and it is easier on the mother. He was the only doctor in Jackson who delivered that way; a doctor in Ann Arbor, Michigan trained him using this method. Dr. Meads used this same procedure when Maxine was born twenty-six years earlier.

On Sunday morning, November 7, 1954, the baby arrived. Maxine was taken back to her room for recovering from the ether and its effects. Jack finally showed up, and said to Maxine, "I went home to get some sleep before I came because I knew I couldn't do anything here."

Maxine asked about the baby and they told her it was an eight-pound-nine-ounce boy, and she cried, "Boys, boys, boys, that's all I ever have is boys."

She felt she had failed her husband because he wanted a little girl so bad and she couldn't fulfill his wishes. She had always tried to please Jack in every way she could. She continued to be so upset with herself and cried and cried.

Jack said, "Mac, it is alright. We will love him."

114

And finally the nurse said, "Let me go get the baby and bring him in to her so she can see him." She brought the baby in and put him in Maxine's arms and as she looked at him she thought, "Oh, what a nice baby, I am so sorry I acted like a spoiled brat," as she held him close with love and compassion. From then on Maxine loved Mark with an extra-deep love, realizing how terrible she had reacted when she found out that he was a boy. The nurse brought the papers in to be filled out and wanted to know what his name was to be, and Maxine said "Mark Clark." Her mother had been so disappointed because she didn't name Danny after her father, so Maxine decided to name him after her younger brother Clark (Corky) who had been killed the year and a half before. This made her mother very happy. Maxine stayed in the hospital for ten days and then went back to their home on Reynolds Road. She was older and wiser by now and knew more about newborn babies and didn't need to go to Vera's this time.

Hunting season was here by now and Jack did his usual hunting when he got out of work. Sometimes he would have friends come out and hunt with him or go hunting with them somewhere else. He was drinking more and more now, and seemed to be discontented. He was staying out late on weekends and not wanting to get up in the mornings to go to work, although he did so reluctantly. Mike and Lillian asked Jack and Maxine to go to a dance with them to help Jack get over his discontentment and maybe have a little fun, and he agreed to go. So Maxine pumped her breast so Mark would have something to eat while she was gone, but at the dance she leaked milk all over her dress and told them she needed to go home and nurse the baby. Mark was such a contented and happy baby, and Maxine was thankful he was so healthy; she loved him so much and was thankful to God for another wonderful and healthy boy. She finally learned that the father was the one who determined the sex of the child, not the mother, so this gave her some peace of mind.

Christmastime was here and Maxine invited all of her family to come to their home for Christmas Eve to celebrate together. It was a big crowd: Henry, Doris and their three children, Linda, Peggy and Lexie; Herman and Gale; Harold and Jeanne with Pamela; Clara and Jim with Sharon and Rick; and finally, Maxine and Jack with their three boys, plus Grandma Bohl and Grandpa Wheeler. Everyone had such a good time and Henry took pictures of the entire group by the big Christmas tree. It was sure good to be together and see how this family had grown, and a blessing to have Grandpa there. Grandpa was so thrilled to be there and have the children sit on his lap. It gave him joy to see these children and to know they were part of him and part of Grandma, the part of life that will continue with his love and blessings through many generations to come.

Here it was another New Year, 1955, and the everyday routines they had become accustomed to continued to keep things in order, especially the nursing schedule and keeping the chores done. The boys were good helpers and kept their toys picked up and their room clean, usually minded quite well, then one day when Jackie was eight years old, he was disobedient and had to be punished. He was sent to his room and he got very angry and told Danny, "I am going to run away." He proceeded to pack some clothes and toys in paper bags.

Maxine went in and asked him, "Do you want me to pack you a lunch?"

He answered with an angry, "Funny, funny."

He finished packing and went out the back door, down the driveway and headed south on the road until he got to the neighbor's front yard and stopped. He sat on a rock for a short time and then decided to go in the other direction.

In the meantime, Danny was so upset and said, "Mommy, he's running away and won't be back."

"He won't go far, Danny, it is a long way down that road and he will get tired soon."

After Jackie had passed the house and started down the road the other way, he stopped in front of another neighbor's yard and sat on another big rock for about ten minutes. Then slowly he got up and started walking, with his head lowered, toward home. As he entered the back door Maxine said, "Home isn't so bad after all, is it? Now you can go in your bedroom and take care of those clothes and toys."

From then on Jackie never thought of leaving home again. Sometimes lessons like these are good for children to let them know they do have the freedom to do some things but there are limits and they need to be able to make the right choices or suffer the consequences, even at an early age.

Springtime came and it was getting warm again and Maxine had to make a decision whether or not she would be going back to work at the shop, as her leave time was coming to an end. If she did go back she would have to go on the afternoon shift to work. That wouldn't be too much trouble; she could nurse Mark just before she left and again as soon as she got home after midnight from work. Maxine asked her mother if she would come and stay at the house from Sunday night until Friday night to help with the children and especially Mark, being only six months old. Her mother said she would, so that problem was solved. Maxine was able to go back to work and it seemed to work out just fine for everyone. She was able to get her housework done, nurse Mark when he needed to be nursed and still get ready for work on time. Grandma Bohl would feed Mark some baby food for his dinner and give him a bottle if he needed one before Maxine arrived home after midnight. He was a very hungry boy by that time.

Sometimes on Friday, Grandma Bohl wanted to go home in the afternoon before Maxine went to work. So, after taking her home, Maxine would wait in the parking lot at the factory for Jack to come out so he could take Mark home with him. On one of these Fridays, it was such a beautiful spring day, warm and sunny, that when Jack came to the car to go home he asked Maxine, "Don't go to work today, it's so nice, let's just go for a ride before we go home to be with the boys." So she went in the shop to tell her foreman she wouldn't be in that after-noon and he thanked her for letting him know. They left Jack's car, the Mercury, in the parking lot and drove the Lincoln. He drove out of the city toward the little town of Brooklyn, on the Brooklyn Road, and spot-ted a dirt road angling off the main road and up a steep hill, so he decided to take that road to see where it led. It led to a small wooded area away from the main road, so he decided to park and wanted to make love, so they walked out a little ways and just down a hill from the sight of the car, with Mark asleep in the back seat. Just after making love, Jack was lying there naked, but Maxine had fully dressed herself and was relaxing when they heard footsteps coming down the hill and saw that it was a police officer.

They scrambled to their feet and looked surprised and embarrassed, and the officer asked, "Is that your car up there with the baby in the back seat?"

They answered in unison, "Yes, it is officer."

He then asked them for their driver's licenses, and they showed them to him. As he was examining them he said, "It's a good thing you two are married. I could take you in for this, and especially the fact that you left your baby in the back seat of the car where someone could have easily taken him, do you know that?" They apologized and said they were unaware of the law and didn't think they were doing anything wrong and that they were not far away from the car. The officer was very understanding and warned them not to do it again and left.

"Please don't tell anyone about this, it is so embarrassing to be caught with your pants down," Jack said.

Maxine answered, "I am so glad I was dressed when he walked up on us. At least you are a man like he is." They laughed as they went back to the car. That was quite a lesson they learned on that beautiful spring day.

CHAPTER TWELVE
FAITH DESTROYED

The temperature was getting much warmer and the summer days were nice. The lakes were warm enough to go water skiing and the family had been busy varnishing and painting the boat so it would be ready to use when the weather permitted. The family was anxious to go water skiing and spend some time at the lake; the boys wanted to learn some of the tricks and learn how to run the boat, too. Even though they were quite young, Jack taught them how to drive it and how to be careful and respectful of other boats.

Usually there was an older lady, Mary, at the lake with her son. She just liked to relax on the shore while Jack drove the boat, and she liked to watch Mark for Maxine while she went out in the boat with the family. One day Jack wanted to put Danny on his shoulders while he was skiing, so he got in the water, put the skis on, and Danny got on his shoulders. Jack took hold of the towrope and Maxine operated the boat. Jack motioned for her to give it the gas and she did, and the steering cable broke and the boat started to go around and around. Jack let go of the rope handle, with Danny still on his shoulders. The boat was still going around and around, and Maxine was so scared she didn't know what to do. Then, finally she went to the back of the boat and grabbed the handle of the motor to steer the boat straight, and of all the places for the boat to head was straight for Jack and Danny. Jack had to push the boat to the side, or otherwise it would have run over him and Danny with the propeller. Maxine was so upset and scared. When it was over and they went back to the dock, Jack yelled and cursed at her.

The owner of the Gibson Boat and Bait Shop told him, "Stop yelling at her, she didn't do it on purpose, can't you see she is really upset? And that is no way to be talking to a lady!"

Maxine was so thankful that Mr. Gibson said what he did because Jack was embarrassing her in front of all those people on shore. He had been drinking a lot that day and was mean when he drank too much. Jack fixed the cable and then took the boys out to ski and run the boat. The rest of the day Maxine was so tensed up she could not relax as she usually did at the lake. She didn't go out in the boat anymore that day, so she spent some time with the others on shore and got more acquainted with Mr. Gibson's wife and daughters. They talked and enjoyed the rest of the day until it was time to go home.

The trip home wasn't very pleasant; Jack kept harping on how ignorant Maxine was and how she almost killed him and Danny. Then Jackie told his dad, "Dad, she didn't mean it, she was scared and didn't realize what to do, just forget about it, you're okay, aren't you?"

Maxine thought, "Thanks Jackie, he thinks he never does anything wrong." Sometimes a day starts out to be so beautiful and so full of fun and joy but trials and tribulations seem to come up and are hard to handle, and words can't be said because they may not set right, especially when the other person is drinking and does not like criticism and reproof.

They arrived back home and took care of the boat and cleaned up the picnic dishes, then Maxine prepared something to eat for supper. The rest of the evening they watched television before retiring, and no more was said about the incident that happened that day.

These days were long for Maxine. With keeping the housework done, nursing Mark and going to work at the factory, she didn't get to see Jack very much. He was taking the boat to the lake in the evenings with the boys while Grandma Bohl stayed with Mark, and sometimes he would go by himself. One evening after Maxine had come home from work and finished nursing Mark, she went to bed, but Jack wanted to talk. He said, "Mac I want you to quit work and stay home or else go on days if you can, because I have met someone I could really get to care for and I am afraid if you aren't around I will."

What a shock! "Has it come to this again?" Maxine thought, and all the trust and faith she had in Jack had just vanished in that one second. She had told him back in 1947, "Don't you ever do it to me again," and she meant it. After these thoughts came to her mind and she was over the shock, she answered him, "If that's what you want I will try to get on days so we can be together. If there are no jobs to bid on I will quit work and stay home with the kids, even if it means less money and changing our lifestyle."

Jack had been turning in some good suggestions at work to save the company money and was getting certificates and rewards for them.

He was set-up man and job leader in his department in "B" building and he was also the union steward. He had responsibilities at work and it seemed to be too much for him and he couldn't handle it. He kept complaining to Maxine about everything going wrong at the shop and said he would like to find work outside of the Michigan. He was getting more and more unsettled, and couldn't cope with his work, although he didn't admit that the drinking was his problem.

The boys were back to school now and Maxine had quit her job and was back being a full-time wife and mother and enjoying it, although she missed the people she worked with and the friends she had socialized with at the shop. It was hard getting along without a paycheck and the independence of having her own money when she wanted or needed it. Jack was drinking more and more and it was harder and harder for him to get up and go to work and he was blaming everyone for all of his troubles. Sometimes Maxine would have to throw water in his face to get him up to go to work, and when he didn't want to go in, he wanted her to call in and lie about him being sick. She refused to lie for him and he would get very upset with her, evidently trying to blame her for his staying out late and not getting his rest. She took him at his word that he would not be attracted to that other person if she stayed home from work, should she have been more cautious and watched out for his meanderings even if she did exactly what he wanted?

Jack was staying out later and coming home drunk and mean, beating on Maxine and pulling her out of bed by her hair and cursing and swearing at her and calling her all kinds of vulgar names. Once, he ripped her nightgown off and woke up Jackie and Danny and told them to come into the bedroom where he and Maxine were. He was holding her down with one hand and spread her legs apart, then pointed at her vagina and said in a loud voice, "That's where babies come from, not from God."

The boys, only eight and nine years of age, started to cry because of what he was doing to their mother, and he yelled at them and told them to go back to bed. Maxine cried and thought, "My God what is he doing? Doesn't he realize the psychological effect this will have on the boys in years to come seeing him do this to their mother?" Maxine was so embarrassed for both the boys and herself, she had never been so

121

humiliated in all her life.

Mark was in his crib at the foot of the bed and when he started to cry and fuss, Jack told him to shut up. Finally, Mark quieted down and went to sleep and so did Jack. In the morning he said he didn't remember a thing that had happened that night before. Many times abusive behavior would happen and he said he didn't remember. Anyway, whenever Maxine confronted him about it, he always used that excuse or if it was true, it was the sure sign of an abusive alcoholic. Maxine didn't have any knowledge about alcoholics and their behavior, but she did know he was getting worse because he was drinking more and not giving any time to sober up in between, even drinking first thing in the morning or afternoon whenever he got out of bed.

In spite of all this, keeping busy with housework, baking, doing laundry that had to be hung up on the clothesline to dry about three times a week, and all the other household chores helped Maxine keep a good spirit; she was happy doing for the family the things she liked doing best. The boys were growing up so fast, and they were now old enough to join the Boy Scouts; this helped them to get acquainted with more of the neighborhood boys. Maxine was able to meet their mothers and help out with some of the scouting activities. Mark was over a year old now and he was a good little boy and never much trouble. He seemed to be able to entertain himself while the boys were away at school or fishing down the road. They would ride their bikes down to the creek about two miles away. Mark liked to play with Blackie, the family cocker spaniel, because the dog would let Mark crawl all over him and play. Mark was never mean to the dogs, he just hugged them and loved them.

Jim and Martha Linsday, with their little boy, Mark, would come out and visit. Both Marks would play together and they became good little friends. Jack and Jim would go hunting sometimes while Maxine and Martha visited and compared the boys' progress in growth and activities. Then they would prepare something for dinner, because the men would be so hungry when they returned back home from hunting. After dinner the men would clean the game: pheasants, rabbits or squirrels, whatever they shot that day and the women would do the dishes and clean up. These were fun days, laughing and joking and enjoying

122

each other's company; it was good to have friends come over to spend the evening.

The next day was a beautiful day, and things had gone so well that Maxine went through the day with a hopeful feeling of things getting better and thinking, "If I can try harder to make Jack happy, maybe he will quit his drinking and we can live a normal life."

She always kept a positive attitude toward her marriage regardless of the abuse. This attitude filled her soul throughout the day and she looked forward to spending the evening with her family. That evening after dinner and when the boys had gone to play with the neighbors, she and Jack decided to watch some television. They turned it on but it kept rolling, the vertical control needed adjusting, so Maxine got behind the television to fix it and Jack, who was sitting across the room on the couch, yelled, "Maxine." So she stood up and he threw a glass at her.

She ducked and wondered, "What in the world is he doing?"

In another minute he yelled, "Maxine," again. Once again, she stood up and this time he threw the beer bottle at her and the bottom of the bottle hit her in the forehead. She saw hundreds of Technicolor stars and almost fainted; blood came gushing out of her head. Without even saying he was sorry, Jack said, "We have to go to the hospital emergency room." Maxine was stunned speechless as she grabbed a wet washcloth and a small towel to soak up the blood.

They arrived at the emergency room and they notified her doctor. In the meantime, they took an X-Ray to see if she had a skull fracture or concussion. While waiting for the doctor in her room, the police came in to take a report of what had happened and she told them, "I am not filing any charges against my husband."

The police officers looked very surprised and asked, "Are you sure?"

Maxine replied, "Yes, I will forgive him, the Bible tells us to forgive seventy times seven." (Matthew 18:22)

During these years they didn't have shelters for women, the abused-wife syndrome wasn't heard of and women didn't have anywhere to go to get away from it, so they didn't have much choice.

After the police left, the doctor came in her room and said, "The X-Ray shows you have a hairline fracture and you will have to stay in the hospital for twenty-four hours to make sure you don't have a concussion"

"Thank you, I feel like I need to," she answered.

The doctor said, "Maxine how much longer are you going to put up with this kind of treatment?"

She shrugged her shoulders and said, "I love him, Doctor."

But she wondered where Jack was; he had not visited her since her entry in the hospital. She slept well that night and was doing so well the next day they decided to release her. She called Vera to come and get her and she did. On the way back home Vera talked to Maxine and said, "You shouldn't have to put up with that kind of treatment from anyone." Vera didn't go in the house with her because she was afraid she would say something she would be sorry for.

Going in the house, Maxine found Jack waiting for her and he was happy to see her and said. "I waited in the parking lot of the hospital for a long time and prayed you would be alright, then decided I better get home to the boys." He had Mark with him in the car that night.

For a while after that, things seemed to be going pretty smooth, but then he was back to his same habits again, drinking so much he couldn't remember what he had done the night before. Several times he took Maxine by the neck and choked her until she could hardly breathe. The older boys would come to her rescue and make him stop. One time, Jack had Maxine down on the kitchen floor and was sitting on her when Jackie hit him in the face real hard and knocked him off of her.

Thanksgiving, 1955 had come and gone and Christmas was almost here. The joy of Christmas helped Maxine to forget the problems she was having at home with Jack and how he had been treating her and hurting her by the physical and verbal abuse, and by telling her she was ignorant and dumb, not to mention the beatings. Anyway, it helped for a while.

After all the Christmas dinners had been attended that weekend, Christmas morning came and it was time for the boys to see what Santa had put under the tree. They came running into their parent's bedroom and begged them to get up so they could open their gifts. So Maxine and Jack went out to the living room with them to watch with

124

anticipation what they had received from Santa. There was a train set for Jackie and Danny, football helmets and kneepads, plus a new football for both of them. They were just learning how to play football and had asked for these things. Mark got some pull toys and a wagon. The day was a good and happy one as the children played and enjoyed their toys.

Jack decided they should have a New Year's Eve party and invite their friends and some of the neighbors over to celebrate the New Year. Maxine made the list and sent out invitations or called the guests to come for the party. She planned the meal, shopped for the food and beverages. She planned for the boys to stay at the Miller's home so they could be with other children and not with the adults. Of course, the children were happy about that. The day of the party was a very busy day, preparing the meal and all the trimmings, but Maxine enjoyed having parties with their friends, they were all so much fun to be with and so willing to help whenever she needed them. The living room floor was hardwood and a good surface to dance on. With all the furniture either pushed back or placed in the bedrooms, there was plenty of room to dance. The evening was fun and everyone had a good time. Time went by fast and before they knew it was midnight and they all kissed their partner first, then others, and yelled "Happy New Year." Then one of the men used Jack's shotgun. He opened the front door and shot a few times, "to make a loud noise," he said. But the next morning Jack noticed he had shot a big hole in the mailbox and was very upset about it. When Jack confronted him about it he said, "I am very sorry and didn't realize what I had done when I shot the gun," but he didn't offer to pay for a new one and Jack thought he should have.

With winter well on its way, time seemed to be going by fast. With homework to be done almost every evening, the boys didn't have much time to play before they went to bed because they had to be up early in the morning to catch the bus. They did get to watch about two hours of television after they got their homework done, they had more time to watch if they did their homework before dinner. When it was time to go to bed they would come in and kiss their parents good night. One evening Danny went to bed first and Maxine asked him, "Why didn't you kiss us goodnight?"

"Bobby Mumma said I was too big to kiss my parents good night!"

Maxine replied, "You will never be too old to kiss your mother goodnight, I don't care what Bobby said."

So Danny came in and gave them both a big kiss. After the boys were in their room Maxine told Jack, "Boy, you never know how much influence other kids have on your children until something like this happens." From then on there was no problem about the goodnight kiss.

Spring came and Jack decided to build a garage. By now the foundation was done and he was framing it. With working at the factory and building the garage he was getting very tired and impatient with himself and others as well. A friend came out to help him on the roof so that was a relief. When the temperature rose enough to take the boat out, he was happy getting some relaxation and fun. Also, he decided to buy a small trailer to take to the lake so the family wouldn't have to stay in a tent. It was so nice to have everything in the trailer: a stove, beds, and a place to sit and eat when it rained. It was only about eighteen feet long, but so much better than a tent. They would take it to Swain's Lake in Concord and Maxine and the boys would stay there on the days that Jack worked, and Jack would drive back and forth to work and enjoy the lake evenings and weekends.

The summer of 1956 was a good one with lots of fishing, boating, water-skiing and just being a family and enjoying each other and meeting other campers at Swain's Lake. Friends and relatives would come out and enjoy the activities with the family and picnics were a lot of fun, too. Jack seemed to be relaxed and happy staying at the lake most of the time, unless he got to drinking too much, then he would get pretty noisy and embarrass Maxine in front of other people. After a while, it became so bad that the campground manager asked them to leave because the other campers were complaining about him and the manager didn't want any trouble, so they left and went back home.

Of course, Jack was very mad about it. He didn't realize that just because Maxine put up with his drinking and bad ways, other people wouldn't put up with it and they didn't have to. The boys were unhappy to leave because they had made so many friends at Swain's Lake and were having so much fun; they loved to swim and fish and water ski when Jack was there to run the boat. Maxine didn't want to run the boat because of the accident that had happened before while she was driving it, and besides she had Mark to look after.

The garage had to be finished so Jack spent time on that. One day the boys were out in back and were playing on the trailer that Jack used to haul supplies. They were running up one end and it would drop down and then they would run to the other end and it would drop. Jack yelled at them to stop it about two or three times and then as they jumped off the trailer Danny bit his tongue almost in half. Blood was gushing out of it and Maxine almost fainted when she saw it, so she said, "We have to take him up to see Doctor Ransom up on Horton Road, now!"

They put him in the car and took him to show the doctor. When he looked at Danny's tongue he said, "There is not anything I can do, any injury in the mouth heals fast. So just give him liquids to drink, nothing too salty and it will heal before you know it."

Maxine looked at him in amazement and she said, "Okay, if you say so, Doctor." Sure enough it did heal and it didn't take long. Danny now had a scar across his tongue from one side to the other and he stopped sticking his tongue out like he used to.

Many times Jack would come home from work and say, "Get a picnic ready we are going to the lake to water ski." So Maxine would get things together and they would take off for Clark's Lake, where Gibson's Boat and Bait Shop was located. This lake was the one they spent most of their time water skiing and boating. One day Jack was pulling Maxine on the skis and as they went past the ski jump, Jack pointed to the jump and Maxine shook her head no and he went back by it a couple of more times and pointed for her to jump and she shook her head no both times. Then he went by it again and pointed to the jump once again and this time she nodded her head yes and he pulled up beside the ski jump. She went up the jump and came off it with her arms spread way out and her legs were wing spread, too. She landed on her face and chest with a big PLOP. Boy, did that ever hurt, and Jack just laughed at her as she got back in the boat. The funny thing was, he didn't know how to run the boat to pull a water skier over a jump. He kept the rope tight and it needed to be loose, otherwise Maxine might have jumped successfully. She never tried it again.

Another experience at the lake was when Danny had climbed a

tree and was coming back down. When he reached the last limb on the tree, he jumped and landed on a broken bottle that lay on the ground. The bottom of the bottle was upright with jagged sharp edges and it cut his foot real bad, so Maxine had to take him to the emergency room to have it cleaned out and stitched up. When they arrived back to the lake, Jack had the boat on the trailer and was ready to go back home and complained about what had happened to Danny. He said, "That kid is always hurting himself one way of the other and messing up the day for me."

Maxine thought, "You always think about yourself and are not concerned about what happened to Danny or anyone else." Then she said to Jack, "It wasn't his fault that bottle was there, someone was careless and it caused the accident, he had a serious cut on bottom of his foot and it wouldn't stop bleeding until we tied a rag around his ankle. So many times people don't think before they do something that may hurt others." Then she added, "This summer Danny seemed to be accident prone, first his tongue and now his foot. Let's hope there will be no more accidents."

It was Danny's ninth birthday, September 1. Maxine baked him a birthday cake with an Indian head with lots of colorful feathers on the headdress. He received a new ball mitt and bat because he and Jackie belonged to the Little League now and loved to play baseball. Although the season was about over and school would be starting after Labor Day, they could still play ball with the neighbor children. They would meet at the empty lot near their friend's house to play. There were enough boys in the neighborhood for a couple of teams.

It was time for Maxine to go shopping for the boys' school clothes and supplies. She didn't have to worry about dress clothes because her sister-in-law, Gale, had a sister who had two boys that were older than Jackie and Danny and she gave her boys' clothes to Maxine for Jackie and Danny, and they wore these dress clothes to church. The Sunday school bus came every Sunday for the boys to go to the Spring Arbor Free Methodist Church. The deacons from the church had visited and asked Maxine if the boys could go to church. She said yes and they were picked up faithfully every Sunday. Maxine was so happy that they were going to Sunday school because she remembered her experience going to Sunday school as a child and wanted them to learn about the Lord. Maxine would attend church at Christmas and Easter but otherwise she didn't go because Jack wouldn't go. Later in life she realized that was a poor excuse. There are many wives who give up their spiritual life because of a non-spiritual husband: they believe in being submissive to their husbands, and Maxine not knowing the truth that she should have gone to church anyway – a believer should not be unequally yoked with an unbeliever because of the spiritual warfare between them.

Soon it was November and Mark's second birthday. Where did the time go? He had grown so much and was a joy to be around, and before one knew it, he would be all grown up like Jackie and Danny. Thanksgiving, then Christmas, the shopping and the dinners all came and were gone and 1957 was upon them. It is true that time waits for no one; it passes you by (as the song states). Routine chores were done every day and Maxine tried hard to keep peace in the family, even when Jack would come home late at night drunk and in a bad mood. She would think, "Maybe he will be better tomorrow." Not realizing that this was a standard lament of nearly every abused woman and wife, it would lead nowhere but to more abuse. But Jack was still unhappy with his job and wanted to go out of state to find work. He talked about going to Florida or somewhere warm. Maxine had talked to a neighbor, who had gone to Arizona and said it was real warm there, and Maxine saw a program on television about how Arizona was the fastest growing state and that there were plenty of jobs there. She told Jack about it and he started looking into it.

This year seemed to go by fairly well. With the boys in school, Boy Scouts, and baseball practice, they kept busy and were doing well with their schoolwork, too. They went to Sunday school regularly every week and seemed to enjoy going. Mr. Orville Fitzgerald was the bus driver and he was kind to them and usually gave them candy on their way home. On Easter, the boys rode the bus to church and on their way home, the bus had to stop very suddenly and Jackie hit his head on one of the bars and it made a large bump on his head. It really looked like it hurt a lot, but he didn't complain about it. Maxine's mother, her sister Clara and her family came over for dinner and they took many pictures.

Jackie didn't want to be in them but we all convinced him the pictures would be a good reminder of the big bump he got on the Sunday school bus when he was almost eleven years old. Sharon Kay was sure growing up to be quite a little girl; she always loved to come over to see the boys and play with them. Little Rickie, who was nine months older than Mark, loved to play with Mark and they got to be good buddies.

Clara and Jim still lived in Lansing and Mom Bohl was living with them and took care of the children while Clara and Jim worked. Clara drove back and forth to Jackson every day. By this time a divided highway had been built, US 127, and it didn't take that long to drive the distance. This made it easier for the families to go back and forth to see each other more frequently because the children had grown so close to each other. Clara's family didn't like boating that much, because they were afraid of the water, but they would bring a picnic lunch to the lake and spend time on the beach so the children could swim.

Summer passed by quickly, as usual, because it was so much fun. Being in the sunshine at the lake gave new energy and hope that the family would be content and happy with life and would enjoy what they had: a home that was paid for, two cars, a boat and motor, a travel trailer and good health. Maxine sure enjoyed her family and loved them very much and was grateful to God for all He had done in her life. Whenever she was upset with Jack, she would go in and kneel beside the bed and pray to God that He would give her the strength and courage to go on. She always remembered her marriage vows she made to God. She meant them and would continue to keep trying to make a go of her marriage, regardless of Jack's outrageous behavior. She really loved Jack, even though the trust wasn't there as it had been, mainly because of the way he treated her.

Another hunting season was underway and Jack would come home from work as usual and have coffee then go hunting. One day he brought a friend out and as they were leaving to go in the field he hollered at Rusty, their hound dog, to come to him. As Rusty came and stood by him, Jack said, "Boy wouldn't it be nice if you had a woman that would mind like your dog and lick your hands?"

They both laughed and walked out into the field to hunt. Maxine had heard that remark and she thought to herself "So this is how he

130

really thinks. He wants me to be like a dog."

She already had an inferiority complex, and this remark didn't help because she had always tried to do things to please and make him happy, but was being degraded for it. Through the years this type of remark had really cut deep into Maxine's heart. His remarks hurt so much that sometimes she would go in and cry to God until the hurt seemed to go away, but they weren't forgotten; it was like adding fuel to a fire that wouldn't go out and it kept smoldering. She would suppress the hurt along with all the other times it had happened and it was building a wall thicker and higher between them. She went over to Clara and Jim's a couple of times to stay for a day or so in order to see her mother and mainly to get away from Jack for a while. Her mother asked her why she didn't divorce him so she wouldn't have to put up with all she had been going through. But Maxine would remind herself of her marriage vows and she didn't want her children to grow up without a father because she knew what it was like to have a father around only part-time. Her mother and father were separated for many years before he passed away and she never divorced him. So, Maxine said to herself, "Why should I? Besides, I don't believe in divorce." Thank God Mother didn't divorce her father, because Maxine would have grown up without knowing her father. Even though he only came home occasionally, she knew him and loved him.

The new year of 1958 was well on its way. Jack turned thirty on February 28 and they went out to dinner at Wynn Schuler's in Battle Creek to celebrate. This was a very fancy and expensive place to eat, especially for this family, but they wanted to make this something special for Jack. It was fairly dark in the restaurant and as they were leaving, Danny said, "How do we get out of this joint?" Those around them just stared at them and gave them funny looks, but Jack, Maxine and the boys all laughed. It had been a fun day for all of them and they decided that from then on they would go to a restaurant closer to home, and the boys said, "Next time let's go to one where we can see what we are eating." They all agreed that was a good idea.

The folks next door, Pete and Anne Lawrence, were good neighbors. Pete was an American Indian from one of the tribes in Michigan and he liked the boys very much and would talk to them and tell them many stories. His children had all grown up and lived out of state so he didn't get to see them very often. Anne had children from her first marriage, also. Mark loved to go over there to visit them and Anne would always give him cookies or candy. Of course, Maxine always had cookies in the cookie jar at home, but a child usually likes someone else's too. The home that Pete and Ann lived in didn't have plumbing or water, so they came over and used the outside spigot on Jack and Maxine's house for their water. Maxine knew how it was to be without water and besides Pete and Anne were elderly and needed help. The boys would help Anne carry the water home when she needed it.

Jack had planted some fruit trees a couple of summers before and they were blossoming. The family was looking forward to eating the apples, pears and peaches from them this summer. They decided not to put in a garden this year because Jack had quit his job and they planned to be going out of state so he could look for a job elsewhere. Jack was discouraged with his job, the state, and any other excuse he could come up with, and he thought if he went somewhere else he would be happy. On the first of July, they packed up their car and boat and headed for Arizona; the neighbors were looking after the house and dogs while they were gone. This was an exploratory trip to see what the possibilities would be for a job and housing for the family.

The boys were excited about the trip and all the new scenery they would see along the way. Maxine had bought some things for them to play with when they were bored: coloring books and crayons, cards, and other hand games. Along the way they would stop and set up the tent at night so they could get a good sleep and a good breakfast before going on. They didn't stop at hardly any sight-seeing places because Jack was in a big hurry to get there and find a job, but of course he would always find time to stop for his beer and very seldom asked if the rest of the family wanted anything to drink. His selfish nature seemed to take over during the whole trip.

July, of course, was very hot and humid and as long as the car was moving it was fine, but the minute it stopped, the heat would hit them full force. A couple of times when they stopped for the night they found a lake and put the boat in the water so they could cool off and relax for a while. They drove the Lincoln and it rode smooth even with

132

the boat behind and in those days there was no speed limit posted in most states, so they were able to make good time on their way to Arizona. They saw many beautiful places along the way, scenery so different than the state of Michigan. Each state had its own beauty and unique landscape – America the beautiful, from shore to shore as the song describes. They traveled on Route 66 for quite a while and it was an experience to see the little towns along the way that the new highways had bypassed and the little concession stands where people were selling their handmade goods and articles, such as pottery, blankets, wall hangings, baskets, leather goods, and novelties too numerous to mention. They finally stopped at one of the Indian-operated stands and bought a pretty orange (variegated with other colors) vase, on the bottom of the vase it said NEMADJI POTTERY USA with an Indian head in the middle. Maxine was very happy they bought this souvenir from the Indians because she wanted a keepsake from their trip along with the memories they would have forever.

They were in New Mexico and Jack was driving too fast. Maxine had just told him to slow down or he would get a ticket and he said, "There are no cops out in this deserted desert land so don't worry so much, the faster we go the faster we will get there."

Well, it wasn't long and sure enough they heard a siren coming closer and closer and the lights flashing on the police car signaling for Jack to pull over. Jack did pull over and was very angry, and Maxine said, "I told you so, you were going ninety-five miles an hour, that is too fast for me, let alone having three kids in the car, too."

The police officer came up to the car and said, "Man, do you know how fast you were driving? Please give me your driver's license." The officer wrote a ticket and said, "You will have to go before the justice of the peace and he won't be in until Monday morning so you will have to stay in the area until then."

This happened on a Saturday and so Jack had to find a camping spot near the town of Blue Water, New Mexico. At least they got to see some of this part of the country besides the highway. They went up on a large mountain to a lake named Blue Water, a beautiful spot to camp and fish. The boys were sure happy to be able to fish and climb the mountain a little higher because they were tired of riding in the car.

Monday morning arrived and they packed everything up and went into town to see the justice of the peace. Jack went in with the ticket to see how much his fine would be; he wasn't prepared to hear a lecture on speeding but did receive one. After the lecture the justice fined him seventy-five dollars and told him to be more careful, especially with a family in the car. Of course, this didn't go over very well with Jack. That was money they wouldn't have for the rest of their trip, so he would have to get a job as soon as he could. From then on when Jack drove, he watched the speedometer much closer and didn't speed. They traveled through New Mexico and on toward Arizona enjoying the scenery, stopping once in a while to rest and eat.

Arriving in Phoenix, they looked for a place to live and found an apartment complex with a pool that wasn't too expensive and, besides, Jack would be getting a job so they could stay there until they found something else. The boys were so happy to go swimming in the pool; it was so hot they could hardly stand it. Jack called about a job and was told to come in and put in an application. He did and was hired. It was a welding job and nothing could be any hotter than welding in 98 degree weather. This job was just too hot for any person to have to work at and Jack worked only one week, just long enough to get a check. He said, "No way will I work in that heat."

So they packed up, left the apartment, and went to a park to set up their tent. Of course the boys were unhappy about moving away from the pool because they had learned how to dive and swim so much better and even Mark got so he could swim across the pool, and he wasn't four years old yet. He sure took to the water like a fish.

One nice thing about being in Phoenix was there were many public pools so the family could at least go swimming once in a while. The pools had diving boards so the family all liked that and would use the high dive the most, especially the boys and Jack. The boys dared Maxine to high dive and so she did, and (oops!) the strap on her bathing suit broke as she hit the water and her suit went to her knees. She grabbed it before she surfaced and held it in front of her so all of the people in the pool wouldn't see her bosom. She was so embarrassed she got out of the pool and fixed her strap with a safety pin. The boys sure got a big kick out of that and laughed at her. She was always taking a dare and usually ended up feeling like a fool, so from then on she decided, "No more dares for me." The rest of the day was fun and relaxing. They had brought a picnic lunch so they were able to stay at the pool most of the day.

They all wanted to go to Flagstaff because they heard it was so much cooler up there, so they drove up that way. It was quite a long drive but was worth it, for when they got there they found that northern Arizona had miles and miles of big pine trees. It looked a lot like upper Michigan with some small lakes around and it was cool, how wonderful. It must have been at least thirty degrees cooler. It felt so good they spent a whole day there just enjoying it. Jack and Maxine talked it over and looked at the map to see where they would go next.

Jack had decided that Arizona was too hot for him to live in so they would be leaving to go back home soon. He said, "In no way would I ever sell our home in Michigan and come out here in this terrible heat to live. I am so glad we made a trial run to see what it was like out here before we made a final move." He decided they would go see a few other places while they were out in the west. They drove on to Las Vegas, Nevada and were so surprised when they came over the mountain and saw all the lights shining. They all sighed and said, "Oh my goodness, so many lights and so bright." The closer they got to the city the brighter the lights were and they stared at all of the gambling casinos as they passed them on the main street. They had never seen such a sight before. Jack said, "Let's go in one of them and see what it is like inside," and the boys said in unison "Okay, Dad, let's go!"

They found a parking place and walked up to the entrance and went inside. They didn't get very far before they were stopped and were told, "We do not allow children in our gambling establishments, so you will all have to leave."

"May we just take a look around for a minute?" Maxine asked.

"No!" The man answered.

Jack looked at Maxine and said, "Lets go then, they don't even want us to look."

This was a disappointment for them, all they wanted to do was look, but the business had their rules and wouldn't break them, and that was good because it might leave an image in children's minds that gambling was rewarding. After Maxine had thought about it, she realized it was for the best, and was just another experience for them all.

They drove back to the park where they were staying and went to bed for a good night's rest, because in the morning they would find a lake they could put the boat in and do some water skiing. When Maxine awoke she stepped outside of the tent and saw a dead coral snake, a poisonous snake, and she thought, "Thank God it is dead, it could have crawled in one of the tents and bit one of us."

She woke Jack up and told him and he said, "We better get out of this place, right now."

They ate breakfast and left as soon as possible. They drove to Lake Tahoe and put the boat in the water and spent part of the day just boating and water skiing on the huge lake; it seemed so good to be somewhere where it wasn't so hot. Nevada had a lot of desert like Arizona and Jack thought it was ugly and hot, so he said, "We better start heading for home now because we are running low on money and I want to make sure we have enough to get back." They packed everything like they had when they left Michigan, a lot went in the boat they wouldn't be using on the way home.

They all had a good suntan and were ready to say goodbye to Nevada and head back home. They hadn't traveled very far before a tire blew out on the boat trailer, so Jack unhitched the trailer and they went to the closest place they could find to have the tire repaired. It was too hot to leave anyone there with the trailer, so they had to have faith that no one would bother it or steal anything. They had to buy a new tire because the old one was damaged beyond repair. That was another setback they hadn't expected, so they had less money now then they had planned on. Jack wasn't in a very good mood by this time and wanted to find some place to find something to drink.

It seemed like a long way back home because everyone was so anxious to get back to Michigan to be in the cooler weather, also, to be in their own beds at night. They drove without stopping to see any sights or points of interest, mainly because of the money situation, wondering whether they would have enough for expenses to get back home or not. They ate dry cereal for breakfast, bologna sandwiches for lunch and goulash, vegetable soup with either hot dogs or hamburgers for dinner, and drank Kool Aid.

The boys talked about seeing their friends, playing baseball and going fishing down at the creek. They loved their home and being out in the country with so much space to play in and to be able to ride their bikes back and forth wherever they wanted to go. As the miles flew by they continued asking, "How much farther do we have to go?"

CHAPTER THIRTEEN

FATHER'S PAST SECRET REVEALED

When they reached the "WELCOME TO MICHIGAN" sign, the children wanted to stop, so Jack stopped the car and they got out of the car, kissed and hugged the sign and yelled, "Finally we are in Michigan." From then on they knew it wouldn't be far to go before they arrived home so they were content to wait. They were thankful to be so close because they were down to about five dollars left for gas and, of course, a few beers for Jack. Although the rest of the family was very thirsty, he didn't buy anything for them to drink. The older boys asked him about it and he said they could wait until they got home to have some good fresh well water.

Home at last! It looked so good and peaceful. After unloading some of the things from the car and boat, Maxine prepared something to eat – thankfully they had left meat in the freezer – while Jack and the boys finished unloading the rest of the luggage and camping gear. Dinner at home, once again, was so nice for them, they enjoyed relaxing and watching some television before going to bed. "There is no place like my home sweet home," Maxine said to Jack as they retired for the night, and Jack replied, "It is sure good to be back here away from the awful heat we just came from. I believe it would be much better to try to find work in Florida."

The middle of August was beautiful. Jack knew he had to find some work soon or sell the camping trailer so the family could eat and pay the utility bills. He looked for a job for a while and didn't have much luck, so he decided to sell the trailer. That money lasted for a while to pay bills, buy groceries, and to be able to go to the lake water skiing and, of course, buy booze. He was drinking more and more every day and getting mean with Danny. Several times he hit Danny in the head and knocked him off the chair at the dinner table because Danny would say something about his drinking or wouldn't answer his dad when Jack yelled at him for something.

One evening when he had been drinking, Jack asked Maxine to go to Horton to buy him some more beer. She really didn't want to go but she knew he had too much to drink to drive so she went. She bought his beer at the tavern where he usually bought it and took it back to him. He looked at the beer and spit in her face and said, "I don't drink that kind of beer anymore, take it back and get me Miller's."

Maxine left, crying all the way back to the tavern, wondering "My God, why?" She wrestled with her reluctance to stand up to him, "Why am I so weak and submissive to him?" She went into the tavern, feeling so intimidated, and told the bartender, " Jack doesn't drink this kind of beer anymore, can I exchange it for Miller's?"

The bartender could tell she had been crying, her eyes were red and she couldn't look him in the eyes when she asked him. He said, "Sure, no problem at all."

She cried all the way back home and thought of what her mother had told her years ago when she accepted the engagement ring from Jack, "No Maxine, he drinks and he will give you nothing but a life of hell." And Maxine answered, "Oh no, Mama, he loves me." She had been so young and didn't realize what she would have to go through if he didn't stop drinking.

September and October had gone by and Jack had worked at a few different jobs, but they didn't last long because he had problems getting up to go to work. He made the decision to sell the Lincoln in order to pay bills and buy groceries, so this meant they had just the one car. November was almost gone by now and they had a good Thanksgiving dinner at Dad and Vera's and enjoyed the family gathering, telling all about their trip to Arizona and showing pictures of their trip to those who hadn't seen them.

Jack wanted to go to Florida to look for work, so they had to go to the bank and put a mortgage on the house so he could have the money to go. They didn't have any problem at the bank because Mr. Aldridge, the banker, had known Maxine's father many years ago and told her, "I didn't know who you were, until I found out that your father was Heinie Bohl. I knew him when he was Sergeant-at-Arms at the Capitol in Lansing. He did a great favor for some delegates that I was trying to find a hotel room for a convention. With a lot of effort he found us one. We were so thankful for him taking the time, and with a cheerful personality, to help us solve an overcrowded situation at that time."

Maxine answered, "Yes, he was always trying to help others. He died running a servicemen's canteen in Dearborn during World War Two. He was only fifty-four years old."

Mr. Aldridge owned the bank and was chairman of the board, so it was a blessing for Jack and Maxine to have someone who had some knowledge of them to help them get the mortgage. Mr. Aldridge said, "The payments won't be too large so you will be able to make them without any hardship." Maxine thanked him and told him how much she appreciated all of his help and friendship.

Jack was thankful also and said to Maxine on the way home, "Boy, it is always good to know someone like that when a person needs to get a mortgage and they don't even have a job."

Maxine replied, "We have always worked hard and paid our bills, so Mr. Aldridge wouldn't think we would do anything different, would he?"

On December 8, 1958, Jack packed his bags and left to go to Florida. It was a big shock to Maxine when he said, "I don't think I will be back. I want to go where it is warm so you and the kids will have to take care of yourselves the best you can."

Maxine looked at him with amazement. Her expression clearly showed what she was thinking, she couldn't hide her feelings and he knew she was very upset. She said, "Why? Jack, what have I done to you that you can just go off and leave the children and me here all alone with no money, no car, no job and a mortgage to repay?" She continued with anger in her voice, "Jack, you must have had this in mind all along when we got the mortgage on the house. Why didn't you tell me? You didn't, because you knew I wouldn't go along with getting the mortgage, isn't that right?"

"Yes, and I didn't want any trouble." He answered.

"You don't call this trouble?" She asked.

He said, "Goodbye boys, behave yourselves and I will write and let you know where I am."

That is all he said, then left later in the morning.

She was depressed all afternoon until she realized she had to get a grip on herself and figure out what to do. First thing was to try to get a job, but how would she get to work if she did find one? It seemed like a dead end until she prayed to God for His help, she really needed it now and believed God would provide for her and the children.

The next day she was talking to Pete and Ann, the neighbors, about her situation and they agreed that she could borrow their car if she found work. Maxine was thankful for their friendship and help. Lillian came down to visit Maxine and said, "I have been cleaning house for an elderly couple in Jackson but I really don't want to do it anymore, would you like to take the job? It is only one day a week and it will help until you can find something else."

Maxine said, "I could go and see if they would hire me, maybe you could go in with me to introduce me to them, would you?"

"Yes I will. I will give them a call and make an appointment," Lillian replied. The couple agreed to see them in the morning.

Maxine said, "I hope they will like me."

"They are Christians and so sweet, you will like them, I am sure," Lillian said,

The next morning after the children went to school, Lillian came over and picked up Maxine and they drove into Jackson, talking all the way about Jack leaving the family the way he did and leaving the family with no money to live on. They pulled into the driveway and parked. Mr. Zoorman greeted them at the door with a cheery, "Hello, come in and make yourself at home." Lillian introduced Maxine to them and told them she would come to work for them if they agreed to have her. The Zoormans asked Maxine a few questions and told her what they expected of her if she did come to work for them. After more conversation, an agreement was made for Maxine to do the job once a week, on Fridays. As Lillian and Maxine left and drove away they were both pleased that the Zoormans wanted Maxine to work for them, at least it was something to help buy groceries.

One Friday when Maxine was working, they invited her to have lunch with them and they always prayed before they ate and read some Bible verses after lunch. Mr. Zoorman was talking about getting a painter to come and paint their home but the man never returned his call and he was getting concerned. So Maxine said, "I have a brother who does painting and maybe he would come and give you an estimate."

"What is your brother's name?"

"Harold Bohl." She replied.

Mr. Zoorman asked her, "Was your father Heinie Bohl?"

"Why, yes he was."

With a surprised look on his face he asked Maxine, "Do you know what your father did in the First World War?"

"All we ever knew was he was just a plain soldier, working on the fire trucks or something."

"Oh, no, I flew the airplane that dropped your father behind the German lines to get secrets for America. He was a spy for the U.S.A. Because he was from Germany and knew the language so well, they chose him and asked if he was willing to be a spy. Your Father was very willing because he believed in the United States as his new homeland and he wanted to do his duty for the freedom he enjoyed. He had to volunteer and not be forced into something he didn't want to do." He continued, "They chose me to be one of the pilots for this mission and it was my plane your father was assigned to fly in to do this mission, to be dropped in behind the lines He was such a brave man to do this against his old country."

Maxine was so astonished, her heart almost jumped up into her throat. It was such a surprise learning this fact about her father, which no one in the family had ever known before, not even her mother. She couldn't wait to get home so she could call her mother and tell her what she had just learned and how by the grace of God she happened to find this out. God wanted Maxine to know this so she could tell the family that her father believed in America so much that he became a spy against his own native country; and that God works in ways that no one can ever comprehend. Maxine loved her father so much, and this was the most wonderful thing she could ever have found out, especially at this time of her life with Jack leaving her and the children. God was able to put the spark back into her life again. After breaking this news to the boys, she telephoned her mother and explained to her from beginning to end how she had found out this amazing news.

Her mother was so surprised, she couldn't say a word for a moment, then she said, "No wonder all those people who spoke German used to come to the house and I had to leave the room. This was in the early 1930s, and he must have been visiting with some of his old comrades that were on the missions with him, and couldn't let anyone know about it."

Maxine continued to work for the Zoormans, although she needed to earn more money, but it was hard to find another job. Then someone called Maxine and told her there was a job opening for a waitress at The Famous Door restaurant and bar in downtown Jackson. So she borrowed Pete and Ann's car and went into town to apply for the job. The owner read her application and interviewed Maxine, and he asked her if she had ever worked in a bar before.

"No, but I really need this job. My husband left me and my three boys and I will really try hard to learn whatever I need to know. I have worked in restaurants before but not in a bar."

The owner, Tony Consalino said "There is another woman that is qualified, but you need the job, so I will sleep on this and get back with you as soon as possible."

Maxine thanked him and left The Famous Door and went home, praying that she would get the job. Christmas was coming soon and it was hard for her to even think about it let alone try to explain to the boys why all this was happening. She would have to leave them at night unless Mother would come out and stay with them.

The boys were on their way to school and Maxine started her housework that had to be done that day when the phone rang; she answered it and it was Tony, the restaurant owner. He said "This is Tony Consalino and I am calling to tell you my conscience tells me that you need this job even though the other lady has the experience, so I am asking you to come into work tomorrow if you are available."

"Yes, I will be there. What time?"

"Could you come in a little early so we can explain the job to you, say about 9:30 a.m.?"

"Yes, I can, thank you so much for giving me this chance."

After hanging up she ran over to see Pete and Ann and she asked them, "Can I use your car in the morning because I will be starting a new job, I am so excited about it. I go in early to learn about it, but from then on I will be going in at 10.45 a.m. to get things ready to serve lunch as a waitress until 2:00 p.m., then go back in at 8:30 p.m to work in the evening. This weekend I will see if my mother will come out and stay with us so she can watch the children for me."

Pete said, "Yes, you can use the car, you know we will help you as much as we can." Maxine had to tell the Zoormans that she got a full-time job and wouldn't be able to work for them any more, but Lillian said she would go back to work for them again, so everything worked out.

Maxine's mother had a very serious operation for a high stomach hernia about six months before, while she was in Lansing living with Clara and Jim. Upon recovering and feeling better, she wanted to move back to Jackson to be close to the rest of her family, so she went to live with Harold and Jeanne. The doctor in Lansing told her not to even lift as much as a broom, let alone anything else, because it would take some time for healing. Harold had remodeled his upstairs into an apartment for Mother and she enjoyed living back in Jackson so she and her sister Millie could go to church together. Mother had accepted the Lord Jesus Christ as her Savior the year before, and was faithful in going to church to worship and praise the Lord. When she got the phone call from Maxine asking her to help, she said she would do it if the boys would help as much as they could. Harold would bring her out there in the morning in time for Maxine to go to work.

The first day at work for Maxine was exciting, yet she was nervous and anxious to do the job well. Tony told her, "Don't worry about the drinks, just make sure you put on the bill exactly what they ask for and I will see to it they get it."

She had never heard of so many different kinds of drinks before and had never seen so much money spent on them. It was an entirely different lifestyle than she was used to; many lawyers, doctors, bankers and businessmen came there for lunch. Lunch was a prime-rib buffet, all you could eat, and some people really filled their plates to overflowing. They could have used sideboards to keep the food on their plates. Lawyers would sit at a big round table and laugh at one another and say, "You got me in court this time, but I will get you next time."

Maxine thought, "They have no mercy or don't care how much it costs people to go to court. It is all about money and their pride, laughing about whose turn it will be to win next time." Her observation was, "This is shameful and not in accord with God's laws of human relations,

144

and they have taken a vow before God to uphold the laws of this land and give a person a fair trial. How fair is that kind of practice?"

After lunch and everything was cleaned up, Maxine left to go home because she had to be back for the evening shift, which would be entirely different: no food would be sold, only drinks. Tony required the waitresses to wear a hair net at lunch time but they didn't need to for the evening shift, so Maxine wore her hair up in a bun during lunch and down long at night. One evening a customer asked her, "Do you have a sister that works here during the lunch hour?"

"No, that's me, we have to wear our hair up during lunch time." He just smiled and went back to drinking his cocktail and listening to the music the band was playing. After the bar had closed and everything was all cleaned up, Tony gave the waitresses a free drink before they went home, anything they wanted, but Maxine didn't want to start doing that because of what drinking had done to Jack.

After a few days had gone by, Maxine was on her way to work driving Pete's car when the car stalled as she was crossing the railroad tracks. Maxine kept trying to start the car and it wouldn't start, so she decided to see if she could push it across the tracks. As she got out of the car, she heard the train whistle and it frightened her. She got behind the car and prayed, "My God, please give me the strength to push this car over the tracks." Lo and behold, she pushed with all her might and extra from the Lord, too, and the car rolled over the tracks and out of the way. "Thank you Lord," Maxine said as she got in the car to see if it would start. It did, and she sat there for a while to get her composure before she went any further. All she could think about was, "My brother Corky was killed by a train in 1953, and I am not ready to pass away yet, because I have three sons who depend on me. And besides, this isn't my car; I am responsible for this, too."

When she arrived at work she told Tony about the experience she just had and he said, "Thank God you had the strength to push that car." Tony was a father of six children. He and his wife were raising them to believe in God and they belonged to the Catholic church.

Christmas was almost here and the children were out of school for Christmas vacation, so Maxine got to spend more time with them during the day before she went to work on the night shift. They got a

Christmas tree and decorated it with ornaments and lights; it brought some cheer into their hearts anticipating the holidays. They played some table games and watched television together that week. Maxine's mother even played games and enjoyed doing it with them. The day before Christmas, Mother wanted to go back to Harold's to spend the day with them. Dad and Vera had invited Maxine and the boys over to Sharon's to have Christmas with their family. Before they left, Maxine told the boys to be on their best behavior because she didn't want to punish them; she was still hurting inside because Jack had just left them a few weeks before, and she couldn't deal with misconduct from them, too. But, after they got there, the day wasn't going very well and the boys were agitating her to no end. So she told them to get their coats because they were going home; she had enough and wouldn't take anymore. This didn't set too well with the boys. It was Christmas and they wanted to be with Grandma and Grandpa and all the other family, but Maxine had warned them earlier and she meant it. This made Maxine full of heartache and disappointment and she felt so alone the rest of the day.

New Year's Eve day was going to be a long one for Maxine. She told her mother not to expect her until early in the morning; she had to work until 3:00 a.m. That day was so busy, starting at 10:45 in the morning for lunch hour and working all day, going home just long enough to shower and change clothes, then going back to work and getting ready for the big New Year's Eve celebration.

So many people crowded in the bar that the waitresses could hardly get in between them to serve their drinks and clean the tables. Such a celebration, entertainment, drinking, dancing, talking and laughing; the noise was very loud that night and it was hard to hear what the customers ordered, but there were very few mistakes considering the noise factor. When it was close to midnight the waitresses handed out hats and noisemakers to all the patrons, and then they started counting down until the clock struck, twelve, when everyone yelled, "Happy New Year!" and the kissing began.

Maxine stood at the bar station where she picked up the orders and the tears were rolling down her cheeks. Tony reached over the bar and kissed Maxine on the cheek and said, "Happy New Year, Maxine."

And she replied "Happy New Year, Tony." He knew her husband had left her and that she was sad, so as a friend he wanted to cheer her up a bit.

They all worked until 3:00 a.m. until the bar closed, then they cleaned off the tables. Tony told Maxine, "I have never seen anyone work so many hours and still have a smile on her face like you had tonight, Maxine." It was good to hear something nice from someone who appreciated what she had done. Tony told them to have a drink before they went home, so Maxine sipped on a fancy drink and then went home.

The next morning, after she woke up, she had coffee and talked with her mother for a long time and enjoyed the day off relaxing and being with family. This was a new year and time to start looking to the future. Maxine was earning money and her tips were good, which helped out with daily expenses and paying the mortgage. They were having problems with the toilet not flushing and they had to carry water from the bathtub to the toilet in order to flush it and Maxine told her mother, "Don't you do that, the boys will do it for you. I don't want you to hurt yourself because the doctor told you not to even lift a broom, so please don't, Mom." Mother had been so independent most of her life, it was hard for her to accept help and to change her ways.

January was cold and snowy and the boys enjoyed playing outside and sledding. They were old enough to go hunting and Pete took them rabbit hunting. My, how happy they were. They loved hunting just like their dad. Pete realized they needed someone to go with because they were too young to go alone. Danny was so happy when he shot his first rabbit, it was a trophy for him, and Maxine was thankful that Pete was able to go with him. The boys would help with the housework every Saturday and continued doing the dishes every night; they tried so hard to be good boys.

Maxine knew she had to buy a car soon so she wouldn't have to use Pete's car so much. Clara and Jim had a second car they decided to sell to Maxine, and she made payments when she could as agreed by them. After working one evening, as usual until 1:00 a.m., Maxine drove home on the icy roads slowly and very carefully. It was nerve-racking and made her very nervous. By the time she reached Reynolds

Road she thought she was safe, until she turned the corner and the car slid in a ditch and she couldn't get it out, so she started walking the two miles home. This was horrible, too. She had to practically crawl up the hills they were so icy, slipping and sliding all the way. There were no cars on the road because it was too slippery. She started to cry and pray, "God! Why am I going through so much? Please get me home safe and sound." She continued praying until she arrived home. Then said, "Thank you God."

The next morning she called a friend to help her get the car out of the ditch as soon as the road was sanded and they could drive on it safely. It was so good to have friends that would help Maxine and the boys because she needed all the help she could get. They understood what she was going through and how hard it is for a woman to raise children by herself. Maxine kept hoping that Jack would come back and they would be a family once again, she would forgive him. But she didn't hear from him and didn't even know where he was, so she had false hopes and didn't realize it. She was so thankful her mother was still staying with them during the week and helping her with the boys while she worked.

Maxine took her mother home on Friday nights so she could spend the weekend with her sister Millie. Aunt Millie would pick her up and they would go shopping on Saturday, then they would go to church on Sunday and spend the day together. Maxine would pick Mother up at Harold's on Monday afternoon, so this gave her a break away from the boys. Mother had just celebrated her fifty-sixth birthday on the ninth and was enjoying her life more than ever before. Since she joined the church she prayed for her children that they, too, would all be saved and accept Jesus as Lord of their life. Maxine had accepted the Lord when she was twelve and still believed in God, she prayed many times for God to help her in many of her trials and tribulations and He did, although she didn't attend church regularly as she should.

One Monday morning after the boys had left for school, Clara and Jim were at Maxine's front door. She couldn't understand why they would come over from Lansing on a Monday, so she asked, "Why are you here today?"

"Mom died early this morning. She was reading her Bible and got a coughing spell and then stopped breathing," Clara said.

"Oh my God, no!" Maxine said. "It is hard to believe this. Mom felt so good when I left her at Harold's on Friday."

Clara said, "They think it was a loose blood clot that hit her heart when she coughed. They aren't sure yet, but that is what it looks like what happened." Maxine's heart sank with grief.

Maxine and the boys went to Bailey's Funeral Home in Jackson to pay their last respects and to greet those who came to give their sympathy and love. It was so cold and snowing that night. Maxine remembered Mr. Bailey's daughter: she had been Maxine's Girl Scout leader and was so kind to her. Maxine remembered, "I had to quit going because Mom could not afford the five cents it cost a week to belong, and I resented it because Mom smoked cigarettes that cost more than that. How foolish we are thinking such things about our parents when they do the best they know how to raise their children." As an adult she realized the error of thinking this way as a child.

The services were held at the Nazarene Church. The pastor told how Mother had changed her life and was a dedicated Christian and he told about God's love for everyone. As he was preaching Maxine was thinking, "If Mom hadn't carried that water to flush the toilet, she would be alive today, it is all my fault." She felt so guilty and so depressed, she cried. She seemed to be in a cloud of discouragement and disparagement when leaving the church. They all went to the cemetery for the service and to pay their last respects.

Afterwards the family went to Aunt Millie's house and talked for a while. Aunt Millie said, "Your Mom, Hazel, and I were together all day Sunday and when we were at prayer meeting that night she prayed out loud, "God, if it takes my life in order to save all of my children, please take it, I am ready to come and be with you.' Your mother loved all of you kids so much." Maxine's cousins were there and they had spent more time with Hazel in the last year than any other time in the past years and had gotten to know her and enjoyed being with her.

Maxine and the boys left Aunt Millie's house and went to see Dad and Vera. Vera had heard from Jack and told him about Hazel's death and he called when Maxine was there and talked to her on the phone and asked if she needed him, she replied "No! The kids and I are doing just fine. I have a good job and I bought a car from Clara and Jim to get back and forth to work with, and besides we needed one being way out in the country. You sure didn't care anything about us when you left, why should you care now?"

Jack said, "I will be coming back soon."

Maxine thought, "You were not here when I really needed you, why should I need you now?" She talked with his folks for a while and then went home so the boys could get to bed as they had school in the morning. As she drove home it seemed like she was dying inside.

The family gathered at Mother's to choose whatever things they wanted that was hers: furniture, dishes and personal items. It was so hard for everyone to go through these things, because they had been a part of Mom's life for many years. Henry and Herman suggested that Maxine have the bedroom set because she needed one, so Maxine agreed and said, "That is all I want, because I want to remember her in my heart." They had decided that Henry would buy the house and he would pay the others their share of the total value which all of the brothers and sisters agreed upon. Maxine knew she would surely miss her mother; she was so helpful these past months and they had grown close.

Life went on, and Maxine had work and the boys to think about, so she kept very busy at home to keep her mind occupied and upbeat. It wasn't long after the funeral she received a phone call from Jack and he said he was coming home. With that in mind, she didn't know exactly when he would be back and she continued to go to work every day. Maxine received good tips from the customers and she had Tony save some of the money for her because she had the mortgage to pay and wanted to keep it paid on time. Anxiety was filling her soul waiting for Jack to come wondering whether he would be any different. One evening while she was working, she looked up and there he was. He was very upset to think that she was working in a bar and pushed her and started to cause trouble, so Tony told him he had to leave. Maxine felt so embarrassed she cried and said, "Tony, I am so sorry."

"It wasn't your fault Maxine. Are you going to be alright?"

"Yes, I will try to handle it when I get home." She answered.

"To think I have been so excited about his return and he had to make a scene," she thought to herself on the way home that night.

He was waiting for her and said, "I never thought that you, of all people, would ever work in a bar. It made me mad when I saw you in there."

"I couldn't find work anywhere else and I had to go to work in order to pay the bills and eat. You didn't send me any money, how do you think we were going to live and pay the bills? You have been gone for over three months."

Jack replied, "I know what I did wasn't a good thing for you and the boys, but to see you working in a bar was a shock to me."

"Your abuse and abandonment to the kids and me has been the story of our lives. How in the world did you think we were going to survive out here ten miles from Jackson without a car, no job, or any means of income to provide for us?" Maxine sure laid it on him with the facts and continued to let him know, "After we went to Dwight Aldrich at the bank, and he willingly helped us get the mortgage on the house because of my Father's reputation as a good man, you then ran off and left. I felt it very important to pay the mortgage payments as we agreed to."

There was no answer or comment made by Jack; only silence and a puzzled stare.

Maxine continued to go to work every day despite Jack's objections, and Jack stayed with the boys most of the time, unless he decided to go out for the evening drinking, then he would be in a foul mood when she arrived home from work. He was usually ready for an argument or confrontation with her about where she worked. She tried hard not to say much to him when he was in that condition, and would only agree with him verbally while thinking the opposite. In the mornings after the boys had gone to school and Jack got out of bed, they would have coffee together and talk; it was so much easier to talk to him when he was sober, but he didn't take her feelings seriously when she tried to explain to him how she felt about what he was doing. Maxine even suggested, "Let's go see a counselor about your drinking, because I have gone to an alcohol program where they explained how it affects the body and mind and how the alcoholic needs help."

"I am not an alcoholic, so get that out of your mind right now. I am not going!"

Again she felt defeated without his cooperation and admission of his problem.

Working at The Famous Door until early morning, one time Maxine arrived home to find that Jack had broken every dish in the house, even a set of service for twelve with all the extra bowls and platters, during one of his drunken spells. These dishes were given to them by Dad and Vera for a wedding present. This was a shock to come home to; the boys were still awake because they had cleaned up all the mess and had thrown the dishes in the garbage. They said he just flung them every which way, including in their bedroom. They had to hide under the bed so they wouldn't get hit by flying dishes. By the time Maxine arrived home, Jack was in bed sleeping it off and, of course, in the morning he said he didn't remember what he had done the night before. At breakfast time, Maxine got out some tinfoil pie tins and placed them on the table and thought, "If this is the way you want to live, I guess we will have to do without dishes. This is just another experience I have to be able to forgive him for. I married Jack, and the vows I promised before God were: for richer or poorer; for better or worse; in sickness and in health; until death do us part, and I meant those vows."

Springtime was here and the signs of new life were seen on the budding trees, the tulips were blooming with a variety of such beautiful colors and the daylight hours were longer with more sunshine. This time of the year was when the family looked forward to a busy summer, because they had been talking about going to Florida so Jack could find work; he liked it there and wanted to take the family. Maxine thought, "This may be the answer: to go with him and try once again to keep the family together."

One afternoon a man came to the door and said he had just run over Blackie, one of the family dogs, and he was dead. Maxine thanked him for letting her know about it and would have Jack go and get him and bury him. This was a sad event for the family because the dog had been with them for so many years and was like part of the family. For several days after the Blackie's death, Rusty would sit on the front porch and howl a mournful sound. He missed his buddy; they had been partners for years, and this was his way of grieving. Maxine had never

152

heard anything like this before and she would go out and pet Rusty and talk to him so he would quiet down. She could sympathize with him because she knew what it was to lose someone. She thought, "Animals do have feelings and express them in their own way."

The pastor and some of the elders of the Free Methodist church, where the boys were going to Sunday school, came over to visit several times with Jack and Maxine and invited them to church. They said they enjoyed having the boys attend Sunday school and thanked Maxine for letting them go. The boys continued to go to Sunday school on the bus every Sunday and also the Kesterson boys invited Jackie and Danny to go to Vacation Bible School with them for a week. They attended faithfully every day and asked Maxine to go with them one day and she did. She realized she hadn't attended church much, only on Christmas and Easter and she felt out of place, but was so thankful the boys wanted to attend. They came home one afternoon and said, "Mamma, we have accepted Jesus Christ as our Savior and we are going to be baptized in the river at Vandercook Lake." They were so excited and happy, and Maxine was happy for them, too.

Preparations for the trip to Florida were being made: an advertisement was placed in the newspaper to rent the house for a year, the television was repaired, articles they didn't want the renters to use were put in the attic and they were packing for the move. They had to wait until the school year ended in June before they could leave, and by then they would have enough money saved for the trip. They also had to think about Rusty , the hound dog. What were they going to do with him? They couldn't take him with them because the hot weather in Florida would be too much for him at his age. So they thought they would ask the Millers to keep him for a year.

The phone rang and when Maxine answered, and a man asked, "Are you the one who has an advertisement in the paper to lease a home for a year?" She said she was and arrangements were made to meet at the house to talk over the particulars of the lease.

The day came and Maxine showed them through the house and explained how things worked and offered them coffee and cookies. They accepted and talked about how nice the house was and that they wanted to rent it so they could look for a home to buy later. They also offered to take care of Rusty and make sure he was fed and they promised to take good care of the house as if it were their own. They agreed on the price and paid a security deposit plus a month's rent and were anxious to move in as soon as Jack and Maxine were ready to go.

Maxine was so pleased to think they had found someone to move in. She felt comfortable knowing these people would take care of the house and would also take care of Rusty while they were gone for a year. It wasn't easy letting strangers move into their home, not knowing who they were or what kind of people they really were, but they had convinced Maxine and Jack that they were honest. They even left some references for Maxine to call if she wanted to, but she never did; she was so naive and believed everyone. She could only see the good in people until they proved otherwise.

Mike and Lillian Miller had a going-away party for Jack and Maxine and invited some of the neighbors and friends over to their home for a good time and fellowship. The children were there also and they had a good time playing outside, it was so nice to be able to see them all before they left for their trip. Maxine was grateful because she had given many parties for the last few years, it was good to be able to be a guest for a change. Through the years the neighborhood had grown close and they looked out for each other whenever any one of them needed help.

Maxine and Lillian were very close friends and could tell each other things they didn't want anyone else to know and they knew it wouldn't go any further. Jack and Mike were best of friends also; they had hunted, fished, worked and had gone camping together for many years. They had known each other years ago when they were just kids in the same neighborhood. Mike was a little older then Jack and he tried to steer him in the right direction even if Jack wouldn't listen, but Jack always had a mind of his own.

CHAPTER FOURTEEN

SEARCHING FOR GREENER PASTURES

Everything they were taking was packed in the Mercury, in the Plymouth that Maxine had bought from Clara and Jim, and in the boat. They planned to be gone for a year so it took a lot of preparation to make sure they had what they needed on this trip: cooking utensils, bedding, towels, dishes and silverware, spices and food staples, toiletries and all they had room for so they would not have to purchase basics when they arrived in Florida. The boys asked if it would be as long a ride as it was to Arizona and Maxine said "No, and besides we are taking two cars this time so you boys can take turns riding with your dad and me." It was the middle of June in 1959, a warm sunshiny day when they pulled out of the driveway and drove down Reynolds Road, then turned left on M-60 and were on their way south. It would be about 1,300 miles to where they were going.

Jack usually took the lead and Maxine followed close behind him in case of any trouble along the way. They would stop and take breaks and eat their meals, cooking on the three-burner camping stove for their dinner in the evening before going to bed in the tent. Arising in the morning to eat breakfast and pack things up again, they drove on toward their destination; they didn't even stop to see any sights along the way. They drove Interstate 75 until late at night the second day and Maxine was getting very tired and wanted to stop for the night, so she signaled to Jack to stop and he did. They found a place to set-up camp just off the road and went to bed. When they awoke in the morning they saw where they were and it was a good thing they had stopped when they did, because they were at the foot of the Appalachian Mountains in Tennessee and as tired as Maxine was, she could have had a bad accident on those roads. She sighed a deep sigh of relief thinking, "Thank God we stopped. Only you, Lord, would know what would have happened on those mountain roads."

After breakfast they filled their cars with gas and checked to make sure everything was all right before they started into the mountains. The weather continued to be nice and the scenery was beautiful

155

in the mountains, even though it was hard to look and drive too, because driving in the mountains wasn't Maxine's first priority. She talked to Danny, who was riding with her at that time, and pointed out to him the interesting sights ahead as she could see them and explained how each different state had its own landscape and interesting places to visit. They had traveled for some hours and it was about time to stop and eat some lunch, so she signaled Jack to stop pretty soon. After eating lunch and resting for a while, they looked at the map and planned where they would stop for the night. It wasn't too far before they would be out of the mountains and Maxine was happy about that. But going down the last decline of the mountain roads, the brakes went out on Maxine's car. She was terrified, but kept cool as the car finally came to a stop since she didn't want to frighten Danny. She said, "Thank you, Lord." By this time Jack had turned around, pulled over by her car and said, "I realized what had happened when I looked in my rear view mirror."

Jack looked for a garage so he could buy some brakes to replace the bad ones. Maxine stayed in the car and relaxed until he came back; she helped as much as she could while he changed the brakes. It was a good thing it was still daylight and Jack had all the right tools to complete the job. There weren't too many things that Jack couldn't do. He was very talented and learned things as he grew up because he liked fixing things himself whenever they needed it, although he wasn't too happy about the timing of this incident. Maxine felt bad about it, but there wasn't much she could do or say to him that would make him feel any better, she was so thankful she and Danny were safe. After doing what she could to help, Maxine decided to fix dinner while he finished and they would not have to stop again so soon.

They traveled on to Georgia and stopped close to Macon and found a place to set-up camp for the night. Jack said, "The trip is taking longer then I expected, but I am thankful we are all safe this far and it won't be long now, we have gone through the worst part of the trip over the mountains."

Georgia was a pretty state but it was very hot and humid so they got up early and were on their way before it reached the heat of the day. Jackie and Mark were riding with Maxine through the rest of Georgia; Mark was worried that the brakes would go out again, but Maxine reassured him, "Your dad fixed them and they will be safe now and you do not have to worry." He said "Okay!" He was four and a half years old now and was a good little boy, so thoughtful and concerned about others, he got along well with his older brothers, and they treated him good, although sometimes they teased him about being so little. The miles flew by and before they knew it they were in Florida with most of the trip behind them. They knew they didn't have much farther to go now.

They stopped in Lake City for a rest and to eat something before they went on. It was a pretty city but warm for them. They were so used to Michigan weather, but would have to get used to this climate now. They decided to stop at a lake near Apopka so they could set-up camp and go swimming, then maybe find a place to stay so they could shower and have a good bed to sleep in. They inquired and found a small cottage to stay in for a couple of weeks and the boys could get out and play and run around for some exercise and get some fresh air after being in the car for so long. They weren't very far from Orlando so Jack could go in and look for a job because their money was running out and they needed an income to keep them going. He tried several days to find work but came back to the cottage without a job, so Maxine went in town to see if she could find work and stopped at the Holiday Inn to see if they were hiring and they were. So she filled out an application and they hired her as a waitress and asked her to come in to work the next day, and she picked up a uniform they furnished her.

The first week she worked she received good tips and was happy with her job and the people she worked with and told Jack and the boys it was a good job. Jack had gone out to Martin Missile factory and put his application in for work and was waiting to hear from them. He waited a few days and went out there to see if he had been hired, they told him he hadn't. He wanted to know why, and they said because of his performance the last months of employment for Kelsey Hayes in Michigan. This made Jack very mad and so he went in where Maxine was working and asked her for the tips she had made that day because he wanted to buy some beer. Of course, she gave the money to him rather then create a bad scene in the dining room of the restaurant. He had left the boys at the cottage alone that day and was drunk by the time he got back there and was not in a very good mood, so the boys tiptoed around so he wouldn't get mad at them.

By the time Maxine arrived home, Jack was asleep, so she didn't have to deal with him in that condition this time. In the morning after breakfast they talked about why Jack didn't get the job and he was still upset about it. He said, "After all those years I worked there and gave them so many suggestions to save a lot of money for the company, they won't even give me a good recommendation to get another job."

Maxine agreed with him because she knew he had worked hard for many years and did win several awards for his ideas and suggestions. Then he suggested, "Maybe they would hire you if you go and put in an application; they would pay you more than what you make as a waitress."

"Sure I can try, will you take me out there to apply for a job?"

The next morning they left early to go to Martin Missile on the other side of Orlando. Jack drove in and showed Maxine where to go to fill out an application. She was nervous, but went in and asked if they were still hiring, and they said that they were, and handed her the papers to fill out. There were a lot of questions because this was a tight-security federal factory and they required people who could pass the security qualifications before they would be hired. After finishing her forms, she turned them in and was told to wait for a short time and they would let her know whether or not she was hired. So she waited for about half an hour and a woman came over to her and said, "You are hired. Come in to work on Monday morning at 7:00 a.m."

"Really? Thank you." As she left the office Maxine ran to the car to tell Jack the good news: that she was to report to work on Monday morning.

"That's good, at least someone in this family will be working there. We will have to see if we can get an apartment closer in town so you don't have to drive so far back and forth to work." On their way back to the cottage they saw a sign that said "Apartment for Rent," so they turned into the driveway and inquired about the price of it and how soon they could move in. The lady was very nice and said it was available now if they wanted it. They told her they could only give her a week's rent for now until Maxine got a check because she was just hired and

158

they needed the apartment.

"Okay, I will take a week's rent and trust you for the rest, because if you were just hired at Martin Missile you must be trustworthy," the lady said.

Maxine went to work at Holiday Inn on Saturday and told them she wouldn't be working there anymore after that day because she had another job. They said they were sorry to hear that because they liked her and how she worked so hard. They said they would miss her and if she ever wanted to work there again they would hire her. After work she knew she had to finish packing so they could move, so they all pitched in and helped after dinner. They would be happy to have a bigger apartment; it was beside an orange grove and they could have all of the oranges they wanted to eat, plus grapefruit too. What a treat for them.

The Sunday evening after they had moved in from Apopka to the apartment, Maxine was getting her clothes ready for work the next day at the factory. Jack had been gone for awhile and returned drunk, then started an argument and hit Maxine in the eye very hard, causing her eye to swell up and turn black. What a way to go to work the first day! Maxine couldn't understand why in the world he would do that to her, she thought, "Could it be because I got a job and he didn't?" That was the only reason she could think of at the time. The boys went to bed early to avoid any scuffle that might occur the rest of the evening.

Monday morning came and Maxine awoke and got ready for work; she tried to be quiet so she wouldn't wake anyone up. Looking in the bathroom mirror, she saw the biggest shiner she had ever seen looking back at her, and she wondered, "What in the world will I tell everyone at work? The truth, I guess. There isn't anything else to say." On the way to work she prayed for the strength to face the people she would work with and help them to understand. "How much more can I take? Doesn't he understand I love him? It isn't my fault he wasn't hired and I was. Besides, it was his idea for me to apply for the job! Will he continue doing this while we are here in Florida?" Her thoughts kept going around and around in her head until she finally drove in the parking lot and realized she was at work.

The minute she walked in the shop everyone looked at her and then looked away, as if to say, "What a way to come to work on the first day." But after she was assigned to a place to work and met her fellow workers and explained to them what happened, the word got around and they all treated her with respect and said she had a strong will to be able to come to work the first day like that. She replied, "I really need this job and I had to come in."

The lady that worked next to Maxine was Eva Suggs and they did the same things, soldering wires on a circuit board for the missiles. It was a tedious job and took quiet nerves to join the tiny wires. Eva struggled and had a few circuit boards returned for repairs and Maxine felt sorry for her, because she was so nervous she would work up a sweat, so Maxine helped her do the repairs. Eva told Maxine they might get in trouble doing that but Maxine said, "We will be careful, you need help."

Maxine continued to work at the Martin Missile plant through the winter;. Even in Florida it got cold at night in the winter and the car windows would frost over . But she worked through springtime and the weather was getting much warmer, especially during the middle of the day. Jack wanted to take the boat out on the lake across the street from the apartment to look around the lake to see if there might be some property to buy. They thought if they found something, they would sell the house in Michigan and stay in Florida permanently. However, Maxine got laid off work at the factory in the springtime because of a cut back. Her foreman told her, "I sure didn't want to lay you off because you are a good reliable worker, but because of seniority I have to."

"I realize that, I've worked for unions before," she answered.

Maxine had to find work again and all she could do besides factory work was waitress work. She answered an advertisement for help in a small fast-food restaurant called The Toddle House; they specialized in breakfast and hamburgers and stayed open twenty-four hours a day. This was a different pace than sitting on a stool and working at the slow pace she had been used to at the factory, but she adjusted quickly, working the afternoon shift from 3:00 p.m. until 11:30 p.m.

It had been over a year since Maxine's mother had passed away and she received a letter from her brother Henry stating she would be receiving her share of the money from the settlement of her mother's estate, which wasn't much after all funeral expenses and other financial responsibilities were taken care of and the remaining divided seven ways. Maxine thought, "I would rather have Mom alive and be able to spend time with her once in a while and to know she was there when I needed her," but life goes on and she had to think about the present and her family situation and the children's future also. Living in Florida, away from her friends and family, was not easy for Maxine and she was getting homesick for them, yet she realized she had to try to make a go of their marriage so she accepted this challenge by going to work every day with an upbeat attitude and a smile on her face to greet her customers.

The day finally arrived when the check from her brother Henry came in the mail; Jack wasn't home and so she decided to go grocery shopping and then deposit the rest of the money in a separate bank account and not tell Jack, because he was still being very mean to her on different occasions whenever he drank too much. She wanted some money set aside in case of an emergency.

Well, that wasn't a very good thing to do because after grocery shopping and depositing the money in the bank, she headed home and the brakes went out on the car and she hit a car in front of her. The kids were with her and she was so thankful they weren't hurt, but she damaged the rear end of the other car. Maxine just lowered her head and thought, "That's what I get for trying to hide that money from Jack, now I have to call him and let him know what has happened."

After the police arrived and she was ticketed, she was told she would have to pay for the damages because she didn't have any insurance on her car. She called Jack and told him what had happened and he asked, "Are you and the kids alright?"

"Yes, but you will have to come and get me and the boys because the car has no brakes." She was very upset and crying and blaming herself for what had happened.

By the time Jack arrived, all necessary information had been exchanged about payment for the damages, and Maxine was so thankful they didn't exceed the amount she had just deposited in the bank. After they transferred the groceries into Jack's car and made arrangements to have her car removed from the street, they headed for home. Maxine told Jack, "I received the check from Henry, my share of mom's estate, and we needed groceries real bad, so I decided to go buy some and put the rest in the bank."

"And you weren't even going to tell me about it?"

"No, because I thought it would be there when we really needed it. The last time, when we received mortgage money on the house, you took it and abandoned the kids and me. Would we be abandoned again if I told you about the money? Don't put such a guilt trip on me!"

But even with that reply, he was very upset to think she would do such a thing behind his back. From then on things began to get worse: his drinking, the arguments, beatings, and his not going to work.

Still wanting to buy property across the highway on the lake, Jack decided to ask the landlady if she knew who owned the vacant lot directly across from her house. She told Jack the man next to the lot owned it and asked, "Do you want to talk to him?" He said he did, so she called the man to see if he would talk to Jack and Maxine about selling the lot. He told her to send them over and he would discuss it with them. They crossed the busy highway and knocked on the door; an elderly woman answered and asked, "Are you Mr. and Mrs. Derr?"

Replying, "Yes," the old woman let them in and motioned for them to go in the living room where a white haired, very long-bearded elderly man sat smoking a long pipe. Maxine was so frightened and thought, "It sure seems spooky in here, so dark and so many old books lying around."

They introduced themselves and Jack told him, "We are looking for some property on the lake because we like to water ski and thought this would be a good place to build a house. How much are you asking for the lot?"

He told Jack the price and then said, "There are alligators in that lake and it wouldn't be a very good place to water ski, especially with children, so I believe you should look somewhere else to build a house." Then he turned to Maxine and said, "He is very hard to get along with, isn't he? And his birthday is in February and your birthday is in October."

Maxine was shocked to think he would know all of this and answered, "Yes, sometimes he is, and yes those are our birthday months, how in the world did you know that?"

His wife informed Maxine he was an astrologist and she showed her some of the books he had written on astrology, and said that he had been a concert pianist at one time and had also written music.

Maxine was fascinated with this couple and wanted to learn more about them. But by this time Jack was ready to leave, and told Maxine, "Let's go back to the apartment." And like a submissive wife she obeyed, but she wanted to stay and talk.

After arriving back at the apartment they told the boys about their experience and how weird it was that this man knew their birthdays, that he didn't want to sell them the lot, and that it was more then Jack wanted to pay for it. It wasn't long after this experience that their landlady told Jack, "I think you should move because of all the arguing and fighting that goes on. It gets pretty loud sometimes and I can hear it and I don't like it. So as soon as you can, will you please find another place to live?"

This made Jack very angry and he told her, "We will move as soon as we find a place, so don't lose any sleep over it."

After Jack told Maxine what the landlady had said, she thought, "I'll bet she was the one that told that old man across the street about Jack's fighting and that he was hard to get along with. How else could he have known?"

Now they had to decide what to do with the car that had no brakes; they didn't want to take it with them, so Jack sold the Dodge so they would have the money to help pay for the rent of another apartment.

It wasn't long before they found another place to live; it was on the other side of Orlando, a small two-bedroom house on a fairly large lot close to a small lake. The boys were happy about that because they could go fishing, and a minor-league baseball field for one of the National League baseball teams was only a few blocks from their place. The day they moved in, they cleaned the cupboards, mopped the floors, and moved their stuff in; they all pitched in to get things settled and put away, so it was late when they went to bed. Maxine awoke in the middle of the night and went to the kitchen. She turned on the light and screamed, "Oh my God, Jack come out here, there are cockroaches everywhere, it is awful, come here, hurry up!"

By his time everyone was awake and came running to the kitchen, the roaches were running in all directions. The boys all shuddered and said, "Do we have to live here?"

Jack replied, "I will go get some bombs to fumigate, but we will have to stay somewhere else for a day or so then we can move back in."

What a mess to clean up after they fumigated. There were dead roaches all over the place, plus all the dishes and cooking utensils had to be washed and scalded good; all the bedding had to be laundered – it turned out to be quite a project for them all. They did laugh about it as they worked and cleaned everything that was affected by the bomb; at least they hadn't lost their sense of humor. It turned out to be a comfortable place to live and they kept roach traps around so they wouldn't have those unwanted pests anymore.

One evening while the family was watching television, Jack spotted a man looking in the window and he ran out the door chasing the man all over the neighborhood trying to catch him, but the peeping tom got away. The neighbors came out to see what was going on and Jack told them and they said, "This has happened before, so be sure you keep your doors locked and report this to the police. They want to know about it, when and where it happens."

"We sure will," Jack said, "I don't like this kind of thing going on where I live." He went into the house and said, "If it isn't roaches invading us, it's peeping toms, I hope we don't have anymore surprises." Maxine and the boys agreed with him unanimously.

The days and the nights were pleasant by now, but Jack was getting restless; he couldn't find any work and the renters who were renting their home back in Michigan weren't sending the rent money as they had promised, so Jack decided to go back there and find out why. With Jack leaving, that left Maxine and the boys there without a car, so she would have to ride the bus back and forth to work. The school was close enough for the boys to walk and a friend Maxine had met working at the factory, Deanne, kept an eye on them after school until she arrived back home from work. A couple of times they skipped school so they could watch a minor-league game at the ball field, but the teachers notified Maxine and from then on they attended school as they were supposed to. It was hard on them being away from their friends in Michigan, the school they had always attended and a home they had lived in all their lives, a home in the country, quiet, secure and away from the hustle and bustle of the city. Plus, they had the freedom to ride their bikes to the river to go fishing and play baseball with all the neighborhood boys up in Michigan. These are things that shape a young boy's character and attitude for the rest of his life and when unpredictable changes occur in the family lifestyle with many changes of residences and schools, often cause boys' attitudes to become insecure and unhappy.

It was hard for Maxine to keep up her cheerfulness and hope for the future because Jack was so unsettled in what he was going to do. She felt so lonely and alone without him. Even though he didn't treat her very nice, she still loved him dearly and missed him. The days were getting hotter now and she was on the second shift, leaving for work in the early afternoon and coming home on the last bus. She didn't like to leave the boys home in the evenings but had no other choice, and Deanne kept an eye on them to make sure they were safe and in the house by nine o'clock. Maxine would call them to talk to them every so often until they went to bed. She trusted them and they promised they would be good for her. By this time Jackie was almost fourteen and Danny was going to be thirteen in September and Mark was five and a half years old.

One evening she called the boys and they told her that their dad had just arrived from Michigan and they would come and pick her up after work. She was so surprised because he had not notified her he was on his way home. She could hardly wait to see him and the boys, and as she waited on the customers she just beamed with a smile continuously and walked about with bouncy steps as if walking on a cloud. She could never hide her feelings; her emotions usually showed on her face. Her customers asked her why she was so happy; they had noticed how excited she had been that day and were curious to find out.

The hours went by slowly, but finally her shift was over and Jack and the boys were there to pick her up. She ran to the car and got in and gave Jack a big hug and a kiss and said, "Hi."

He replied with a "Hi" and then added, "I believe we need to move back to Michigan because those people have moved out of our house and they owe us almost three months' rent, so we better start thinking about it very seriously. You can give your boss two week's notice and we should have enough money to move by then. It is hard for me to find work down here and we can't live on what you are making."

Maxine wasn't too happy with what he said. They had been here for nearly a year now, she liked it in Florida and really didn't want to move back to Michigan, but she always let him make the important decisions.

Jackie had turned fourteen on June 6 and the family started to make arrangements to move back to their home. They notified Dad and Vera they would be there in a week or so and notified the landlord they were moving out. Jack did a lot of the packing while Maxine worked the last week or so. The children were out of school by then for their summer vacation and their plans to move seemed to be timed just right up to this point, the middle of June. They only had the one car and the boat to haul everything they had brought with them, so it was packed solid. They hadn't planned on using the boat for skiing on the way home because they wanted to get there as soon as possible and it would be too much trouble to unload and load it up again. They had to be sure the camping equipment, the stove, the cooking utensils and paper products were within reach whenever they stopped to camp or eat. They carried the groceries in an ice chest and put it in the trunk of the car so they could snack whenever they wanted.

Finally everything was ready to go. They said, "Goodbye, house," as they drove out of the driveway and headed for the highway for home. Maxine thought, "It has been a year since we arrived in Florida. It didn't seem that long. It went by so fast and with many experiences seeing the beautiful sights and enjoying the warm weather and sunshine. It was something to remember for a long time and she would remember her friends through the years. Memories are so precious and they will remind me of those happy times I had with each friend I became acquainted with."

The boys were busy in the back seat with some games and activities Maxine had bought for them so they wouldn't get bored. They did need something to do besides just look at the scenery all the time.

As the miles passed by and they were moving into other states, it seemed like they were making good time, Maxine had been driving for some time while Jack and the boys had all taken a nap. When Jack woke up, he looked around and said, "Where are we now?"

"We are still in Georgia heading home," Maxine replied.

"Do you know you are heading back to Florida? You must have taken the wrong turn. What in the world are you doing?"

"Oh my goodness, I didn't realize that. When I stopped to go to the bathroom and started out again I must have turned left instead of right and didn't even notice it."

"I wonder how many miles you have gone back, let's stop at the next station and check it out. How could you be so dumb?" he asked.

"Well, it was dark and none of you were awake to help me with the signs. I am sorry, maybe you had better drive now," she answered.

They had gone over fifty miles back toward Florida, so that meant they went one hundred miles out of their way. They could have been one hundred miles closer to home. Of course Jack wasn't too happy about that, so they turned around and headed in the right direction again. It was getting late, so they hunted for a camping ground to set up the tent so they could get some rest before going on any further.

Georgia was hot and humid the same as it was a year ago when they were headed toward Florida and it made everyone cranky and short tempered unless they were in the car driving with the windows open. They tried to drive as many miles each day as they could in order to get home faster; they just wanted to be home in their own beds to sleep. Jack was drinking and Maxine drove as many miles as she could so he wouldn't drive while he was in that condition. Of course, he didn't really mind at all; he was enjoying it.

They had traveled through Tennessee, Kentucky and spent another night in Ohio camping and resting before they continued on for the last miles. It seemed good to be closer to home and to know it wouldn't be much longer before they would be there. The boys kept asking, "How much farther do we have to go? We're tired of being in this car."

"It won't be long now. We are near the Michigan border and you can get out and kiss the sign like you did when we were coming back from Arizona," Maxine said.

Maxine thought, "It is so hard traveling, especially when you haven't much money and can't stop to see the interesting sights along the way that cost so much for a family. We have to hurry home before the money runs out. Although the bright side of this is getting to see the different states, the mountains, the plains, and just being able to go traveling wherever we want to whenever we want to for as long as we want to. In America, we have that freedom and no one is checking us at the borders of each state. That freedom is so wonderful as long as the laws are obeyed and a person lives an honest life keeping God's commandments and doing unto others as you would be done by. Even though we don't have much money, there is so much to be thankful for that is free."

What a sight to see: the Michigan border and the sign once again that read, WELCOME TO MICHIGAN. As Jack stopped the car, the boys got out and ran up to the sign, and as before, they kissed the sign and jumped up and down with joy, yelling "Michigan, my Michigan."

Oh, what relief for the family to be so close to home. They returned to the car and headed north. It wasn't far now, only about two hours away from home. Maxine drove the rest of the way because Jack wanted to stop and get some beer to drink because it was so warm and, "So I can relax the rest of the way," he said.

By the time they drove in the driveway at home he had finished all six beers. They were all so happy to be home once again. They began unloading the car and boat of the things they would need to get meals, their clothes and other important things they needed. Jack turned on the television and it didn't work; he was very upset and said, "We went out of our way to have that fixed before we left and now it isn't working for us. I wonder how much more there is wrong around here. I am going in the attic and get the rest of our electric appliances."

What a shock to find that all the appliances were gone from the attic. And then they couldn't find Rusty, so Jack called his dad and asked, "Do you know anything about Rusty?"

Dad said, "The last time I was out there Rusty was running all over the neighborhood and was so skinny from not being fed, I took him

168

in and had him put away because those people who were renting the house had moved out about three months ago. They moved about a mile from your house and no one was feeding the dog."

They couldn't understand why Dad didn't tell them; he could have called them in Florida and let them know in advance about Rusty. By this time Jack was furious and told Maxine, "I am going over to their house with this gun and make them give me the money they owe me and ask them why they didn't feed the dog like they had promised they would do."

"Jack, wait and get a lawyer. You will get into trouble going down there on your own, please wait!"

"No! They didn't wait, they are going to pay, now!" he yelled.

Maxine was so upset, she cried and thought, "To think that those people would do that to us, and I thought they were such nice people." The boys were upset, too, because of Rusty; they loved that ol' hound dog so much and would miss him. Soon Jack came home madder than ever before. He had tried to force his way in their door with the gun and they slammed the door in his face and told him they were going to call the police, and they did. The next morning the police came to the house with a warrant for Jack's arrest.

CHAPTER FIFTEEN

LIFE OF HELL PREDICTED

With Jack in jail, going for a hearing at court the next day and not knowing if the judge would release him on bond, Maxine was about fit to be tied, and she was in knots. The family had just returned home from Florida without any money; she was so discouraged she didn't know where to turn. "Why didn't he listen to me? Now what am I going to do? I need help and who can I turn to?" All these questions filled her thoughts as she kept busy putting things away, doing the washing and trying to explain to the children what had happened the night before and why their dad was in jail. She told them, " No matter what those people did to us by not paying the rent and all that, it gave your dad no right to go down there and threaten them with a gun. We live in a civilized world now, and we need to do things in a civilized manner."

At the hearing the next day, the judge announced the amount of the bond and Jack was given a date to appear in court for a trial because Jack wanted to fight the charges they had against him. After they left the courthouse Jack told Maxine, "Go over to the Sheriff Department and see if you can get your gun back in our possession." He had used the shotgun he had bought her for Christmas the year before and thought the police would return it, but they told Maxine that since it had been used in a crime Jack had committed and was evidence, it would not be returned at all. Of course, Jack got very upset about that, too, and stopped to buy some beer to drink. That seemed to be his answer to all his problems, but it only made things worse. He drank until the early morning hours and made Maxine sit up with him to listen to all of his complaints about the government, work, people, and just about anything he could think about that irritated him. She sat there and just nodded her head in agreement with him, all the while thinking the opposite, in order to keep from having an argument or having him calling her stupid because she didn't agree.

The next morning after he had sobered up somewhat, he was still furious about the matter and said, "They are the ones who took our things, didn't pay three months' rent and let Rusty starve, and I am the one who has to pay. That's justice?"

"I told you to wait and we would get a lawyer and take them to court, but you wouldn't listen to me, so now you got us into this and are the one in the wrong and in a mess," Maxine answered.

Jack really got mad at her and slapped her face very hard and told her, "You are so stupid to think the law will do anything for us and, besides, it takes so long to get our money they owe us. Those people used the money they owed us for rent to help pay for the down payment on a house they bought, that is the same as stealing, isn't it?"

"Yes, it is, but we live in a civilized country and should not use force to get someone to pay their bills, and just because they do wrong doesn't make it right for you to take revenge. Two wrongs never made a right; this is what I was taught in Sunday school. To love thy neighbor as thyself, it is up to God to judge people, not us."

A few days later Jack decided to go look for work and wasn't very successful, so he went to a friend, Ken Robinson, who was working on a highway job to see if he could help him get on the crew, and Ken said he would help him get a job. Jack was hired and he rode back and forth to work with Ken most of the time. They were so thankful to have him working again because they needed the money for bills, groceries and school supplies, as the boys would be going back to school soon.

Later that month, Jack decided not to go to trial and appeared before the judge for sentencing. He was found guilty of a misdemeanor and paid a substantial fine to the court.

The summer was beautiful and it seemed good to be back in their own home once again, plus it was delightful seeing and spending time with family and friends. Absence does make the heart grow fonder and makes a person realize how important it is to have those around who care about you and your family. Daily chores had never been a burden for Maxine; she loved her family and doing things for them was natural for her and made her happy knowing this was what she wanted in her life: being a housewife and mother. Joy filled her heart as she settled back into the daily routine. Even with all the problems that had risen with Jack, she was hopeful of the future and tried to stay above it all.

On weekends the family went to the lake to go boating and water skiing; they usually went to Clark's Lake, out by Brooklyn or to Swain's Lake out by Concord. Jack usually was the one to choose where they would go. The whole family loved to water ski, the boys were getting pretty good on them, dropping one ski, jumping the waves and other tricks. Jack was teaching them how to run the boat while pulling a skier and they caught on fast because they liked to drive it fast and try to dump each other. Sometimes after it got dark they would fish if the fish were biting – they didn't have the patience if they weren't.

The boys were so happy going to their friends and playing ball, going fishing or helping with the chores at the Jordan's farm. Maxine would call to see if it was okay or not, and tell the parents when the boys were expected back home. The same was true when their friends came over to their house; it was a good bunch of kids and they were all easy to get along with and very seldom did they fight.

Summer was passing by fast and Clara, Maxine's sister, called and asked if the boys would like to go up north to their farm in Cadillac with them for the weekend. This would be the last weekend before school started, and she knew the boys liked to go there to fish and camp out. Clara and Maxine took turns taking the kids on the weekends so they would grow up knowing their cousins, because Clara and Maxine didn't know their cousins very well until after they were older and went to the family reunions.

Clara and Jim arrived back in Lansing on Sunday evening and decided to keep the boys until later in the week. On Monday, Clara was fixing lunch for all of them and Danny asked for another peanut butter and jelly sandwich and Clara said, "No, we don't have enough bread."

That made him upset and he walked out of the house and kept on walking; he was determined to walk home, so he headed for the highway and walked and walked. When he got close to Jackson, he called his Grandpa Derr and told him where he was and asked him if he would come and get him.

"Of course I will. You stay where you are and I will be there soon." Dad and Vera were so astonished to think that a boy that young, thirteen years old, would even start to walk that distance. They took him to their home, fed him and let him take a bath before they took him home. Upon arriving, Grandpa told Jack and Maxine they had better get their act together and pay more attention to the boys, to stop thinking of themselves and start thinking of what the kids are going through. Danny had told Grandpa many things that had gone on with Jack's drinking and that Jack would hit Danny along side of the head and knock him out of his chair.

It was Danny's thirteenth birthday, September 1. He was a teenager now. They had moved into this home when he was a newborn baby and so many things had happened through these past years. At the moment things seemed to be going pretty smoothly and peaceful between Maxine and Jack. He had a job now and was doing much better with his attitude, and was not drinking as much as usual. Maxine made a birthday cake and they celebrated that day with joy and had fun playing games. Dad and Vera came out later that evening to give Danny his birthday gift and to visit. They were so faithful about giving the boys a gift on their birthday. Vera teased Danny about being born on Labor Day when they were up north fishing that he couldn't wait for them to get back in town.

School started after Labor Day and the boys were anxious to be back in school, as they liked sports and being with their friends. They had really missed their friends the year before while the family was in Florida. Things seemed to be back to normal now: the children were back in school, Jack was working quite regularly and Maxine was staying at home keeping house and trying to make sure everyone was happy. But that didn't last. Before long, Jack started drinking again and staying out later at night and wouldn't get up to go to work. He was back in his old routine once again, making everyone be cautious around him. When he drank too much, he got mean and talked about the time he had to go to jail and other woes. He just wasn't the same person when he was drunk and Maxine began to get discouraged; she wanted him to get help but he wouldn't.

It was just another day of drinking and lying around the house for Jack. Jackie, Danny and Mark had gone to play softball with the neighbor kids and it was getting past time for them to be home for dinner and Jack was upset about it. The boys were about twenty minutes late, and as soon as they came in through the back door, he grabbed Jackie and started beating him in the face and head. Maxine thought, "You may beat on me, mister, but you better leave my kids alone."

As she thought this, she spotted the baseball bat in the corner where Danny had placed it. She was so mad, she picked it up and put it on her shoulder, thinking like an old mother bear, "Kill him, kill him," and with his back to her, she swung that bat and hit Jack over the head. This pushed his head through the kitchen door window and broke it; then he fell to the floor unconscious and she placed the bat back on her shoulder and continued thinking, "Kill him, kill him."

"Don't, Mom, you will kill him," Danny yelled.

Something snapped in her mind and she thought, "My God, what have I done?"

Fear struck Maxine like never before and she ran over to the neighbors, Pete and Ann Lawrence's and told them what she had done and Pete went over to see if Jack was all right. By this time Jack was on his feet and decided he had better go to bed. He told Pete, "I am okay. I must have really tied a good one on and fell through the kitchen-door window." Pete left and the boys came with him; they and Maxine stayed all night at Pete and Ann's because she was still afraid to be in the same house with Jack.

The next morning Maxine and the boys went back to their house so the boys could get ready for school. Ann told her if there was any trouble to send one of the boys back to let them know and Pete would go and calm Jack down. Jack was drinking coffee and eating breakfast when they all came in and asked, "Where have you all been? I must have really tied a good one on last night and put my head through the kitchen-door window."

Maxine decided to be truthful and said, "No, I hit you over the head with the baseball bat because you were beating Jack in the face and head just because they were late getting home from the ball field last night."

"No wonder I have a big lump on my head," he answered.

They sat together and had coffee talking about disciplining the boys when they needed it and Maxine said, "I don't mind discipline, but they have a bottom for that; you don't need to knock them in the head."

The rest of the day was quiet and civilized, for a change, between them; apologies were made and a sense of peacefulness and contentment seemed to be present. "If only this could continue it would be an answer to prayer," Maxine thought as they watched television. After the baseball-bat episode happened, things were pretty calm and the days passed quickly while Jack was working, then he started drinking heavy again and didn't want to get up to go to work, so he was fired.

He wanted her to go back to work because he had lost his job, so she called Tony and asked him, "Could I please come back to work? Jack isn't working and we need the money."

"Maxine, that will be fine but he must stay away from here; I don't want any trouble," Tony answered. So she went back to work at The Famous Door in October.

November was here and Lillian had a little girl that they named Roberta. She was a sweet one, of course, and she got so much attention from all of the other children. Lillian was very happy as she loved having a new baby to care for; she was content with her family and the way things were going now.

One day Maxine called Lillian and asked her, "Can I come down and talk to you?"

When Maxine got there, Lillian greeted Maxine at the door and asked, "Is there something wrong?"

"Yes, very much wrong. I am pregnant and Jack doesn't know it yet and I am afraid to tell him. You know we use the diaphragm, and he is going to wonder what happened, and so do I."

Lillian said, "I don't know why men are so selfish about us women getting pregnant. I guess they don't think we have enough love to go around to everyone. Those diaphragms aren't one hundred percent guaranteed anyway, others have gotten pregnant using them."

" Thanks Lillian for talking to me, I feel much better getting it off my mind, you are a good friend."

Maxine knew she had to tell Jack sooner or later, but she wanted to find the right time, especially when he wasn't drinking, which didn't leave much time. She cooked an extra-special dinner and was very happy the evening she decided to tell him, so that anything he might say wouldn't crush her spirit. After dinner they all went into the living room to watch television and to enjoy a quiet evening together as a family, although it was rare anymore that Jack wouldn't be drinking and they could have a time together like this without some conflict happening.

After watching *Gunsmoke* and *I Love Lucy*, it was time for the boys to go and get ready for bed, so they left the room, returning a short time later for their goodnight kiss. Maxine was very apprehensive about telling Jack the news, but she knew it had to be done one way or another and now was as good a time as any to let him know she was pregnant. She thought, "What will I say? Oh Lord, help me!" So between the show when one of the commercials was on, she said, "Jack, I have something to tell you and it is very important."

He looked at her and said, "Yes, what is it?"

She said very softly, "I am pregnant."

He about dropped to the floor with surprise and with astonishment written all over his face, saying, "How can you be? We've used the diaphragm faithfully and it has never happened before, why now?"

"Jack, I don't know how or why, all I know is I am pregnant. I do remember the doctor told me that they were only ninety-nine percent safe, so maybe this time the odds were against us. It has been safe for us for seven years, before Mark and now almost seven years since Mark was born, God only knows why."

Jack's face flushed red, his eyes bulged out and he said, "God had nothing to do with your getting pregnant, and we don't need this right now, me with unsteady work and you won't be able to work long now either. Get real Maxine."

Silence filled the room for quite a long time between them. The only movements were their glancing and blinking eyes at each other until Jack said, "Maxine you know we can't afford another child, we don't have any insurance and I just don't want any more kids."

Maxine lowered her head and answered, "Jack, maybe it will be a girl this time. You wanted one so bad when I got pregnant with Mark, and I am sure things will work out for us, they always have."

He looked at her with a disgusted look on his face and said, "I am going to get some beer."

Maxine knew what she was in for the rest of the night with his drinking, and now with this on his mind, so she said, "Please, Jack, not tonight. We have had such a good evening together without you drinking, don't let this get you down."

Of course this was just another excuse for him to drink, so he left the house to get some beer.

By the time he returned Maxine was in bed, still awake, dreading what was in store for her after he consumed a few beers. He got so he was drinking more and more bottles because it took more to get him drunk. It was after midnight when he went into the bedroom and grabbed Maxine by the hair and pulled her out of bed, yelling at her, "Get out of bed. I want to talk to you now about this pregnancy."

Letting go of her hair, he gave her a robe to put on. Sitting in the living room, he started in again saying all kinds of mean things: calling Maxine all kinds of bad names and ranting and raving about not being able to afford this baby and that they shouldn't even consider keeping it because he didn't want any more kids. He went on and on about when you have kids you can't have other things. Maxine sat in silence, nodding her head once in a while, otherwise Jack would slap her if she happened to say something he didn't like, and she had learned not to say anything that would upset him.

Finally, he decided to go to bed because he ran out of beer and the beer garden was closed by this time. Fear filled Maxine because he would want sex, and when he was drunk he wasn't able to perform as usual and then he got violent and mean, calling her bad names and treating her like a dog, blaming her for his impotency. Maxine thought, "I hope and pray that I never hurt you like you do me with such tongue lashings, it hurts deep." Finally he gave up and went to sleep.

In the morning Maxine got up and fixed the boys their lunch for school, then called them for breakfast. She sat down with them and Danny asked, "Are you alright, Mom? We heard Dad yelling at you again."

"Yes, I am okay. Your dad got mad at me because I told him I am pregnant and he didn't like that at all. I guess he realizes he might have to go back to work because I won't be able to work much longer."

Working at The Famous Door, Maxine received good tips because she tried to please the customers and always had a smile for them and a cheery, "Hello." But Jack would get into her purse at night and take her tips so he could go buy his booze. Maxine finally got wise and asked Tony if he would put some of her money away for her because she needed to save enough money for the mortgage or they would lose their home.

"Sure, Maxine, I will gladly do that for you, and whenever you need it just let me know."

So, every night after hours, Maxine would give Tony at least five dollars to save for her, sometimes more if she could without Jack suspecting something because she didn't have as much money as usual. This is a survival tactic for an abused spouse.

Thanksgiving had gone by and the Christmas decorations were in the store fronts all over town and Christmas music was being played wherever you went. It was good to hear the music and to sing along with it and to look forward to celebrating with all of the family. Although Christmas would be a slim one this year for Maxine and Jack, they knew with all of the relatives the kids wouldn't go without. Maxine was getting extra-good tips and was able to save more each day and that was helping her with the assurance she would have enough by the time the mortgage was due.

One of the ladies that came in The Famous Door had just had her hair cut and styled, and it looked so pretty, Maxine asked her, "Where did you have your hair done?"

"Down the street at the Beauty Shop. It is a new style, do you like it?"

"I sure do," Maxine replied. "I think I will have to wait until after Christmas to have it done. You won't mind if I copy you do you? I am getting tired of this long hair. My husband is the one who wants me to keep it long. But he is not the one that has to take care of it, and I do have a mind of my own." Maxine kept this idea to herself and planned to have it done after Christmas.

Many regular customers and Christmas shoppers were coming in The Famous Door for lunch to enjoy the wonderful roast-beef dinner being served with the all-you-can-eat salad bar. They went away full and content.

These were busy evenings also, and the customers were very generous with their tips as she took their coats and hung them up for them and seated them with a cheerful, "Good evening, may I help you?" The Christmas season brought the joy of giving to the customers and they were generous with their tips and she was able to save more money.

Jack continued drinking more and more and was getting very mean again, treating Maxine worse than ever before: calling her terrible names, knocking her down and choking her until the boys would take a hold of him and pull him off. One evening when he was doing this, Jackie just punched him in the face, knocked him with a hard punch and he fell off her. Jackie said, "You get off of my mother and leave her alone, now!"

Jack looked up at him and said, "I needed that."

Maxine had an inferiority complex and thought she deserved punishment because of things she had done and she felt were wrong. Jack called her stupid and said other things that hurt her. She didn't argue with him because he would get upset.

Thank God the boys were there many times or he would have killed her. He was so drunk he couldn't remember what he had done the night before, and when Maxine told him, he wouldn't believe he had done those things to her. Throughout this time there wasn't much money for fuel oil and they closed off the bedroom and slept on a hide-a-bed in the living room.

It was Christmas Eve and Jack was really drunk. Maxine was in bed and he jumped on her, grabbed her throat, and choked her until she could hardly breath. Jack and Danny ran in and jumped on him and dragged him off of her and told him, "Leave our mother alone. You're going to kill her."

She sat up to catch her breath and thought, "He could have killed me and the baby. Oh, I can't take anymore of this. He needs help."

Maxine had gone to different places to get information about alcoholics to see if she could do anything to help him but to no avail; they said he had to want to help himself. She even went to a psychiatrist to see if she had a problem, and he said, "The only thing that's bothering you is your husband's drinking."

When she went home and told Jack she had gone to see a psychiatrist and what he said, Jack laughed and said, "I could have told you that!"

CHAPTER SIXTEEN

WHO IS AT FAULT – GOD ONLY KNOWS

January was a very cold month and Maxine was still working at The Famous Door trying to keep the bills paid and food on the table. Jack had agreed to go for some help for his drinking and behavior, and Maxine told him he needed to be present, so they made an appointment to go after she got off work. The appointment was made for January 4, 1961, at 3:00 p.m. Somehow Jack thought it was for January 3 at 4:00 p.m. She was late getting home on the third because she went and had her hair cut and styled. As she walked in the door the boys said, "Ma! Is that you?"

She looked entirely different with her hair short and styled. She asked them, "Do you like it?"

"We liked it long, Mom," they answered.

"It's too late to change it now," she said.

Jack was very upset and he said, "We have missed our appointment because of you going to the beauty parlor."

"We aren't supposed to go until tomorrow at 3:00," she replied.

He argued with her about the date and time and said, "I refuse to go now, and I am going to go get something to drink."

"If you do I will not be here when you get back." Maxine said.

"That's fine," he said.

"When you find out what is causing a problem, don't you usually get rid of it?" She asked.

"Yes!" He replied.

"Then I am leaving," she said,

When he heard her say this, Jack had the gall to go out and re-place the good tires on her car with a set of old ones.

The money she had saved would help her, although she had intended it for the mortgage. She decided it would be a chance to make a change in her life because she couldn't take much more and she knew what he would be like after drinking again. The one hundred dollars she had saved would help her to get to Florida, but she knew it wouldn't be enough if she took the older boys along. She explained to them, "As soon as I have the money you can come on the bus. I will call you at least once a week to see how you both are. Also, I will send letters to you at Pete and Ann's house so your dad won't know where I am. This is a hard decision to make, leaving you boys, but I feel you boys need to be in school, so keep in contact with Grandma and Grandpa Derr. If you need anything or if your dad is treating you harshly, let them know right away. I have to take Mark along because he is so young and you boys can't be responsible for him." Danny was almost fourteen and Jackie was going on fifteen; they were physically capable of handling themselves around Jack. Mark was only six at this time so she had planned on taking him with her.

When Mark heard this he ran in and started packing his clothes and some toys right away. It was a hard decision to make and she was crying while she packed her bags, knowing she had a long trip ahead of her, but she didn't know any other solution to this problem. She phoned Tony and told him, "There is trouble and I need to come in and get the money. I will explain to you later." They were all crying when they said their goodbyes and she reaffirmed to Jackie and Danny, "I will keep in contact with you and as soon as possible will let you know where I am."

While driving to town she realized her heart was broken to think she couldn't save their marriage; she tried hard in so many ways but had failed. Remembering what her mother had told her when Jack gave her the engagement ring, "He will give you nothing but a life of hell. He drinks and you don't believe in drinking." She thought about how Mother was so right.

It was cold that day, and Maxine was thankful for a good heater in the car as she drove to town to see Tony and to explain what had happened. Tony said, "Maxine you have gone the extra mile with Jack and it is too bad things didn't work out for you. I do want to give you my blessings for a safe trip."

Crying, she said, "I didn't realize when I was saving this money that it would be used for this, but I am thankful I did. May I use the phone?"

"Sure, go ahead." She phoned her ex-sister-in-law, Jeanne, to see if it was possible for her to stay all night with her and Pamela, her daughter. She told Jeanne, "I'll explain to you what has happened and what I plan to do. I don't want to leave on a trip this time of day."

"I agree with you, come on over now." Jeanne had married Harold a second time and they adopted Pamela in 1954. Later on, Jeanne divorced Harold because she met and fell in love with her manager at Stillman's Clothing Store. They lived together until he passed away. She and Pamela stayed in his apartment.

Maxine thought, "Here I am, leaving the very thing I believed was my answer to prayer and it turned out to be a nightmare. Now I realize when I asked God many years ago about marrying Jack and He answered , 'It is what you need, not what you want,' what He really meant."

Maxine and Mark arrived at the apartment house and went upstairs to Jeanne's to spend the night. She explained everything to Jeanne and she sympathized with Maxine, knowing the history of the marriage.

They arose early and realized how much colder it was, so Maxine went down to start the car and couldn't even get the door open; it was frozen shut. She went back in to call someone and Jeanne gave her some spray that would melt the ice and loosen the lock. After a few tries it came loose and she was thankful, even though she was almost frozen from standing in the cold. The car was like a refrigerator with the windows frosted solid, it would take some time for it to thaw out.

Jeanne and Pamela hugged them and said their goodbyes to Maxine and Mark and wished them, "Good luck and a safe journey." Maxine was four months pregnant with her baby and this wouldn't be an easy trip with just her doing the driving all the way to Florida. Before they left, Maxine asked Jeanne, "Can I send letters to the boys here and have you put them in another envelope and send them from Jackson? This is so Jack won't know where I am, and later on when I can afford it, I will send them bus tickets. Jack doesn't need to know about that either."

"Yes, I will do that for you so Jack won't know where you are," Jeanne replied.

By this time the car was warmed up and they left, heading for Florida. As the miles flew by that day, Maxine felt freedom from the turmoil of the drinking and the beatings Jack had inflicted on her, plus the awful things he spewed out of his mouth that would hurt her so deep. Only God would know her heart was broken because she had left the boys behind.

Mark was a joy to have along; he was so concerned, never asking many questions about where they were going to stay that night or anything. The first night they stayed at a motel and when they awoke and were ready to leave, they spotted a flat tire on the car, but thanks be to God, a gentleman was willing to change the tire for them right there at the motel.

They found a garage, had the flat tire fixed and they were ready to continue on their journey. Heading south toward the tollbooth, just before they got there, another tire went flat, so Maxine pulled over to the side of the road and another gentleman came over and changed the tire for her. God's angels were looking after Maxine and Mark. They drove on for the day until it was early evening and then found another motel, ate and rested for the night. They were both very tired and slept well. The next morning they decided to stop at a service station for gas and oil, plus get that flat tire fixed, and as they were pulling into the station there was a loud BANG.

"Oh my Goodness!" Maxine said, "We just had a blow out." So she purchased another used tire and had it mounted so they could be on their way. She was disturbed and wondered, "How many flat tires must we have before we reach Florida?" She got a grip on herself because she couldn't let Mark know how she was feeling. He commented on the way out of the service station, "Boy, it's a good thing we needed gas, Mom."

"How true that is son, and God's looking out after us all the way to Florida."

As they traveled south the weather was getting nice and warm, a far cry from where they had come from. It was great to see the "WELCOME TO FLORIDA" sign and to know it wouldn't be long before they would be in Orlando. But first Maxine must call Eva, her friend, to see if they could possibly stay with her until she could afford a place for Mark and herself. Maxine found a phone booth and called Eva and she was so happy to hear from Maxine and answered quickly, "Why yes, you surely may, I'll have the room ready for you when you get here, it will be so good to see you and Mark again."

How pleased and thankful Maxine was to hear this positive answer. Eva was a friend she had met at the Martin Missile factory working on the assembly line soldering circuit boards. Eva had told Maxine that, "Someday I will repay you for helping me so much and if there is ever anything I can do for you, just let me know." Maxine thought to herself, "Maybe this is the reward I will receive for being a friend to her a while back."

They drove into the driveway and Eva came out with her arms wide open and happy to see them. Maxine said, "Eva, real friends are very hard to find and I am so grateful that you will take Mark and me in like this. When we are settled I will fill you in on everything."

"You don't have to explain anything, I know what you went through when you and your family lived down here before and you worked with me," Eva replied.

After a good night's rest and a delicious breakfast, they lounged around, drinking their coffee and catching up on all the news about some of the people that Maxine had worked with at the factory and Eva's family. Maxine mentioned that she wanted to go and see if she could go back to work at The Toddle House, a breakfast restaurant she had worked at before Jack had decided to move back to Michigan.

Eva suggested, "Maxine, why don't you call the manager and see if they need anyone, it will save you a trip."

So Maxine called and was told, "Yes, we would love to have you come back to work, it would be on the midnight shift from 11:00 p.m. to 7:00 a.m."

Maxine agreed and told them, "That would be the best time for me, thank you very much."

Everything was working out well for them all. Mark stayed with Eva nights while Maxine worked and Eva's husband, Len, watched him during the day while Maxine was sleeping. Then in the evening she was able to help Eva get dinner and do the dishes and still have time to spend with Mark. Len worked out in the yard a lot and had hundreds of chickens to care for. He raised them to sell to Kentucky Fried Kitchen, so Mark kept busy helping him and enjoying a man who was so sweet and kind. Eva had a son, Butch, who was grown by this time and didn't live

184

at home, so Len enjoyed having Mark around. They both loved children and catered to Mark; he was a good boy and never caused any trouble. Maxine was happy to be back to work and it was good to see the people she had worked with before and to know she was safe from Jack's abusive behavior.

Maxine made a doctor appointment because she was four months' pregnant and hadn't seen a doctor yet. She told him she had driven down from Michigan and was separated from Jack and wasn't feeling too good. He puffed on his pipe and looked Maxine in the eyes and said, "Young lady, you are dying from a broken heart."

She thought, "Yes I am, I miss my sons I had to leave behind in Michigan because I didn't have enough money for them to come here with Mark and me, Mark is only six years old and the boys are teenagers. Mainly, I am so hurt by Jack's failures. I still love him and am committed to our marriage, but can't take his abuses any more. He almost killed me and the baby by choking me to the point I was gasping for air to breath, when the older boys pulled him off of me."

But she answered the doctor by saying, "Yes, I am."

In one of the letters she sent to the boys, she gave them the phone number where she worked so they could call her and let her know how they were doing, and she could also reassure them that she was saving the money for their bus tickets to come to Florida. After staying a month with the Suggs, Maxine felt she should get a place of her own to stay so she wouldn't be a burden on them. They said she could stay longer if she wanted to, but she didn't want to wear out her welcome. First, she had to find someplace where Mark could stay all night and she would pick him up in the morning after she got off work. Eva told her about one of the ladies she had worked with who might do it for Maxine. Eva called her and asked her if she was available and she said she was. The arrangements were made for Mark to stay at Sandy's. Now the next step was to find a church school that would take Mark for the day while Maxine slept. Finally she found a church that would take Mark and found that the bus would drop him off at their apartment when school was over. She asked the bus driver if he would honk his horn when he dropped Mark off so she would wake up, as she didn't have an alarm clock. Mark enjoyed school very much and was happy with this arrangement. They would have dinner and sometimes go to the park or go fishing at a nearby pond.

One evening the phone at The Toddle House rang and it was Jack. He said, "I have been trying for two months to find you, and my mother told me that she bet you had gone back to Florida and got your old job back. I called during the day and they said you worked the 11 - 7 shift, so I knew you were there." As he went on, he swore, calling her all kind of bad names, ranting and raving on and on.

"Mister, you are 1,300 miles away and I don't have to listen to this!" Then she hung up. He tried calling back and she wouldn't talk to him.

Another two months went by and Maxine had enough money for one bus ticket for the boys; she let them know that it wouldn't be long now and they could all be together again. The rent was due again, so Maxine paid for April rent and a day later a neighbor came over and said there was a phone call for Maxine and told her, "She said her name was Vera, your mother-in-law." Maxine had let Vera know where she was because they, too, were real good friends. Although Maxine didn't have a phone, she had asked the nearest neighbor if she could give Vera their number and they were willing in case of an emergency.

Many things came into her mind on the way over to answer the call: Are the boys okay? Has something happened to Jack? Maxine picked up the phone and said, "Hello, Vera? Is anything wrong?"

Vera answered "Yes, Maxine, you had better come home. Jack is selling everything he can get his hands on for drinking money, and he is a mess, and I am afraid for the boys. They need you here."

"Vera, I just paid my rent but I'll go ask for it back and explain why. Then we will be on our way back to Michigan."

"Okay, we will be looking for you. Call when you get close and you can stay here with us. Drive safely, we love you, Maxine," Vera said.

It was a task to get the landlady to return the rent money, but with Maxine's persuasion and pleading, she reluctantly returned the money. Maxine thanked her for understanding the situation, then packed their belongings, called The Toddle House and explained to them what had happened, and then they headed back for Michigan. Driving through

Florida and on to Georgia, the miles flew by, then there was a strange noise coming from the transmission and Maxine knew she had better stop and have it checked. Sure enough it needed new bands. After a few hours it was fixed and they were on the way once again. It seemed like it was taking a long time to get back home because of the worry and wondering what was ahead of her and trying to keep her concern from Mark. Then it happened again: another flat tire as they were pulling out of the motel parking lot. "Could anything else go wrong?" Maxine wondered. "I need to get back home safe and sound. Thank God for gentlemen willing to change tires for a seven months' pregnant lady and a little boy."

The man who changed it said, "You know, if this was my wife I sure hope someone would do the same for her. That is the way it should be in this world of ours." Then he suggested that the tire should be fixed so there would be a spare, just in case of another flat.

"My husband took the new set of tires off my car before I left."

He shook his head and said, "He sure must have a mean streak in him."

Back on the road again, thanking God for the helpers along the trip and silently praying for a safe journey back, Maxine tried to instill into Mark that God had been with them all the way and they were going on a wing and a prayer, trusting they would arrive safely. They entered Michigan, evening was drawing near and they were getting closer to the little town of Spring Arbor, which was about fifteen miles from Jackson where Jack's folks lived. Maxine knew there was a telephone booth by the firehouse and she would call from there to let the folks know where Mark and she were. It was about 8:30 p.m. when she phoned them, Vera answered the phone and said, "We are so thankful you're safe and we'll see you soon."

"It won't be long now," Maxine told Mark.

"Okay, Mama. That's where I went to Sunday school isn't it?"

"Yes, Mark, it is and maybe you will be able to go there again soon," she answered.

Spring Arbor was a little town inhabited by many Christians, and at the time there were no alcoholic beverages or tobacco products sold in the township, so consequently, no bars were permitted to do business in the area. The Spring Arbor College was located in the middle of town along with the main church, Free Methodist Faith. Jackie, Danny and Mark all attended Sunday school at this church every Sunday. The bus would pick them up at the house and bring them home. For years, the bus driver was Orville Fitzgerald, one of the elders at the church.

Remembering how the pastor and a couple of elders came several times to visit at Maxine and Jack's home and to invite them to church, she would go at Christmas and Easter with the boys. They called them CEOs (Christmas and Easter Only) attendants. She thought because her husband didn't go to church, she wouldn't either, not realizing each one is responsible for his or her own individual actions and beliefs toward God and will stand alone with Jesus Christ interceding for them to God. She had so much to learn and understand about God. These memories brought tears to her eyes and she thought how lucky she was to have in-laws who were understanding and ready to help when she needed it. Mark was so excited these last fifteen miles driving to Dad & Vera's home, he said, "It will be so good to see Grandma and Grandpa again, won't it Mama?"

"It sure will, Mark!" she replied with a happy note.

The yard lights were on and the folks came out with their arms wide open to greet Mark and Maxine, tears filled their joyous faces with excitement and gratitude. Vera said, "We are so glad you made it safe and sound, Maxine, and thanks for coming when I called you, those boys need you so much."

Maxine replied, "I am so thankful you called me and told me about what is going on. We left as soon as we could."

This was a family that had always been good to Maxine from the first day she met them. They showed her the real meaning of love throughout the years, and to the boys, especially, taking them for the weekends. They were very good grandparents.

"For a long time we have been worried and concerned about Jack and his drinking problem and what it was doing to his health and to you and the boys Maxine," Dad said as they went into the house.

Vera said, "The boys want to come in to see you in the morning and wanted you to call them when you got here."

Maxine went to the phone right away. It was so good to talk to them knowing she would be seeing them in the morning when Jack brought them in. Vera made coffee and had a snack for them to eat and they caught up on a few things that had been happening these past months. It was getting late so Vera cleaned up the kitchen while Maxine showered and got ready for bed. Mark was so tired and relaxed to be in familiar surroundings, he kissed everyone goodnight and went to bed; it didn't take him long to go to sleep. Maxine was relieved to be back in Michigan so she would be with the older boys again. As she lay in bed she thought, "Thank God for a safe trip and for wonderful caring in-laws, may the next day go well with the boys and especially with Jack, hoping he won't cause trouble."

A good night's sleep and a hearty breakfast in the morning seemed so good, it was bright and cheerful as they conversed more about what had been happening. The folks said, "We have gone out to see Jack and the boys several times to take food and check up on them to make sure they were alright. Jack's drunk most of the time, so the boys needed you to be there for them, that's why I called you. They need adult supervision for their welfare and Jack is in no condition to give it to them."

"I felt so guilty for leaving, but I couldn't take it any longer," Maxine said. He almost killed me and the baby on Christmas Eve. If it hadn't been for the boys, Jackie and Danny, he would have killed us in his drunken stupor, and as a mother I had to protect the baby I am carrying."

"We didn't know this had gone on to that extent and agree that you did the right thing for the sake of the baby and yourself," Dad said.

Maxine replied, "The day I left, Jack kept blaming me for everything that has happened, so I said to him, 'Jack when you find out what the problem is, don't you usually get rid of the problem?' and he answered, 'Yes' and I replied, 'Well I am going then, goodbye'."

The folks just shrugged their shoulders and said, "You did what you thought you had to do, and no one blames you for it. You are here now to look after the boys and they are so happy knowing that."

A car drove in the driveway and they heard the doors slam shut. The boys ran in the house and grabbed Maxine and hugged her for some time, and Mark also. They were so happy to see their mother and

Mark they stayed by her side a long time. A happy reunion, oh how thankful Maxine was to see them and hold her boys again and thinking, "I will never do that again, wherever I go they will go with me from now on."

Jack said, "Hello, it's good to see you again." No embrace between him and Maxine, but he did kiss and hug Mark and tell him, "Hi son, it is good to see you, and I sure missed you." They talked and filled Maxine in on some of the events that had happened, how school was going and how they had gone hunting earlier that year. The morning went by fast and Vera suggested, "I will fix lunch for you later on if you all want to stay?"

Jack spoke up and said, "I've got everything to make goulash at home if you want to come out and fix it."

Maxine hesitated before she answered, half scared to go out there with him, then the boys said, "Yes, come on Mom, we want you to cook it for us."

Maxine thought, "With a plea like that what mother could refuse?" Maxine went into Vera's bedroom to get her clothes and Dad followed her in there and said, "Now if anything happens and he gets out of control, you call me and we will come out and pick you and the boys up. Don't hesitate one minute, Maxine."

"I will, Dad. Thanks," she replied.

The boys wanted to ride with their mother out to the house so they could talk to her some more and fill her in on some of the things Jack had been doing and Jackie said, "We wanted to ride with you, Mom. Dad is drinking his beer, like always, and it is so good to see you and Mark." They were all so happy to be together again, looking forward to having dinner together at home. They reached home and Jack was there waiting for them and it seemed like everything was going along okay. Nothing was mentioned about Maxine's leaving or what had been happening since she had left. As Maxine fixed the goulash, the boys set the table and helped as much as they could to get ready for dinner. It was a joyful time, laughter and hugs, so good to be together again as a family. They all sat down to eat and started to pass the goulash and Jack got up and went into the bedroom and got his 12-gauge shotgun and loaded it with two shells, and as he was racking the shells in, he pointed the shotgun at Maxine. Instantly, the older boys grabbed the gun and took it away from Jack and unloaded the shells out of the gun. He got very upset, but the boys knew how to handle him.

Maxine got on the phone and called Dad right away, she said, "Dad, you need to come and get us right away. Jack threatened me with a loaded shotgun and the boys took it away from him and unloaded the shells. We are all upset."

Dad answered, "I will be right out there and get you all, stay calm."

Maxine cleaned up the kitchen as the boys stood by her protecting her from Jack. She felt so much tension and hopelessness. Dad arrived and talked to Jack for a while and tried to reason with him, but to no avail. No one could talk to him; he knew it all. So Dad said, "Let's go now, Maxine. You and the boys aren't going to stay here with him in the condition he is in."

Arriving back at Dad and Vera's house, Dad said, "We have to discuss the possibility of having Jack committed for his alcohol problem and we need to do it as soon as possible." Maxine agreed.

They went to the court the next day to sign papers for his commitment; they both signed, so if Jack would ever say anything about it, they agreed they both would take the responsibility. It was for himself and the family's welfare that this had to be done. The police picked up Jack the next day and he was taken to the Ypsilanti Hospital for Alcoholics. With him gone from the house now, Maxine and the boys could move back in and live there even though she didn't know if Jack had kept the mortgage paid or just what the status was. She would have to soon investigate this matter.

Maxine was informed that she had to go to the hospital and talk to the psychiatrist about Jack and the particulars about why he was committed. The doctor said, "This should only take about an hour." By the time he had finished talking to Maxine it was two hours. She told him everything she had been going through all these years and he asked, "Why in the world did you take it so long?"

"Because I love him," she replied.

The doctor said, "Mrs. Derr, we can keep him here for six months and put him through the program, but when he gets out and starts drinking again, that's his own free will. We can't make him stop drinking; he has to want to." Maxine left with hope in her heart that day thinking that Jack would want to.

Settling back in the house and the routine of housework, Maxine began thinking about the future: the mortgage on the house, the expense of the baby coming soon and other expenses. It wasn't long before she discovered Jack had put the house up for sale and found a buyer, Jack had bulldozed Maxine into signing the papers for the new owners and placed the remaining equity into an escrow account. Jack began borrowing money on it because he wasn't working. She and the children would have to find a place to move to because the new owners would be moving in within thirty days.

A good friend of her sister's, Sally Emerson, came over to visit Maxine one day to check to see if she was okay and said that there may be some places in Spring Arbor for rent. Also, Pastor Dunkel stopped by for a visit and said, "I will try to help you find a place to live if you decide to move to the Spring Arbor area. We are concerned about you and your family, Maxine. Your boys have attended our church for many years now." She thanked him and gave him permission to look for a place. There were a lot of good memories as well as bad memories living in that house through the years and it was very emotional knowing they had to move away from their neighbors they had so many years. Fourteen years in one place puts down a lot of roots to have to pull up and move. Maxine thought, "It will never be the same. The hope for a successful marriage has vanished and I don't know if it will ever be revived again."

CHAPTER SEVENTEEN

THE LOST RETURNING HOME

Spring blossoms were in full bloom and so beautiful; new life had sprung forth for another year and the pastor had found a place for Maxine and the boys to move into. So the time came to move. It was hard in one way but a relief in another, because of the things that had happened over the past year were not very pleasant and maybe moving would help erase them from their minds: a new start. The new place was a small two-bedroom apartment in a duplex converted from barracks that the army had moved there many years before for the servicemen to use while going to college. The couple in the adjoining apartment was the pastor's son and his wife, a nice young couple and their baby. Although they kept to themselves, they were very friendly whenever they did appear. A widow and her sons, Phil and Don Webb, occupied the house on the east side of them; they were close to Jackie and Dan's age. The boys got acquainted right away and played baseball at the field across the street, which was very handy for them. And there were other boys who were Mark's age living close by that he could play ball and go bike riding with in the neighborhood.

The family received some help from the food surplus – flour, cheese, canned meat, powdered milk and beans. Maxine made fresh bread, cinnamon rolls, and even homemade noodles. The boys were so happy to have their mother's home cooking again and even enjoyed the whole-wheat bread she made. Maxine was getting acquainted with some of the neighbor ladies and enjoyed their company and someone to talk to. She didn't have a telephone so the neighbors up the block, Jerry and Gilbert Roller, would let her use their phone whenever she needed it, and the Roller's would take calls for Maxine when necessary.

Vera arranged to have a baby shower for Maxine because she didn't have anything for the baby to wear or any of the necessities needed. It was a very nice shower and it was so good to see many of the family and friends once again and fellowship with them. With much gratitude, Maxine thanked everyone so much for their gifts and friendship toward her and marveled at the beautiful things she received for the baby. This gave her spirit a boost knowing that the love she received was a blessing and helped fill her sad heart with joy for the coming of the baby. She had no preference for either a boy or a girl. Knowing how she had her heart set on a girl when she carried Mark, this time she was going to accept with love and gratitude a healthy baby. Her due date was getting close and Maxine was ready for it any day now; she had made arrangements for the boys while she was in the hospital so whenever the baby was ready, so was she.

June 6 was Jackie's fifteenth birthday and he thought the baby would be born on that day. Well, the baby almost was – just one day earlier, on the June 5 …it had to have its own birthday. On Saturday night Maxine went into the hospital because the baby started to come but held back until Monday morning. Finally, the doctor said, "It is time to go into the delivery room and I won't be able to deliver this baby like I did the boys, feet first, because the hospital being run by Catholics wouldn't allow it." He was speaking about the unique method that he used to deliver all three of the boys.

"I want a natural birth without ether this time." Maxine said.

"You will have to really push hard when we tell you to," the doctor said.

So she pushed and pushed, then here came the baby after the last big push, and the nurse said, "It's a girl."

Maxine almost sat up – bouncing her buttocks up and down, so happy and thinking, "Maybe Jack will be better now that we have a little girl." She was in seventh heaven.

The doctor told her, "Settle down Maxine, you've just had a baby."

They showed the baby to Maxine and weighed her, cleaned her up so Maxine could hold her when she got back in her room. Oh, how happy she was and so sure Jack would be, too, because he wanted a little girl. She thought, "This will finally be the answer to our problems."

Returning to her room, she decided to get in touch with the authorities so Jack could come to see her and the baby. She had previously arranged for him to have a leave of absence when the baby was born, because he didn't like to wait around in the hospital before delivery; it usually made him uncomfortable. He wanted to be there the day before the birth, so when he got there on Monday he came in to see

Maxine and the baby girl and he was very upset.

"Why didn't you arrange for me to get here before she was born?"

Maxine explained that she couldn't have known the exact day of her delivery, but he was mad at everyone and left to go out and drink. It was just another excuse to get drunk while he was out of the treatment facility. When he got back to his dad's house where he was going to stay for the few days of his leave, his dad was very upset with him and took him back to the hospital and told him. "I don't have to put up with this drunken habit of yours, and I am not going to."

Vera went to the hospital to visit Maxine and told her about what had happened and why Jack wasn't coming to visit. She said, "Jack said he was upset because he couldn't be there before the baby was born, no one had asked him when he wanted the leave." Vera added, "Oh, well, just another excuse for drinking, that is all it is."

The state paid the hospital bill and they sent an agent in to see if Maxine wanted to adopt the baby out because of the circumstances and the family situation with Jack, an alcoholic committed to Ypsilanti State Hospital. Maxine said bluntly, "In no way is anyone getting my baby girl. She is mine, so don't any of you even think about it." Maxine named her Cynthia Gale, Mark wanted to name her Cindy, so Maxine said, "We will name her Cynthia and call her Cindy, and her middle name will be Gale, after Herman's wife."

After a week in the hospital Maxine went home and it was so good to see the boys and to be home again. They were surely glad to see her and their new baby sister too. The boys were so willing to help whenever they were told to do something, like the dishes or just picking up around the house. School was out and they usually were close by at the ball field or at the neighbor boy's playing games. Mark liked to go fishing in the pond about a block away and catch frogs and snakes, which Maxine didn't mind because she wasn't afraid of them.

One day a friend, Marlin, came to get the older boys and when he stepped into the house he saw the cage with a couple of snakes in it and he screamed and yelled, "There are snakes in there, I am afraid of them!"

Mark laughed and said, "They won't hurt you. They are just garden snakes."

"I'll wait outdoors," Marlin replied.

One time, one of the snakes got out of the cage and Maxine found it on top of the cooking stove, so she placed it gently back in the cage. Mark also had a couple of rabbits in a cage outside the house; he loved to be around little critters.

The family was content being in Spring Arbor, even though the apartment was small. It was good for the boys to have close friends and to be able to go to the college gym and play during the summer months. Also, Lime Lake was not too far from where they lived; they went swimming as often as they could get a ride. It was good not to have strife and tension and to be able to enjoy the children without Jack's harsh discipline with them. They seemed to be doing quite well as far as Maxine could see, and if they did get into any trouble the town sheriff, Mr. Glare, would let her know. He was an elderly man and was very understanding and would give them a warning not to do it again. Maxine would talk to the boys and ask them not to give her any problems because she had enough as it was.

Jack had written to Maxine and told her, "I was disappointed that I couldn't be there when the baby was born and so I went out and got drunk. I don't know if I want to come there and live with you and the children or not; I have been doing a lot of thinking about it since you were here last time to visit."

Maxine was very upset and her hope of his returning was crushed. All day Saturday she pondered over the letter and grew more discouraged as the day passed. She tried to keep busy so she wouldn't think about it, but it just wouldn't leave her thoughts. She didn't sleep well that night and was exhausted in the morning, but she arose and fixed breakfast for Mark and nursed the baby, then helped Mark get ready for Sunday school. While thinking of what she would prepare for dinner that day, she bathed Cindy and held her until she went to sleep, then quietly laid her in her crib.

After their Sunday pot-roast dinner, Jackie and Dan did the dishes and then left to go to Marlin's house, which was on the next street behind the house. Marlin's mother, Ethel McMinn, was their Sunday school teacher and she loved to have them come over and play games and just talk and get acquainted. Most of the neighbors went to the church there in town and knew who their neighbors were, so when new people moved in they would visit and get to know them by name and maybe invite them to lunch or dinner. One of the families that lived two doors away from Maxine was the Sheldon's; Gene, the father, was attending the college to become a minister and his wife, Betty, taught Sunday school and took care of little children during the weekdays along with her two daughters, Shelly and Julie, who had both been adopted when they were newborns. Gene and Betty had accepted the Lord Jesus Christ as their Lord and Savior of their life and were on fire for the Lord.

Betty came over to visit Maxine that Sunday afternoon and Maxine told her, "I have been so upset about our family situation and I don't know what to do." Crying so hard she could hardly talk; she went on to explain the situation to Betty.

Betty looked at her with such loving eyes and said, "Maxine, Christ is the only answer!"

A bright light went on in Maxine's mind, as she thought, "That's what I need!" The seed had been planted in her mind and heart as child of twelve years old, when she accepted Jesus into her heart, that seed of truth had just broken open to a realization of the need that had to be met in her life. Betty invited her to go to church that evening for services, and Maxine said she would.

Mark went to his class that evening and Maxine took Cindy in her bassinet and sat in one of the very last rows of the auditorium at the college. There was a new church building being built, so the church services were being held at the college. Many people were in attendance and many songs of praise were sung before Pastor Vernon Dunkel preached the sermon, then songs of invitation were sung, such as "Just as I Am, Without One Plea, That Thy Blood Was Shed For Me."

Then the Pastor gave the altar call, "Those who are seeking God, please come forward."

Maxine stepped out into the aisle and it seemed like her feet never even hit the floor. As she went down to the altar, the weight of the world was lifted off of her shoulders. "What a glorious day this is. I am set free from my sins and shame, a day I will never forget as long as I live," she thought as she kneeled on the altar. By the grace of God through faith in the Lord Jesus Christ, Maxine was "Born Again." The elder saints of the church sang, "Hallelujah, Hallelujah, Hallelujah." Many members had been praying for Maxine and the family for a long time. The Free Methodist Church in Spring Arbor, Michigan was the right place and time for Maxine to be, and by listening to Betty, one of God's family members, she took that advice and went to church where she found the answer. The love of God is never-ending and He will never leave you or forsake you, as long as you listen to that still small voice within you, and never underestimate the power of the Lord working within your life.

Maxine went home with the joy of the Lord in her heart. She couldn't wait to tell Betty and Gene; she hadn't seen them there that evening. Betty and Gene were both happy for Maxine and greeted her with a big hug and praises to God when she arrived. Also, Betty had a pot of coffee ready so they could talk about that evening. Maxine couldn't stop praising God and saying how she believed everything was going to be all right now, because she would go over and ask Jack for forgiveness of all the bad she had done and she didn't doubt a minute he would forgive her. Ever believing that forgiveness would solve all her problems and with Jack having some type of reciprocal change, her hopes were ever so strong again. Some of the other neighbors dropped in, also, and praised God for Maxine's commitment to God. What happiness and blessings God has in store for each one, if only they would believe Christ died for them, to wash away their sin and their guilt.

Maxine wrote Jack a letter and told him they would be up to see him the next Sunday and would bring a picnic lunch, and that she would like to tell him something that has happened to her. Maxine still had the car and it was running pretty well, good enough to drive over to Ypsilanti to see Jack. They woke up early and prepared a lunch to take with them and everyone helped Maxine pack up the car with the diaper bag, blankets and anything that she would need for the baby. The bassinet was placed on the back seat and the older boys sat back there also, Mark sat in front as they left for the day. As they were traveling on the highway, a car pulled up beside them and a man motioned for Maxine to pull over. She didn't like the looks of him, so she told the boys, who were slouching down, to sit up straight, and they did. As soon as they did, the man slowed up and got behind them; the boys tried to get his license-plate number but they couldn't. Maxine was quite shook up and told the boys, "I am so thankful you boys were with me because I don't know what he would have done to me."

Arriving at the hospital, Maxine went in for a pass to see Jack and was informed he was out on the grounds somewhere. So they drove around for a while and spotted him with a woman lying on the grass making love. What a sight for the whole family to see! When Jack saw them, he got up and headed toward the car. Arriving at Maxine's window, he started making excuses that it was hot and they were just trying to cool off in the shade.

"Yeah, right," the boys said, "Dad who do you think you are fooling, surely not us."

Jack got into the car and told them where they could find a picnic table and said, "Maybe we can talk." By this time it was too late for talking as far as Maxine was concerned.

All she did was listen; not believing a thing he said. "The experience we had on the way over here and how scared and nervous I was for our safety, then to come and find you with another woman was about all I can take for one day. I came over here anxious to see you and to tell you I was sorry for all of the things I have done and to try to make amends with you, and also because I didn't call you sooner to come home when Cindy was born and this is what I find."

Jack didn't say much more to Maxine, but spent some time with the boys, asking them, "Do you like living in Spring Arbor? What do you do in your spare time?"

They said, "It's alright but we like Reynolds Road better, of course."

Mark told him about all of his little critters and playing baseball across the street. They were all restless and didn't seem to be enjoying each other's company so Maxine suggested, "We better get things ready to go back home." The boys wanted to leave because there wasn't much for them to do and they were getting bored.

There wasn't much discussion on their way home that evening except a couple of remarks about their dad's actions and attitude that day. Jackie asked, "Is Dad coming home after he is released from the hospital?"

199

"That is up to him," Maxine replied. "The psychiatrist told me they could keep him there for six months and dry him out, but if he decides to continue to drink, he probably will and there isn't much we can do about it. He will also be the one to decide if he wants to come home and live with us or not, and I will have to decide if I want to accept him back after this scene today, right? We will have to wait and see; that is all I can tell you right now." Maxine was thinking, "This has been another discouraging day for us all," as she continued to drive home.

The summer was passing and it wouldn't be long before it was time for Jack to be released and Maxine still didn't know if he would come there to live with them or not and if she would accept him back if he hadn't changed. All she could do was wait patiently for his commitment to change. A month passed by and she received a letter from Jack saying he would come there to stay and see how things worked out for the family. He also stated he would have to find work so he could help provide for them and he would make arrangements for his dad to pick him up because his car was at the folk's home. Nothing was said about whether or not he was planning to quit drinking.

The days seemed to go by slower than usual. Cindy was growing and very alert of her surroundings and the boys were getting attached to her, paying attention to all the new things she was learning as babies do. They had forgotten when Mark was a baby, how fast babies learn to smile and cry for attention. The boys were good baby-sitters whenever Maxine had to go grocery shopping or pay bills. The neighbor boys liked to hold Cindy and didn't even think about teasing Jackie and Danny about baby-sitting, but they did tease them about being called Jackie and Danny, so from then on the boys insisted we call them young Jack and Dan. Jack arrived home in the middle of August and it was very warm that day, so the boys had gone to the lake swimming with their friends and that didn't go over too well with Jack. He said, "They should have waited for me until I came home so I could go with them."

"They wanted to go with their friends, because they didn't know for sure what time you would be here, and it has been so warm all day they wanted to cool off. You know how the boys like to swim and be with their friends," Maxine answered.

"I guess you are right. I should stay here a little while so I can acquaint myself with our baby girl, then I will go to the lake and find the boys."

Mark was there and he sat down beside Jack for a little while and told him, "I have been playing baseball across the street and have been going fishing down at the pond, but I don't catch many fish, but I caught a couple of snakes."

Jack said, "That is good Mark, that you can find things to do here and that you like it so well. It won't be long before you will be going to school, will it?"

"Not much longer, I will be in the first grade and the school is right over there," Mark answered, pointing to the school across the baseball field, on Melody Lane.

Maxine had given Jack a large glass of iced tea, and as he finished drinking it he said, "I'd better go to the lake now before the boys decide to come home. Mark, do you want to come with me?"

"No, I think I will stay here with Momma," Mark replied.

Mark was still uncertain about his dad and had been away from him for quite a long time, since January when he and his mother had left for Florida. Jack left and Mark told his mother, "I am afraid to go with Dad alone."

Maxine replied. "That is alright, Mark, I understand how you feel. After he has been with us for a while, we will see if he is going to be good to us.

Betty came over to see Maxine and asked, "How are things going?"

"So far they are going good. Jack just went down to the lake to see the boys and go swimming for a while. He asked Mark to go with him but Mark didn't want to go."

"We will pray for you all and maybe Gene and I will come over later and meet Jack. Gene would like to talk to him," Betty said.

"That would be great, he will need some male friends to neighbor with so he won't feel alone. He sure seems distant since he arrived home. Thanks Betty, we will see you later." Maxine nursed Cindy and thought about what she would fix for dinner that evening and how things would go with them all. She bowed her head and prayed for God to help her to do and say the right things from now on. After they all returned home from the lake and had dinner the boys went to see their friends and Maxine asked Jack if would like to go over and meet Gene. He agreed so they went over and visited for two hours.

It was Monday morning and Jack wanted to get up early so he could go look for a job. Maxine set the alarm so she could fix breakfast for him and wish him good luck. Cindy woke up and wanted to be nursed; when she was finished Jack got to see her for a few minutes before he left. It was good to see him spend time with her. He dressed up in his good clothes, white shirt and tie, and Maxine wondered, "Why is he getting dressed up when he is just looking for a job?"

As he left he said, "I don't know how late I will get back, I may go to Detroit to see about a job, I read an ad in the paper yesterday."

Maxine gave him a kiss and said, "Good luck and be careful driving to Detroit."

The day seemed to go by slower than usual and Maxine decided to make some homemade bread and cinnamon rolls, this was always a big hit with the family. As the day went by Maxine thought about Jack and wondered if he had found work or not. She thought, "I am so happy he is back with us and I hope things will work out for us. This is my prayer, God, please help our marriage be successful so we will stay together now." It began to get late and the boys came from a ball game and had something to eat before they went to bed. Maxine waited up for Jack but when he wasn't home by midnight she went to bed concerned about him.

Cindy woke up early and wanted to nurse so Maxine got up and noticed that Jack had not come home and was worried that something might have happened to him. She thought to herself, "There I go again, anxious over him and he does not even call and let me know if he is alright or not." Maxine made coffee and read her Bible; she needed some spiritual food for the day to keep her on top of things. When the boys got up for breakfast, Maxine told them, "Your dad didn't come home last night and I am worried that something happened, an accident with the car and besides he doesn't have any insurance at all."

Young Jack said, "Mom you should know by now that Dad can take care of himself, so you shouldn't worry so much about him."

202

"Yes, I know. It is easier said then done. You know me, it seems if I worry then nothing usually happens, but if I don't worry, it does." She added, "Sometime this week we will need to go shopping for your school clothes. It won't be long before school starts, so let me know what day is best for you guys. I will plan on it but we won't be able to get as many clothes as we usually do, so be prepared to have your mind made up what you want or need the most."

It was laundry day and Maxine was getting clothes separated and ready to be washed when the front door opened and it was Jack.

"Boy, I have been all night trying to fix my carburetor, it went out on me on my way home from Detroit. Look at me, I am all dirty from working on that old car and I am so tired, I didn't get any sleep at all. I couldn't call you because you don't have a phone." As he was talking, he was undressing so he could take a shower.

"Do you want something to eat before you go to bed?" Maxine asked.

"No, I had some breakfast, I am just tired and need sleep," Jack answered.

Maxine took his dirty clothes and put them in the sorted piles she had ready to wash. She noticed something red on the collar and on the front of his shirt and took it into the bedroom and showed it to him and said, "Since when did they start packing carburetors in red grease?"

Shock is the only word to describe the look on his face, and nothing was said to answer the question, only the remark, "I am tired and I would like to get some sleep now, okay?"

Maxine walked out of the bedroom with the shirt and threw it on the white-clothes pile to be washed, disgusted at Jack for his behavior, and with herself for being so trusting.

The boys left and said they were going up to the college to play in the gym for a while and would be back later in the afternoon for lunch. Maxine did the laundry and hung it out on the line; it was a beautiful day for drying clothes and she sat down and enjoyed the sunshine for a while and meditated. Mark cleaned the rabbit cage, fed and watered the rabbits and then decided to stay in the back yard to keep Maxine company, because he knew she was upset with Jack. He sat down beside her and talked about his rabbits, and that he wanted to go fishing that day if he could. Maxine told him, "It is fine, just don't stay too long because lunch will be ready in a couple of hours"

Then the neighbor lady came over and talked for a while and wanted to know how things were going with the family and how the baby was getting along. As Maxine got up and went in to see if Cindy was still sleeping, Maxine said, "I will bring her out so you can see her, she is really doing fine and such a good baby, too. We all love her so much, and I am afraid we are going to spoil her, it is so hard not to."

Cindy was awake and just looking around in her crib when Maxine went in to get her, so she took her outside so the neighbor lady could see her and hold her for a while. "Well, Maxine, I had better get back home, it is so nice outside and so nice to talk to you and get more acquainted with you, but I need to get some work done. You come over and visit me sometime." After the clothes were taken down and folded Maxine prepared lunch for the family and they were all ready to eat as they came in one by one from their activities. Jack was still sleeping and everyone had to be very quiet, walking more or less on eggshells because the apartment was so small and he didn't like to be disturbed, even though it wasn't their fault he was up all night.

Jack finally woke up and came out in the living room late in the afternoon and said, "I better get up now or I won't be able to sleep when I go to bed tonight." He turned on the television and watched the news. There was not much conversation between them (one could almost cut the air with a knife). Maxine thought, "It is up to him to explain to me what is going on, although I can just imagine it is the same as usual – another woman and drinking again. I have lost all faith in him."

Soon he said, "There is no use trying to get a job in Detroit, that is too far and my car wouldn't hold up driving that many miles, so I will try to find work in Jackson tomorrow. There just aren't many jobs to be had around here and I am sure we aren't going to live in this little place for long, it is too crowded and confined for me." Maxine agreed with him.

September was here and the boys had to go back to school; young Jack and Dan were happy to go back because they were getting bored and needed to be busy. Mark was a little reluctant about going the first

204

day and wanted his momma to go over with him, so she went and asked the teacher, "Is it alright if I just stay with him for a few minutes? Mark is very shy and insecure at this time and I am sure he will be content to stay by himself." The teacher agreed it would be fine with her. Maxine sat beside Mark and said, "Mark, the other children don't have their parents staying with them, are you sure you want me to?"

Mark looked around and said, "You can go now Momma, I will be okay." From then on Mark was contented and looked forward to going to school every morning.

Eventually Maxine talked Jack into going to church with her, although he wasn't very happy about it and his attitude wasn't the best. Of all things for the preacher to preach about that day was the need of money for the church, and that people should be willing to give more. Jack got up, walked out and went back home. Maxine was very embarrassed and didn't stay long after church. She walked back home, and of course, Jack wasn't at the house when she got home. Dan said, "He didn't come home so he must have gone after some beer. You might know, Mom!"

Maxine explained to the boys, "He got up and walked out when they preached about money, and he doesn't understand the church needs money for all their expenses like utilities and office supplies. He thinks buying beer and drinking will solve his problems, but they just get worse each time he does it and he won't go to church and find out the truth." Maxine added, "He is drinking again whenever things don't go just right for him and is spending too much time in Jackson with his mother at the bar.

CHAPTER EIGHTEEN

ABANDONED AGAIN

The year was passing by quickly. September 1 was Dan's fourteenth birthday and the children were all back in school and busy with friends and sports. Mark's seventh birthday was on November 7. It was a happy time with family and friends that day. Thanksgiving was celebrated with turkey, dressing and a few of the traditional trimmings; bread and pies had been baked the day before and it turned out to be a peaceful day for the family as they all relaxed and watched television. "It sure seems good to be here all together and enjoying each other's company like we used to," Maxine thought, as she finished nursing Cindy and was about to lay her down in her crib for the night. Jack's behavior was a little rocky: he had his ups and downs, occasionally drinking around the house, but Maxine, with hope in her heart, was happy to have him there. Christmas would be here soon and Jack still didn't have steady work, only odd jobs here and there. He was getting more discouraged then ever. Maxine signed up at the Salvation Army to get gifts for the children and the church gave them a bushel-basketful of groceries for their Christmas dinner and with the family giving gifts, also, they had a very nice Christmas. The children were happy and thankful for the presents they received. This had been a year of mixed experiences – trials and tribulations and the future was uncertain for this family, but Maxine trusted in the Lord and had faith everything would turn out all right. "All I need to do is take one day at a time and believe God will work it all out for us and hope a new year will be better for our family. I will try my hardest to do my part to see that it does."

The new year was here, 1962, and Maxine and the children continued to attend Sunday school and church. Sometimes the older boys would skip going because most of their friends from school didn't attend and made fun of them saying, "Those church people are just as bad as anyone else but won't admit it, yet they think they are high and mighty above anyone else. Some of their kids do things their parents don't know about and you wouldn't believe."

Young Jack and Dan said to Maxine, "Mom, some of it is true

because we see it at school and around other places too." Dan said it and young Jack confirmed it.

Maxine replied, "You know I have always taught you that just because someone else does something bad, that is no sign you should do it. You will be punished or rewarded for what you do in life, not what someone else does. So don't judge all of the people that go to church with those who do wrong because most of them are trying to live a good life and be good examples."

Jack continued trying to find steady work but was unable to, so he spent time in Jackson with his mother, Helen. They would go out drinking together, crying on each other's shoulder about their problems and he would come home whenever he felt like it. He said to Maxine, "I don't like the place we are living in, it is too small for our family. Besides, there is no work for me around here and I can stay in Jackson to look for work."

Maxine said, "I know of a nice mobile home for sale over on Howe Street, maybe we could go to the bank and get the rest of the money we have left in escrow, from when we sold our home and make a down payment on the mobile home. We have to be moving from this place soon, because the owner sold this apartment we are in and they want us to move soon."

"We can go over and look at the trailer to see if it will be big enough for our family and how much they want for it," Jack replied.

They made an appointment and went over and looked at the mobile home, and finding everything to their liking, Maxine called the banker, Dwight Aldridge, and asked to set up an appointment. She told Jack, "Dwight will see us in the morning to go over cashing out the escrow contract on the Reynolds Road property, and he can set up a contract on the mobile home for us."

"That's good. Now we will have a place to move if it goes through. I don't have a steady job, so it may not, but we will see if it does in the morning."

The mobile home was empty and the owners said they could move in even before the papers were final if they needed to, and they did need to, because they had to be out of their apartment in a couple of days.

It was a beautiful spring day to drive over to Concord, which was west of Spring Arbor. Jack and Maxine talked about all the times they has gone to Swain's Lake with their boat and water skied, some good memories, they agreed. The bank was a family-owned bank and it had a board of directors. Dwight had to answer to them for decisions of great value, but this was not a big transaction. Dwight was waiting for them when they arrived and motioned for them to go into his office. The papers had been prepared for the final payment to be paid from the escrow contract. Jack and Maxine signed and dated all the designated places and were told that $3,000 remained on the contract after all charges were paid. Dwight said, "Now we can get the contract drawn up for the mobile home, and you said you wanted to use this money for a down payment."

Jack looked at Dwight and said, "I don't want to buy that mobile home!"

"What do you want?" Maxine asked Jack.

"I want the money and my freedom," he replied.

Crying, Maxine said, "Okay, we will pay what bills we have, then whatever money is left, we will split it half and half. You can have your freedom. I will take the children and you can go your way and I will go mine."

He looked at Maxine and said, "That is what I want."

Dwight was surprised, and the look on his face was a sympathetic look for Maxine. He said, "I will have my secretary get the checks ready for you both." There was silence in the room until he returned with the checks and handed them to each one. Jack left first, and Dwight said to Maxine, "I am so sorry for you, but I wish you and the children well."

Not a word was spoken all the way back home by either one until they went in the house and Jack went to the refrigerator and got a bottle of beer. Maxine said, "I knew someday that beer would come between you and I."

"Well it looks like the beer won. I am not going to stop drinking and nobody is going to make me. Goodbye, it's been good to know you." He didn't have much to pack because Maxine had been packing for the coming move and it was already done. He left, saying goodbye to the children as he went out the door.

"Now what are we going to do for a place to live?" Maxine wondered. "I thought all along we would buy that mobile home and we have to move out of here in just a few days. Our time is up." Maxine got a newspaper and looked at the ads for places to live in the same school district so the children wouldn't have to change schools again; they had enough problems as it was. She went to look at a home in Spring Arbor and talked to the landlord, but he said, "You have too many children and children seem to tear places apart. Anyway, that is the experience I have had and so you better find some place else to rent." She called a few other places and had no luck. They said the same thing; "I don't want to rent to you because of the children." Maxine was about fit to be tied. She went in the bedroom and got on her knees and prayed, "Lord, what am I going to do? We need a place to live, please help me."

It was late afternoon and Maxine thought about calling her brother Harold to ask him if he had a trailer she could use to move their belongings. She went up to the Roller's to use the phone and called him about the trailer.

"Where are you going to move when you get it loaded?" Harold asked.

"I don't know, no one will rent to me and the children, but I have to be out of here in just a couple of days. Jack led me to believe we would buy a mobile home and move into that, but he backed out and wanted his freedom, so here I am."

"Mac, why don't you and the children come in here and live with me? Jeanne has left me for another man and I have this big house all by myself. I will bring the trailer out there and we can take one load today and get the rest tomorrow, okay?"

With tears in her eyes, she answered, "I wanted the boys to stay in the same school district. Maybe I can, and I will have to check it out later. Yes, we will come in there with you; there isn't anything else I can do, thanks. I will make sure the boys are here to load the trailer up when you get here." Walking on her way back home, she thought, "Thank you, God."

The boys were ready to help. Dan said, "Mom, what about my wrestling at Western. How am I going to get back and forth, I don't want to go to any other school."

"I believe the school bus goes as far as Woodville and I can take you and young Jack there in the mornings and I will pick you both up there at night if I get permission from the school. They may charge tuition; I will have to call and find out, okay? Mark can go to the school that is just a block away from Harold's house."

Maxine knew it was gong to be hard on them, but she was so grateful for a place to live and someone who really cared about her and the children. It was another load lifted off her. Harold was there by this time and told the boys he couldn't lift anything that was real heavy as he had a bad back. But they didn't have anything heavy, only the hide-a-bed, so they asked some of their friends to help with that. They loaded the trailer as full as they could and left with it. In the meanwhile Maxine was cleaning up the stove and refrigerator so it would be clean for the next person who lived there. She would come back the next day after everything was moved out and clean the bathroom, mop the kitchen and run the sweeper.

Harold's home was a big one with a long front porch, on the corner and close to a mini-mall within walking distance. There were plenty of bedrooms for everyone, which seemed so good after being in a two-bedroom apartment. There was also a parlor, living room, a dining room and large kitchen. It was so spacious and comfortable. It was good to have more room and privacy for each one of the family and a phone in the house to use when needed.

Maxine called the Western School District and asked about the bus and if the boys could ride it from Woodville, explaining why. The principal told her it was fine and they could finish out this year without paying tuition, but that she would have pay starting the next school year because they were not in the district. She thanked him and agreed to pay when the boys started back the next semester. She had the money from the settlement and felt this was very important for the boys to continue their school, and to be with their friends and the sports they participated in. Every morning she took them to the bus stop and went back to get them, unless they had practice, then one of their friends would bring them home. Daniel was on a strict diet so he would lose weight to be in the lightweight class the wrestling coach wanted him to qualify for. He almost starved himself so he could make weight, because he was so dedicated to the team and the school.

Harold and Maxine made an agreement on helping each other when and where it was needed. He had been laid-off from work for some time and with the food surplus items she received, she helped with their groceries. They worked out a budget and stuck to it as close as they could. Maxine's family was content to be there and felt at home. Cindy was over a year old now, walking around the house and growing so fast. She loved Harold because he spent time with her.

Maxine hadn't heard from Jack in some time and someone mentioned that he had gone to Florida with his mother, Helen. Maxine kept the life insurance paid on the children and when the insurance man came for payment he talked to Maxine about insuring Jack, because he didn't have any life insurance at all. He told her it was more important to have Jack insured then it was the children. Maxine told him, "Jack and I don't live together anymore and I don't know if he will sign for insurance or not."

"Ask him if he would at least sign for a one thousand-dollar policy, if only for burial so you wouldn't be responsible for the cost."

"I will as soon as he comes around." Maxine said.

Less than a month later, after he came back from Florida, Jack came to see the children. Maxine told him about the insurance, and he agreed to sign and thought it was a good idea. So she called the insurance man to come over to take care of it.

Before Maxine realized it, months had gone by. She kept busy and enjoyed being in Jackson. She was beginning to have problems with her teeth; she suffered bad toothaches but didn't have the money to go to the dentist. Daniel would come into her room and sympathize with her and try to do what he could for her, but to no avail. There wasn't much anyone could do, except the dentist. She prayed and wondered why she had to suffer so much; she was trying so hard to do what was right.

Harold went out to socialize once in a while and he met a lady he begin to like real well, her name was Jean, (not Jeanne his ex-wife) and he brought her home to meet Maxine and the children. She had two children, a son David, who was Dan's age and Vickie was a few years younger. David and Dan got to be good friends and ran around together, driving Jean's car around having a good time, until one time they went too far. They were out at Ella Sharp Park and David was driving around and around, then, of course, Dan wanted to drive also. He hit a rock and the car rolled over on the side and damaged the body, somewhat, and David was scared to go home and tell his mother.

So, they decided to hitchhike to Kentucky where some of David's family lived, not realizing that would be one of the first places David's mother would tell the police to look for them, and sure enough, that is where they were. The family called Jean as soon as the boys arrived. Painting the fence for Harold was their punishment, and this was a good lesson for them both not to run away from responsibility. It slowed them down so they would think twice before they tried anything like that again. David's mother didn't allow him to run around with Daniel any more; she thought he was a bad influence on her son, when all the time it was David who drove the car to the park and started the whole episode of driving recklessly. Some people don't take the time to find out the truth of a situation before they jump to false accusations against another person, which causes unmerited consequences and false judgment of the innocent person.

The new school semester started and Maxine went to the high school so she could pay the tuition for the boys to attend, also, to make arrangements for them to be picked up at the Woodville School every morning. The principal was happy because he said, "Dan is one of our best wrestlers and we sure need him on our team."

When she arrived back at Harold's she told the boys, "Everything is all set for you to attend high school again this semester and they are happy you both will be back."

"Gee thanks, Mom, how much did it cost for the tuition?" they asked in unison.

"Fourteen hundred dollars, seven hundred each, and that is all the money I have from the settlement of the house on Reynolds Road. Your dad got half and I got half; which amounted to about fourteen hundred and seventy five dollars each. I know it is best for you both to go to school there because of your friends and sports, and I understand how you feel about them. You're only young once and I don't want to be the one to stand in your way of having a memorable time at school. I feel so guilty about leaving you boys when I went to Florida, when you had to go to school every day without a mother there getting your breakfast, putting up your lunch and being there when you got home, I know it wasn't easy for you and I will try my hardest to make it up to you."

Even forgoing a trip to the dentist, Maxine would spend the money on the needs of her children; they were first and foremost in her life.

The beautiful colored leaves were falling from the trees: gold, red, brown and orange ones, crackling as you walked through them. It was a good sign winter was well on the way. Everything seemed to be going pretty smoothly, with the help of food surplus coupons she received and Harold's generosity; they had plenty to eat. Thanksgiving would be here before long and Maxine purchased the groceries for the occasion; it would be nice to celebrate Thanksgiving this year with others. Harold had invited Jean and her children over and they accepted. Maxine thought, "It is so nice to have a large kitchen and dining room again to entertain on holidays and I will certainly do all I can to make it a nice one for everyone with all the trimmings included."

As the time passed the family became more accustomed to living in town with Harold and adjusting to city life. Maxine, Mark and Cindy walked to the Jackson Free Methodist Church about ten or twelve blocks from the house on Sunday mornings and evenings, and usually attended prayer meetings on Wednesday evenings; young Jack and Dan did not attend anymore.

Everyone had a beautiful day on Thanksgiving and their stomachs were full, coffee and dessert had been served and everyone was sitting around talking and visiting with each other. Dan was on a strict diet because of wrestling; he couldn't gain any weight if he stayed in the same weight class as he was. He was very determined and had his mind set to accomplish this for the school. Sometimes he would get angry with Maxine because she wanted him to eat and told him he looked so thin and tired, and this was one of the times he got angry because she wanted him to eat better especially on Thanksgiving.

Harold told Dan, "Your mother is concerned about your health and you don't need to have such an attitude about it, it is for your own good."

Of course, Dan didn't think so, he was young and idealistic about

213

what he wanted and how to go after it. He left the table angry and went to his room and David followed him upstairs. They stayed there and talked most of the afternoon. Young Jack and Mark went upstairs to see what they were up to.

Wrestling for Dan was his thing. He got a lot of anger out and used his energy to compete in the sport; a challenge for him and his determination to win was uppermost in his mind. Each time he wrestled in his weight class, no matter what weight class his opponent was in, he figured the bigger they were, the bigger the challenge. Many times he won, which gave him a positive sense of accomplishment. Other boys in the class looked on in amazement at his strength for such a small guy, and even the coach was impressed with Dan's moves, quickness, flexibility and takedowns resulting from his strength and quick movement. Many matches with other schools throughout the district were scheduled and the winners would go to competition with other districts throughout Michigan for the Regional Championships, then they would go on the State Championships. Daniel wanted to make it to State, and with his strong will and determination he would surely make it with the right coaching and qualifying, and he did.

The church choir was practicing for a Christmas cantata and the choir conductor asked Maxine if she would like to be in it and she said, "Yes, but I am not a very good singer."

"That will be fine, we will teach you what you need to sing," he answered.

It was so beautiful, the songs were not hard for Maxine to sing and she enjoyed it, especially the song about Mary, the mother of Jesus, "My Soul Doth Magnify the Lord." It was so heartwarming and left a wonderful feeling in Maxine's heart and soul. As it grew closed to Christmas, the weather got much colder and it was hard for Maxine to attend the practices. She had to walk to and from the church and because of leaving the children so long in the evenings, she decided to tell the choir director she wouldn't be practicing with them anymore and stopped going. She felt very sad about it but her family came first and in no way would she neglect them; they needed her at home with them. She pondered in her heart, " Maybe some other time I can sing in a choir, Lord, please forgive me." Maxine continued to speak to the Lord in silence,

214

"I have tried so hard to please you, Lord, and I don't ever want to stray away from you, Lord, as I have done before. Help me to do the right thing, I love you, Lord."

Listening to the Christmas cantata in church the Sunday before Christmas was so inspirational, Maxine just sang silently along with them, tears rolling down her checks, praising the Lord for all He had done in her life, her soul was magnifying the Lord and her spirit was rejoicing in Him. "Praise God," she said out loud, as the singers continued to sing and finish the cantata. When the church services were over and Maxine spoke to some of the singers, she told them, "Your singing was so beautiful, it turned out so well. I sang along silently with you. At least I got to learn the songs even though I couldn't be in it." Walking home with Mark and Cindy, Maxine felt like she was on cloud nine, so lifted up spiritually. She was thankful for so many things and also tried hard to instill in her family the same attitude of being grateful to God for His blessings.

A huge Christmas tree was brought into the living room. It had to be cut because it was too tall; it hit the ten-foot ceiling. Finally, after all the adjustments were made and it was put in a tree stand that would hold it, the decorating began. Everyone was anxious to help, even little Cindy, so with Christmas music playing on the radio and the joy of the Lord in everyone's heart, the tree was getting the trimmings applied to the branches from top to bottom. Cindy, at a year and a half, did the bottom to the best of her ability, as she wanted to help, too. The tree looked so nice after the family finished putting all the decorations on. They even strung popcorn, and when they turned on the lights, "Wow!" they all said.

Harold said, "It is so nice to have a tree this year. I didn't have one last year because there was no one here but me and I didn't see any sense in putting one up."

"The one we had in that little apartment was so small it didn't even seem like Christmas, so I am sure happy, too, Harold," said young Jack.

The holidays were bustling with excitement of what was under the tree and who was it for? The children looked at every package that was placed there to see if it was for them or not. Little Cindy just couldn't understand why she couldn't open them now, but with a lot of explaining why and many "No, No's" she finally got the message that she had to wait and they were not all for her. Maxine thought, "It is hard for adults to wait, let alone a child with so many packages there to tempt them and being so curious to know the contents."

Mark said, "Mommy, I don't keep looking at the packages, I know we have to wait until Christmas and I can read the tags with names on them."

Maxine smiled and said, "Yes, Mark, you have already read the tags, I know." And Maxine thought, "Although this Christmas the presents are not plentiful, we have a place to live, a huge tree, plenty of food and we are all well and God help me to make it be a happy one."

It had snowed during Christmas Eve, and Christmas morning was beautiful, so white and pure looking; snow clung on the limbs of the trees everywhere and covered the ground enough to make a big snowman. As Maxine glanced out the window, she was thankful for a white Christmas. She thought, "Soon the children will be up to open their presents, I will make some coffee and start getting things ready for the dinner."

Sure enough, it wasn't long and here they came saying, "Merry Christmas everybody." Wrappings and ribbons flew all over the living room, words of "Oh!" and "Ah!" were heard from them all, then, "Thank you, Mom. Thank you, Uncle Harold, these are great gifts." Amongst all the paper sat little Cindy tearing open her presents and then reaching for another one to open.

"It is so good to see them happy and thankful," Maxine said to Harold as they sat at the table drinking their coffee.

CHAPTER NINETEEN

TRUTH IN ALL CIRCUMSTANCES

The holidays were over now and it was a new year: 1963. Things were going smoothly, the boys were happy in school, Harold was back to work in the afternoons, and Maxine was going through her routine of taking the boys to the bus stop with Harold's car in the early morning, getting Mark off to school, and then her regular housecleaning chores until it was time to take Harold to work and then pick up the boys. Then, after midnight she would go pick up Harold at his shop. January weather was very cold and the roads were icy and slippery, especially in the morning when driving was hazardous until the roads were salted. Each weekday the routine was the same and Maxine was trying to be content with it because she knew it was best for all of them.

As the months went by and springtime was well on the way, Harold came to Maxine and told her, "I have asked Jean to marry me, what do you think about it?"

"Harold, if that is what you want, I wouldn't say a thing, only that I wish for you to find happiness and if you believe Jean is the one, you should marry her."

"Mac, I do believe she is the one for me, I do love her a lot."

As he was talking, Maxine thought to herself, "I do know there wouldn't be enough room in this house for two women and all the children, so I had better prepare myself for moving back to Spring Arbor if I can find a place."

"Mac, I don't know yet when we will get married. We haven't set a date," Harold said.

"Harold, I will start inquiring about a place to live back in Spring Arbor so we won't be in your way and Jean can start moving her things in."

"Mac, there isn't any hurry, and I don't want you to think I am pushing you and the kids to move, because I explained it to Jean about the setup and agreement we have, and she was very understanding about it."

Maxine explained to Harold, "Jean has two children and I have

217

four, how long do you think before there will be arguments over the children, cooking and cleaning? It is best that we move as soon as possible so she can move in with her things."

Harold agreed with her and said, "I will do everything I can to help you move."

"I sure do appreciate all you have done for us, helping us when we needed it the most. Soon it will be another school year and I don't know where I will get the money to pay for the boy's tuition, so maybe in a way it's a good thing we are moving back to Spring Arbor."

It was a happy day when Maxine found out that the apartment next to the one they had lived in before was empty, and the owner said she could move in any time she wanted to. The boys were so enthusiastic about moving back. They began packing right away and couldn't help Maxine enough with her things that needed to be sorted and packed. They were good boys when it came to helping around the house and doing their chores, and they knew it was another big move the family was making to be together even if it was a small place. So much had happened these past two years and Maxine thought, "I know it hasn't been easy for the children and all I wanted was what was best for them."

As they packed the trailer getting ready to move, they were all happy and young Jack said, "Mom, it sure will be nice to be back in Spring Arbor, again, with all our friends and the gym at the college to go to play in. We can go to the lake swimming, too. There isn't much of anything to do here."

Maxine agreed with him and said, "We are thankful Uncle Harold let us come and live with him, because we didn't have anywhere else to go, but now we need to move back."

When everything was packed and they were ready to head out, Maxine told Harold, "Thank you so much for everything you have done for us. I don't know what we would have done without you, Harold. I sure hope you and Jean have a happy marriage. You deserve it, because you are always doing so much for others, it is time you had some real happiness."

"Thanks Mac, now we had better get this trailer on the road to your apartment," Harold said.

"Back on Harmony Road, in Spring Arbor. Boy, thanks, Mom." Danny yelled out, and the other boys said, "Yes, Mom, thanks." As they pulled into the yard and stopped, the boys all got out and started to unpack the trailer, they were so anxious to get moved in. The landlady came over and unlocked the door and welcomed them back. She had been a missionary in Africa for many years and decided to buy this duplex and live in the apartment they had lived in before; that was why they had to move and now this other side was empty so they could move into it. Maxine was happy and thankful the landlady was willing to let them move in because it was hard to find a place to rent with four children.

Some of the neighbors came over to visit and welcome them back to the neighborhood and invited them back to church and prayer meetings, which was a pleasant surprise and encouragement for them all. The boys let their friends know they were back. Young Jack applied for work at a small factory that hired teens for certain jobs during the summer. Mark played ball and went fishing as much as he could; it was so good to see him happy and contented being in this environment once again. Boys need some freedom to associate with others their own age and to be able do things they like to do as boys and there was plenty for them to do in this little town.

Maxine was again cleaning house for Buelah and others there in Spring Arbor because she was able to take Cindy with her and didn't need a baby-sitter. She also took in ironing that she could do in her own home. With the food surplus given to them, they were able to make ends meet, without any luxuries, of course. They received cheese, beans, white and whole-wheat flour and real good canned beef and pork. Maxine made all of the baked goods: homemade bread, pies, cakes and donuts, and the boys appreciated them.

Danny came home one day and said, "Gary Britton, Randy Lucas, and I are going to go on a road trip. I have earned some money doing odd jobs around town and I want to go with them."

"I think you are too young to be going away like that with those boys," Maxine replied.

"Mom, they are older than I am and we will be taking a Greyhound bus. Nothing can happen to the three of us, we are all wrestlers

219

in good condition. We will call you every once in a while and let you know we are okay. The other guys' folks are going to let them go," Danny pleaded.

Maxine didn't like the idea very well and called the parents of the other boys to check and see if they gave their permission for their sons to go. They did and with Maxine's reluctant approval, the boys were off on their adventure.

All the while they were gone Maxine kept them in her prayers, but also worried about Danny being so young. They wanted to go to Disneyland in California, and that was a long way to travel by way of Greyhound bus. Danny called a couple times a week to let Maxine know they were okay and were having a good time. When they got to Disneyland, he called to let her know they had gotten there and then Maxine called the other mothers and let them know. Then they called and said they were on their way back, but got just so far and ran out of money for the bus and food. Danny asked Maxine to wire him some money for the bus because one of the boys got mad and left the other two by themselves. So she wired Danny money for the bus so they would get home safe and have some money for food also. Danny had said the other boy would pay her back as soon as he could. In the meantime, Maxine prayed for the boys' safe return and waited patiently for Danny's phone calls to let her know they were all right and where they were. Danny assured her they were well and that it wouldn't be long before they were back home, and would she please let the other boy's mother know, too. It was a happy day when the boys returned home. Maxine was so happy to see Danny, she said, "I don't think I will ever let you go that far while you are so young again, young man. You don't know how much I worried about you guys."

"Gee Mom, we were okay except when we ran out of money. It was a good experience for us. We saw a lot of country and met a lot of good people on the way down and on the way back too," he answered.

Maxine thanked God for their safe return and good health.

Jack stopped over and visited once in a while. Usually he had been drinking and didn't stay long, only to see the children if they happened to be home at the time. If they were, he would take them for a ride or go visit someone they knew. One day he stopped over and suggested to Maxine, "How about me coming back here to live?"

"Absolutely not!" Maxine replied. "For sixteen years it was always you first, number one Jack, and you wanted your booze and your freedom, you got them both. I chose the four children to look out after. That is four to one, you are outnumbered by three."

"Then give me a divorce!" Jack said.

She quickly replied, "No, I do not believe in divorce. You have what you wanted. I have always tried to make you happy, but this time I will not go against what I believe. You can go and have your freedom all you want, but you are not coming back here to live with us."

With a surprised look he said, "I guess I had that coming." He turned to leave and said, "Okay."

After he was gone, young Jack said, "Mom, I am happy you wouldn't let Dad move back in."

"He still wants his cake and eat it too," Maxine said. "He just won't quit drinking. He told me, 'There isn't anyone going to make me quit drinking.' It is his choice and I can't put up with it anymore. I am all done trying to get him to realize what he is doing to himself and to us." Maxine thought, "It is about time I had some backbone and put my foot down, standing my ground instead of letting him rule over me."

September 1 was Danny's sixteenth birthday, "Sweet sixteen and never been kissed," was the old saying and the family kidded Danny about it as they celebrated with a cake and ice cream. They also talked about school starting the day after Labor Day and that they wouldn't have many days left to go swimming and to just 'goof off' as the boys said. There wasn't much money to buy new clothes for them but Maxine was doing housework for some of the church members and taking in ironing, so the boys would at least have some new things to wear when they started the new semester. She did the best she could and the boys weren't too discouraged about it because they were so happy to be going back to school on the school bus that picked them up close to home with all their friends, instead of the one from the Woodville School when they lived with Harold in Jackson. Mark was happy to go back to Warner School, which was just across the ball field from their home, with his little buddies from the neighborhood.

One day a young lady named Sharon came to the door and asked

Maxine, "I know you have cleaned for my Aunt Beulah and I would like you to come and talk to my mother about cleaning her house."

Maxine agreed to go with her to meet her mother and to see about the job. She told Mrs. Siefkin, "I will have to bring my daughter Cindy with me because I can't afford a baby-sitter."

"That will be alright with me; I like children and you can call me Ethel, Ben is my husband, he is Beulah's brother." Mrs. Siefkin said.

Sharon thanked Maxine and as she drove her home and she said, "My mother works so hard at the Goodyear Tire factory every day and she needs help with the house work. I am so glad you will work for her, she will pay you good wages."

This turned out to be a weekly job for Maxine and it helped with the bills that had to be paid. Maxine was thankful to God and his goodness to provide for her and the family because one job would lead to another. Maxine always did an extra-good job cleaning for her employers; she believed in doing the work well and having the satisfaction of a job well done. Ethel referred Maxine to three different families, to clean for a week, plus the ironing she did at home in the evenings.

It was October 8, and Beulah Weiman had invited Maxine over for dinner that evening to celebrate Maxine's birthday. When she arrived there were many people in the room and they all yelled out, "Happy Birthday, Maxine." What a surprise – she had no idea they had planned this party for her. They gave her many gifts and cards wishing her a happy birthday. She had tears running down her checks because she didn't realize they all cared for her. This was her thirty-fifth birthday and she hadn't known these people very long but they wanted to let her know they appreciated her and that she deserved to have a surprise party. The whole evening was so much fun with laughter and getting acquainted with the families and their friends from church. The Weimans had three daughters and a son. Marvin was around young Jack and Dan's age. Their daughters were Barbara, Shirley and Marilyn. Barbara and Jack liked each other and were boyfriend and girlfriend for a while until Barbara decided to break up with Jack because he was getting too serious with her and she thought they were too young for that. She broke Jack's heart. He was very hurt and cried about it and couldn't understand why she quit going out with him.

Maxine comforted him and said, "Jack, you are still young and someone will come along who will be as serious about you as you are about her and will love you for who you are."

"But Mom, I really like her a lot," he answered.

"Yes I know, Jack, but we can't make someone love us, either they do or they don't and we have to accept it and go on from there." Maxine understood just how he felt.

Everyday routine was the order of things throughout this fall and the boys usually went hunting on Saturdays down by Lime Lake. On one of these Saturdays, Danny and young Jack came home with faces whiter than snow.

"Mom, we just saw a dead man, he stinks and is all shrunk up. It really scared us, we are going to go call the police," Danny said frantically.

"Maybe it is that young boy that is missing. He escaped from the mental institute and they haven't found him yet," Maxine explained. "Yes, you better call right now!"

So they called and waited for the police to come so they could show them where the body was. Later on they found out that it was that young man and he had committed suicide with a gun they found by his side. This made quite a lasting impression on Dan and young Jack, but they didn't talk about it much at all, only that they didn't get any recognition for finding the body.

The boys worked on their schoolwork whenever Maxine could get them to settle down long enough to do it, they had so many other activities. She got after Danny and told him, "You should do your homework, and you haven't been doing any lately."

" I get C's without even trying," Dan replied.

"But wouldn't you like to have better marks on your report card by studying?" she asked.

"Not really," he answered.

She thought, "I used to try so hard to get good grades, I can't understand why these children don't even want to try. It is so hard raising children without a father being around the house. They take advantage of their mother's kindness, especially when they are teenagers and they think they know it all."

223

It was the evening of Saturday, October 26. Maxine was ironing and Jack knocked on the door and she let him in. He had been drinking. She asked him, "Would you like a cup of coffee?"

"No thanks, I just thought I would come and see how you all were."

The boys had been getting ready to go out for the evening and as they were leaving they saw their dad and said, "Hi, Dad, bye Dad, we're going out. This is Saturday night."

"Hi boys, do your thing, I'll do mine."

They left and Jack picked Cindy up and put her on his lap and talked to her for a little while. She didn't know him very well and was wiggling around a lot on his lap. Mark just sat and watched television most of the time he was there because Jack didn't ever say much to him, besides Mark was very apprehensive about being around him for very long. Maxine continued to do the ironing because she had promised it would be done that evening and the people would be there in an hour or so to pick it up.

Jack put Cindy down, went to the door and said, "I guess it is time to go, there isn't much for me to do around here. I am going over to see Stan Hunt, a guy I met that one night I was in jail. He was accused of horse theft, if you can imagine something like that this day and age. He lives on Howe Street here in Spring Arbor. Bye now, see you all later." Then he gave Cindy and Mark a big hug and kiss and said, "Goodbye, and be good."

They all said, "Goodbye," when he left the house to go see his friend.

Maxine thought to herself. "This guy Stan lives over on the same road that Elry, Beulah, and the Siefkins live on, I wonder if they know who he is?"

Mark interrupted her thoughts and said, "Dad has been drinking, hasn't he, Mom?"

"Yes Mark, he has. It's too bad he can't leave it alone long enough to come and see you kids once in a while."

"He smelled awful when he kissed me goodbye," Mark said.

"Mark, your dad has a drinking problem and he doesn't want anyone telling him what to do, so he thinks drinking helps him forget his problems, but it just makes things worse. I have tried to help him in many ways but he doesn't want help, he wants to go his own way. You kids need me now. He lives with his mother and I guess she can help him now."

After the people picked up the ironing and paid Maxine for her work, she got Cindy ready for bed and told Mark, "It is time for your bath and to get ready for bed now, we are going to Sunday school in the morning."

Mark obeyed and asked, "Can I have a snack before I go to bed?"

"As soon as you're ready."

It was around nine o'clock when he went to bed and he never had any problem going to sleep. Maxine decided to read her Bible for a while as long as it was quiet and peaceful and she could concentrate on what she was reading. She hadn't done a lot of reading before she went back to church and she had to read slowly and sometimes go over it more than once to understand it, because she had always spent her time with house cleaning and other things, and didn't take the time to read.

There was a knock on the door and when Maxine answered it, a man stood there and said, "I am Stanley Hunt and I have some bad news for you."

Maxine looked at him and asked, "Is it one of my boys?"

"No, it is your husband Jack. He and another young man were in the middle of the road and were hit by a drunken driver, by the name of Richard Oberlan. The eighteen-year-old young man with Jack was killed instantly and Jack was thrown up into the bed of a pickup. He has been taken to the Lansing General Hospital. He is in very serious condition and they don't know if he will live. He came over to my house and I was going raccoon hunting, I had gone home to get a large flashlight and that is when Jack pulled in the driveway behind me. He wanted to go with me and I told him he had good clothes on and Jack said he had some other clothes in his car he could change into. So I told him to follow me, and he followed me to a road near Eaton Rapids where my friends were hunting. Arriving there, we parked in behind the other trucks and got out of our vehicles and were talking to the young man getting out of his truck, going across the road to join the other hunters. And as we were walking, this guy came over the hill and didn't see us. I was able to avoid getting hit but Jack and the boy weren't able to get out of the way. I'm so sorry Mrs. Derr, I feel just terrible about this and I knew I should come and tell you about it and let you know just what happened before you heard it some other way."

Maxine was shocked and couldn't say anything for a while and said, "I should try to find a way to get to the hospital and see him. He was just here tonight to see us. Thank you so much for coming over and telling me, I appreciate it very much."

"That is the least I could do, seeing I was with him when it happened; it was a terrible accident. I don't think I will ever forget it."

As he was leaving, Maxine thought, "I feel so guilty, because I wouldn't let him move back with us, oh my God, what have I done?" She knew these feelings were misplaced, because she had done everything she could to make her marriage work, but she had a weak streak in her. She would always feel she was the one at fault even when she wasn't. That's how Satan works, giving Maxine a guilt complex, a weak flaw that invades her life with an inferiority complex that only by the Grace of God she will overcome in time as she studies the Word of God and learns about the spiritual warfare that goes on in a Christian's life.

She went to the Roller's home to see if they were still up so she could use their phone to call Dad and Vera to see if they would take her over to the hospital. They were still up so she knocked on the door and when they answered the door she cried out, "My husband has been in a terrible accident, one eighteen-year-old boy has been killed and Jack is in the hospital in a coma and I need a ride to Lansing General Hospital. May I use your phone?"

Jerry let her in the house and she nervously dialed the phone and when Vera answered, Maxine told her about the accident and as much as she could in her state of mind.

Vera said, "Maxine, we will go over to the hospital right now. You said it was Lansing General? We think it would be best if we go directly to the hospital. We won't be able to pick you up tonight, but maybe you can get a ride tomorrow with someone."

Maxine's heart dropped, she thought for sure they would come and get her.

Jerry hugged Maxine and said, "I am so sorry Maxine, is there anything we can do for you?"

"I better go home now. Mark and Cindy are there alone, and I have been gone long enough now." As she walked back home she cried and asked God, "Help me get through this terrible ordeal. Why another life taken from me. I had loved him so much and tried so hard to make our marriage work, but I have failed so many times. God, help him." All she could think about was, "How am I going to find a way over to Lansing to the hospital?"

When the boys got home she had to tell them about their dad; they were shocked and could hardly believe it. They wanted to go right away to see him, too, but there was no way for any of them to go, so they stayed up most of the night waiting for some news from Dad and Vera. Finally, the next day, Sunday afternoon, Dad and Vera drove out to tell them how he was. Maxine was very upset thinking, "Why did they wait until the next day to come and tell us? They have the Roller's phone number."

Dad said, "Mac, he is in a coma and his head was crushed when he was thrown into the truck bed. They don't know if he will come to or not. We decided to come back home because we couldn't do anything for him."

Vera said, "We thought it would be best if we went when we did and we knew you have the children to look after and it wouldn't be good to take them to the hospital." Maxine agreed with her. They decided to go home so they could go to bed for a while; they had been up all night and were tired and so sorrowful.

After the folks left, a good friend of Maxine's sister, Sally Emerson, had heard on the radio about the accident and came over and asked Maxine, "Do you have a way to the hospital? If you don't, get ready and I will take you and the children now." Maxine thanked her and got the children ready to go. It seemed like they would never get there.

Sally said, "Maxine, I will drop you and the older boys off at the hospital and then I will take the younger ones to stay at Clara's house, is that okay?"

"Yes, that would be fine with me," Maxine answered.

Sally thought it was very unkind of the folks not to come and get Maxine until she had explained the details to her. They arrived at the hospital and went in and sought help where they should go to see Jack. They were told to wait in the waiting room until the doctor came, and that he would talk to them and take them in to see Jack. Danny got restless and couldn't figure out why it took so long and Maxine explained, "They are very busy and the doctor would have to be paged because he has many patients to look out after."

Finally, the doctor arrived and explained, "Mrs. Derr, your husband's condition is critical, his head was crushed and he is in a deep coma. We don't know if he will survive or not. He has destroyed his body with cigarettes and alcohol and we don't think he will ever come out of this coma. Will he ever come out of the coma? God only knows the answer to that question. You can go into see him, but I don't think the boys should go in, it would be a big shock to them as young as they are."

Danny said, "I am going in to see my dad, you can't keep me out." Jackie agreed with him. They all entered the room.

Jack's head was bandaged. His eyes were swollen black and blue; he lay so still for a while and then he tossed around, then was still again as if he was trying to come out of the coma. Maxine thought, "It is as if his soul was fighting for God's acceptance of his soul or as if the devil's hold on Jack would take over.

Danny was upset to see his dad in this condition and cried.

Maxine and the boys went to the chapel to pray for God to save him. They stayed and meditated for a while and cried that he wasn't responding to treatment. The time passed into late evening and Maxine decided to call Clara and Jim to come and get them so they could get something to eat and get some rest. After dinner a discussion about the accident and the events leading up to this point was foremost in their minds to talk to Clara and Jim. Sally had told them some of what happened earlier.

After breakfast on Monday morning, October 28, Jim took Maxine and the boys back to the hospital to see if Jack had improved any during the night and to spend time there with him. They were able to go in the room to see him for five minutes each hour, one at a time. In-between,

228

they would read or go to the chapel and pray.

It was about noon when a nurse came in and told Maxine she had a phone call and that she was to call her sister Clara. Maxine returned the call and Clara invited them over for lunch. Jim picked them up and as soon as they got to the house, Clara said, "The hospital called and said Jack passed away right after you left the hospital. They asked me to tell you to go back and give them some information they need."

Maxine was shocked, and she thought, "I never should have left the hospital."

Clara decided to take Maxine back to the hospital, and on the drive back there Maxine kept thinking, "I should have let him come back home to live and maybe this wouldn't have happened. So many things have gone wrong, and I just can't seem to understand it all."

Then Clara broke the silence and said, "This is the same hospital where Mom had her operation six months before she passed away, so it is hard for me to come here because it brings back memories of Mom. I think she should have stayed here in Lansing with us instead of going over to Harold's to live. She had those stairs to climb every day and I don't think that was good for her. Death is so hard to grasp and none of us knows why these things happen but they do and we have to keep going on no matter how bad we feel, Mac."

"If I would have stayed at the hospital, maybe he would still be here. I feel so guilty about it," Maxine answered.

"Maxine quit blaming yourself. Jack did what he wanted to do and he was in the wrong place at the wrong time when this happened to him. You had nothing to do with it, so stop feeling guilty," Clara said.

Clara was right. No one ever has to take the blame or feel guilty for what another person does, where they go, or what they say. Each one of us will be judged individually for our own choices of what we think or say, where we go and what we do. We alone will stand before the Judgment Bar of God, with Jesus Christ, who is our mediator, pleading our case whether or not we believed He died for our sins. He took our place on the cross, was buried and rose again to free us from the guilt and shame.

Maxine made arrangements to pay the hospital bills with monthly payments, because she was still Jack's wife and she felt it was her duty as his wife and she was legally obligated to pay them. She had to decide which funeral home in Jackson he would be sent to from the hospital in Lansing. She called the Patience-Montgomery Funeral Home and they agreed to have the services for Jack, and then she told the hospital office about the arrangements she had made in Jackson. They gave her all of his belongings he had on him when he arrived, even the bloody clothes they cut off of him. By this time she felt as if she was in a daze and couldn't believe this was happening to her but she knew she had to get herself together, go back home and get all the important papers, marriage license, insurance policy, and other papers to take with her to the funeral home. She thought, "This is October 28, he was born on February 28, 1928, how ironic."

The entire family wanted to meet at the funeral home: Don (Jack's dad) and Vera, Helen (Jack's mother) and her mother, Grace Ort, to discuss the funeral and a place for him to be buried. As they gathered, they were discussing where he should be buried, in a plot that his dad had or one his mother had, and as usual whenever those two got together there was conflict. In the midst of the argument Mark whispered to Maxine, "Momma, why don't we bury Daddy out in the Spring Arbor Cemetery?"

Maxine put her finger to her mouth and said, "Shhhh" to Mark.

Then the funeral director tapped Maxine on the shoulder and asked her to come into his office with him.

"Mrs. Derr, your son was right; you should see about getting lots in Spring Arbor. They are very reasonable and that would calm the discussion the parents are having. And besides, you are still his wife, you are paying for the funeral, and you certainly have the say about this."

"It seems like they shouldn't argue now. It is all they had ever did while he was alive. Yes, I will inquire about a lot and let you know as soon as I get one. Thank you so much for letting me know this," Maxine replied.

Then she went in and told everyone he would be buried in Spring Arbor, so the conflict was settled once and for all. Maxine bought three cemetery lots for fifteen dollars and the opening of the grave was free because she was a member of the church. Hallelujah ...a win for

230

Maxine.

When it was time to view Jack's body, his mother Helen and Grandma Ort were there and insisted they take the bandage off his head before the public viewing. They didn't like the way he looked and said many negative things about it.

The director said, "It is very hard to reconstruct the damage done to him and we thought it best to cover it with the bandage."

But Helen said, "In no way should he look like that." So the bandage was removed. Maxine didn't say a word, because they were separated and he was living with his mother. She just looked at him and the way he looked to her wasn't very pleasant. In her eyes it wasn't the handsome man she was used to seeing. It left a bad image in her mind. Grandma Ort interrupted her thoughts and asked Maxine, "Will it be all right if I buy a head stone to be put on the gravesite for Jack?"

"Yes, Grandma, I think that would be kind of you to do," Maxine quietly answered.

Many flower arrangements and sympathy cards were sent to the families, and the people at Kelsey Hayes, where Maxine and Jack had both worked, had taken up a collection for Maxine and the children. Her friend Doris brought it out to them. Much love was given during this time of grief. Neighbors brought in food and did everything they could to help the family. The Spring Arbor Free Methodist Church had a big dinner after the funeral and those who wanted to attend did, so they could give their condolences to the families. People Maxine hadn't seen for many years came, friends and family from miles around. It was so good to see them once again even under these circumstances, and many tears were shed talking about how hard it was to believe Jack was gone. Many told Maxine if there was anything she needed to let them know, they would help in any way she might need. This was encouraging to her and she thanked them for their thoughtfulness and concern.

It was nearing the end of November and Maxine was over visiting Stan Hunt's wife in her home on Chapel Road to see if she knew any more about how Jack had been killed and who the other boy was, because Maxine wanted to send a card to his parents. Mrs. Hunt said, "They are very good friends of Mark's friend, Jerry Watkins, who had grown up with him."

As they were visiting, the news on television announced that President John F. Kennedy had been shot and they showed the rerun of the action as it had happened. What a shock to see the president of the United States shot in his car, in a motorcade in Texas. It was happening right before their eyes, live on television. The discussion about Jack was forgotten as they viewed what was going on in Texas with the president's life at stake and trying to find out who had done this terrible thing. As time went by they had a man in custody, John Harvey Oswald, who they thought had fired the shots at the president and many questions were raised about why he had done it.

CHAPTER TWENTY

HOME EVER HOME

It was January of 1964 and at long last, the Social Security Administration informed Maxine she would be receiving checks for her and the children as long as she didn't go to work. The life insurance policy on Jack had paid double indemnity: two thousand dollars. This paid for the funeral and some of the hospital and doctor bills; the remaining balance was paid on a monthly basis. The insurance company for Richard Oberlan, the driver of the pickup that killed Jack, informed Maxine that they wanted to settle and how much money she would be receiving. Maxine's brother Herman was on the Sheriff's Department as a process server and he had a friend who was a lawyer. Herman asked the lawyer to investigate to see if they should be paying more for Jack's death. As he investigated, he found out that Jack and the other young man who was killed had been fighting in the middle of the road, so they were in the wrong also, so there was no way his insurance company would pay any more than they were legally obligated, that being the amount the insurance policy stated.

When Maxine received the check, she paid the lawyer his bill, and then started looking for a home to buy for her and the children with the remaining monies. There was a house for sale not far from where they lived. It was a two-bedroom bungalow, with a garage and a big yard for sale for sixteen thousand dollars. Maxine went and looked at it and talked to the owner about the down payment of four thousand dollars and financing. He told her, "If you can get the bank to loan you the money to pay me off, I will discount the balance to eleven thousand, five hundred dollars. So Maxine went to the bank in Spring Arbor and asked them and they wouldn't even consider it.

"Because you are a woman and we don't want to rely on your social security for the payments of the loan you would have to make, we are going to have to say no. We are sorry, but that is our policy," the banker told her..

So Maxine prayed about it and decided to go over to see Dwight Aldridge in Concord about buying the contract. Here was another block in the road she had to get around and with God's help she would.

Dwight told Maxine, "Go and see if the owner would still give you the discount price of eleven thousand, five hundred dollars on the contract after you have paid on it for a full year. If he will, we will buy the mortgage for you and you can still have your home at the discount price."

Maxine asked the owner and he agreed with the terms Dwight had made with Maxine, which made her happy to know all bankers were not against a woman concerned with having a home for her children and buying a home with social security money. Mr. Aldridge was so sympathetic and understanding. He was a man who didn't judge women as second-class citizens, like some men do.

Joy in the morning, oh what joy and happiness there was in the family as they packed and got ready to move into their new home. It would be so nice to have more room and a place of their own to live once again. Once again they borrowed Uncle Harold's trailer to move, and on the last trip the boys turned the corner of Melody Lane and Teft Road and the refrigerator leaned and fell off the trailer. What a time they had getting it back on the trailer. They were thankful it wasn't damaged much at all. Maxine wasn't too upset; only glad that the boys weren't hurt. They now had a basement to store things in that they didn't need right away and a backroom for coats and boots; this seemed so good to them all after living in the little apartment on Harmony Road.

"Thank you, Lord, this is My Home Sweet Home," said Maxine.

It didn't take long to get things settled, by now they were almost experts on moving from place to place. Maxine was thinking of the Bible verse, "The joy of the Lord is your strength," found in the book of Nehemiah, chapter 8 and verse 10. She knew it was true because even after so many trials and tribulations this family had gone through, they still had the joy of the Lord in their hearts and would continue to praise God for all He had done for them. Maxine had learned how precious life is and can be enjoyed fully.

For some time now Maxine had been teaching the Sunday school class for two-year-old children because when it was time for Cindy to go into the class she wanted Maxine to stay with her. As time went on Maxine was asked to teach the class, so she accepted the position and enjoyed it very much. Two-year-old children are like little sponges; they soak up whatever you teach them. They love to learn because their minds are open and ready to be taught in their innocent way of learning.

Maxine wanted to go to college but first she had to pass her GED test in order to get a diploma from high school, so she made arrangements with her Aunt Millie to take care of Cindy while she went for the tests at the Jackson High School. There were five different tests, one each day, and she passed each one with average and above average marks. It made her so happy to think she did it, because Jack always told her how ignorant she was and she had began to believe it. But now she had proof that she wasn't dumb after all and with the diploma she could go on to college. She would be attending Spring Arbor College, which was only two blocks away from home.

It was time to enroll for the spring session, so she went to a counselor to help her decide what classes she should take the first semester. She pondered in her heart, "My eldest son was about to graduate from high school this June, nineteen years from the time I had to quit school and now I will be able to go on to college! It will be hard going to work, keeping house and going to school, but I can do it." Maxine was determined to better herself even though it meant studying late at night.

The graduation exercises for Jack were exciting for Maxine to attend. It was hard to believe that so many years had gone by and now he would be going out to get a full-time job. Planning Jack's graduation party was a lot of fun, and her friend Loretta Siefkin helped her with planning and preparing the food and being there that day to help with so many other things that had to be done. Most of the family members and many friends came to celebrate and congratulate Jack. There was a houseful; at times there were people coming and others were going all evening. Pastor Sebree and his wife came also, which made Maxine feel good to think they would attend. Jack was impressed and happy to see them because one of their daughters had graduated also that day, but her party was to be held the next week.

Jack got a job at Dowling Manufacturing, a small plant that was not far from home and by this time he was going steady with a young lady named Sharol Conklin. One day he came home from work and told his mother, "I am going to ask Sharol to marry me."

"Have you asked her folks yet?" Maxine asked him.

"No, Mom, they don't do that any more," he answered.

"Maybe they don't, but you are going to be a gentleman and ask her parents," Maxine answered quickly.

So he said that he would. After he had asked Sharol to marry him, and she said yes, he purchased an engagement ring for her.

Then one evening he went to her home and asked Sharol, "Can I talk to your dad? I want to ask him for his permission to marry you." They went into the living room where Mr. Conklin was sitting and Jack asked him, "If it is alright with you, I would like to marry your daughter."

Mr. Conklin answered, "It is okay with me, but you will have to ask her mother first."

Then Mrs. Conklin came into the room and Jack asked her the same question and she answered, "Jack, you just graduated and have a new job. I think you should work for another year first and get established, then we will see if you still want to get married, okay?"

There wasn't much more he could say but that it was okay, then he turned to Sharol and he asked her, "Would you like to go out for the evening with me?"

"Yes, I would."

That evening, he gave her the engagement ring he bought for her and told her, "I will do as your mom asked me to do. I was really surprised your dad was the one that was so agreeable; he said he didn't care but for me to ask your mother. Boy, you don't know how nervous I was going to your house tonight asking your parents for your hand in marriage. My mother told me to do it because it was the proper thing to do, and now I can see why."

With everyone busy doing his or her own thing it seemed like the time was passing by so quickly. Helen, Maxine's mother-in-law, bought a flower urn for Jack's gravesite and every time someone put flowers in it she just pulled them out and threw them away. It was usually Dad and Vera's flowers because the urn was always empty whenever they visited the gravesite faithfully in the springtime. Maxine also tried to place flowers in the urn but they were gone, too, and she couldn't understand what had happened to them until Helen called and said, "I bought that urn for me to put flowers in, not anyone else."

It was still a battle between the two of them and it made Maxine feel bad being in between his folks' battles, so rather than have any arguments Maxine decided to go to her friend, Virginia Rainey, because her husband was in the evergreen nursery business and he would advise her on the best plants for the grave site. Maxine bought two beautiful evergreen trees, one for each side of the head stone, and thought to herself, "Now the trees will be there for a long time, evergreen, and they will be easy to maintain and certainly there won't be any more arguments with Helen. I know Dad and Vera will just plant their flowers in the ground in front of the head stone."

Summer was here and things seemed to be going fairly smoothly. There was a woman, Mrs. Fisher, who owned a little gas station on the main street who was murdered when someone broke into her store and robbed it. The police asked questions of the people who lived close by and of anyone who may have any clues to this horrible tragedy. Someone came forward and said, "We seen Danny Derr and Loretta Siefkin's son, Larry Abbott, walking around through the cemetery that evening, which is directly across the street from the Fisher's station." So the police arrested Danny and Larry and put them in jail as suspects not even waiting to hear their story why they were there that night.

Maxine was about fit to be tied when she heard about this. She said to her friend Loretta, "Danny was home that night about the time this had happened, and besides I know he would never do anything like that."

"And I know Larry wouldn't even think of such a thing, why do they have to blame our kids for this?" Loretta said.

A couple of days later the police had some clues about who the person was that had robbed the station and killed Mrs. Fisher. He was a man who lived about a half mile from there, a farm hand working for the Videto family and living in a house they provided for him and his family. He had been stealing ice cream bars and other food for his children and Mrs. Fisher had found out about it and told him she was going to turn him in, so he went there that night intentionally to kill her. He found out the police had a warrant for his arrest and he committed suicide by hanging himself in the barn.

Danny and Larry were released from jail and apologies were given, although it was an awful embarrassment for those two teenagers to have to go through the experience of false arrest and the gossip of the town that week. Maxine and Loretta were so happy to see the boys come home and that the murder was solved. Now they could hold their heads up and smile knowing what they had believed all along that the boys did not do this terrible thing. The boys were glad to be home with their families and a good bed to sleep in, plus their moms' home cooking. They never knew just how many people in that town believed the boys had any part of this, but whoever it was who told the police about them being in the cemetery that night must surely have to ask God to forgive them for even the suggestion of it when they found out the truth. Thank God, " The truth will set you free," and it did for the boys.

Jack and Sharol were beginning to plan their wedding and she asked Maxine, "We want to have Cindy be our flower girl, will it be okay"

"Why yes, thank you for asking," Maxine replied.

"My mother is going to buy the material and wants to make her dress so she will have to get Cindy's measurements and wants to know when it will be convenient for her to come over." Maxine told her to have her mother call her so they could set a time.

"I can't believe that my eldest son will be getting married soon and my youngest will be his flower girl," Maxine said.

Jack said, "Mom, I know, it doesn't seem like I am at the age of marriage either, but I am a man now and it's time for me to get married."

Sharol's parents helped them purchase a beautiful mobile home and had it placed in the Sunny Del Mobile Home Park on Chapel Road, Parma Township, which wasn't far from home and was close to where Jack worked, so he wouldn't have far to travel to work each day. Planning the wedding was fun; Maxine went shopping for a new outfit to wear as mother of the groom. She hadn't shopped like this in a long time and it was very important to her to look nice.

The time had come for Jack and Sharol to be married, everything was all planned. Cindy's dress was done, Mrs. Conklin had done a beautiful job making it and it was so pretty on her, she looked like a little doll. Mark and Dan's tuxedos fit well and they looked so handsome in

238

them. Jack seemed to be so calm for a man about to be married, he went in and lay down on the bed and Maxine thought, "Boy, he is sure calm and cool, resting in there taking a little nap before the big moment, but that is Jack, he has always been quiet, peaceful and patient most of his life." Everyone else was trying to get ready so they wouldn't be late, and of course Maxine was very nervous and excited about the wedding and she wanted everyone to look their best. She finally went in and asked Jack, "Are you ready to go?"

"You all go ahead, I will be there on time, don't worry about me," he answered.

The church was decorated beautifully, and people were filling up the seats on both the bride's side and the groom's side of the church. Mark and Daniel were ushers and so were Sharol's brothers, seating the guests as they arrived, so Daniel took Maxine by her arm and escorted her to her designated seat. The pianist played some lovely music until it was time for the wedding to start and Maxine's eyes filled with tears as she thought of her wedding day and the vows she had made to God, and what she told herself, "I will make a go of this marriage if it kills me." Well it almost did. She had tried so hard because it was what she wanted, but a marriage has to be a bond between two people wanting it to work, not just one. "Well I had better stop thinking about that now, it is all past history, this is the wedding day for Jack, our son, one of the good things God has given me to be thankful for and Sharol, his bride-to-be."

Cindy came down the aisle spreading the flower petals on the floor as she walked, slow and easy, looking all around at the guests with her big blue eyes just about popping out because she was scared until she saw Jack standing up in front with Dan, Mark, the ushers and the best man, then she relaxed the rest of the way. By this time the maid of honor and the rest of the bridesmaids were on their way to the front. Then the pianist played the wedding march and everyone stood up as Sharol and her father came down the aisle. It was a beautiful ceremony and Henry, Maxine's brother, took many pictures afterwards. He didn't believe in taking pictures during the ceremony because a wedding is a spiritual occasion and with God's presence there shouldn't be any interruptions with a camera's flashing lights.

It was a big wedding, many friends and relatives from other towns came also, many whom Maxine hadn't seen since Jack's funeral, it was a happier occasion this time and she was able to visit with them a little longer to see how their families were. The reception was held in the basement of the church and the bride and groom greeted the guests and were congratulated by them. After dinner Sharol and Jack opened their gifts with thanks and appreciation for each one attending and for the gifts they had received.

Everything was back to a normal routine once again and it wouldn't be too long before it was time for school to start again, so Maxine had to make up her mind about continuing with college. She needed to talk to the dean about finances and how she could pay for her classes before the semester started. Most of the professors and teachers at the Spring Arbor College attended the same church as she did and so she knew some of them quite well, as church members, that is. Pastor Dunkel was on the staff also, he was always so pleasant and friendly to Maxine, and she felt very comfortable whenever he was around.

He told her, "Go to the dean and make arrangements, I am sure he will set up a plan so you can continue." Maxine made an appointment, then went and discussed her situation and it turned out to be disappointing because they didn't have any way for a payment plan that she could apply for. So she went back home and knew she would have to continue doing housework for others if she wanted the extra money to pay for school. She could still draw her social security as a widow and mother of underage children if she didn't go over the limited amount of earnings they allowed. She thought, "It seems good to be able to get to sleep like I should instead of studying all hours of the night, so maybe it is God's will that I don't go back to college so I can spend more time with the children and my housework here at home, I need to be content with what I have, so I must decide not to go on with school."

The year was slipping by and the beautiful multi-colors of fall, red, orange, yellow and beige leaves had faded and fallen, the trees were bare and the frost appeared every morning on everything. It was so pretty to see and she was thankful for God's picturesque scenery. No man could paint a scene as beautiful. This Thanksgiving would be the first one in their new home and they would have room to invite some-

240

one to dinner this year, so Maxine invited Clara and Jim and their family and her other brothers and their families, also, because it had been a long time since she had them over for a holiday celebration. The other families had made plans to go somewhere else but thanked her for the invitation and asked for a rain check for future celebrations. They had a grand time at Thanksgiving.

Christmas was about here and time for the Christmas program at church to take place. The committee asked Maxine if the two-year-old class wanted to participate. Maxine thought, "What can I do with these little children in this program?" Then she remembered how each time one of the children had a birthday she used an imitation cake and lit the candles and they all sang, "Happy Birthday" to that child, and she thought, "I can get one of those candles you can't blow out and when we all are in front of the audience I will light the candle and we will all sing, "Happy Birthday to Jesus," then have the children try to blow the candle out a few times, without any luck. Then I will say, "Jesus' light will always shine and we can't ever blow it out." She practiced with the children on Sunday mornings and when the time came to do it, the children were very good with their performance and the audience was so pleased to see these little two-year-old children participate in the program.

The year 1965 was well on its way and the routine seemed to be going smoothly so far for everyone. Winter was about as usual, lots of snow and cold, but beautiful to look at. The children all seemed to be happy with their lives doing what they wanted to do. Dan had met a young lady in school named Cynthia Breton and was dating her now; she was the eldest of ten children and a very pretty girl. They called her Cindi. She was a likeable young lady and paid a lot of attention to little Cindy when she came to visit with Maxine.

"Time seems to fly by so fast and before you know it, it is the end of the school year and Daniel is about to graduate, another son grown up. It doesn't seem possible, where has the time gone?" Maxine contemplated in her mind.

She didn't have a spouse to talk to, so she talked to God and let Him know what was on her mind and just how she felt. When she needed answers she would get down on her knees and pray, asking for His help. She realized, "I have to decide if I am going to continue going to college in the fall or not, but I will think about it this summer and make up my mind."

The day of the Dan's graduation, Pauline, Maxine's cousin, came over from Lansing to attend the graduation with Maxine. Western High School was so crowded with parents and relatives, one could hardly find a seat. This was one of the years of the "baby boomers," children born to parents whose fathers were in the Second World War, and who came home to their wives or got married after the war. There was an explosion of births for a few years in a row. So now those children have grown up and are graduating from school to go on and live their lives, marry and have children also. The cycle of life just keeps going on year after year with more knowledge to make life easier for everyone along with inventions and technology, even going into space and back, gathering vital information man has never known before. God only knows just where these graduates will be another twenty years from now or what they will be doing. Their children will be graduating, too. Maxine had to wipe away a few tears; it always hurt her knowing she couldn't graduate from her high school, but God only knows the reason why and she is attending this graduation of Daniel's, which is one of the reasons for her not completing high school.

The party for Daniel was a success; many friends and relatives came to the house to congratulate Dan and give him some very nice gifts.

"I believe I should have that diploma for getting him to go each day and keeping him encouraged," Maxine said.

Everyone just laughed and agreed with her. Dan was so appreciative of each one of the gifts he received and thanked each one personally. He thanked Maxine for such a nice party and her patience with him throughout this last school year.

Loretta stayed to help Maxine clean up and do the dishes; she was such a good friend and helper in so many ways. Maxine tried so many times to get her to go to church with her but she just refused to go, she had been raised Catholic and wouldn't attend a Protestant church.

During the summer Daniel worked on his cars to get them ready for the races, he loved to race his cars. He brought many trophies home he had won during the seasons of racing. He worked long hours chang-

242

ing motors, fixing transmissions and whatever had to be done to make them go faster, whenever he wasn't working for a building contractor earning the money needed to buy all these parts. Sometimes he would get mad because things wouldn't go back together like they should and he was too tired; not getting the sleep he should didn't help matters either.

The neighbor man across the street, Walt Huffman, came over to help Dan one day when things weren't going too well getting the parts back together. He told Dan, "Any time you need help, just ask and as long as I am not busy, I will help you."

Dan was sure happy to hear that after all the struggles he had been through with this car. He loved to race and the living room was filling up with trophies he had won, although he said, "It isn't the trophies I like, it is racing, going fast and the challenge of winning against those who have expensive cars." His whole life seemed to be wrapped around the racetrack, doing everything he could to get his car to go faster then anyone else's.

It was a beautiful day to do the washing and to be able to hang the clothes out on the line to dry, so Maxine was bringing in a basketful of dry clothes when she heard Dan in the garage getting so mad at the car he was working on because things were not going well at all. He got mad and threw something; it hit one of the windows of the car and cracked it. Maxine said, "Well that didn't do any good to lose your temper, did it?"

So then he really got mad, jumped up on the hood of the car and smashed the windshield and said, "There, now I really lost my temper."

"Now do you feel any better? Being out of control undoes all the hard work you are trying to accomplish, you should remember where anger took your dad," Maxine said. She went in the house just shaking her head and sighing, thinking, "It seems like he is fixing that car more then he is racing it."

Working for Ethel and Ben Siefkin once a week continued to be one of Maxine's steady jobs. Ethel usually came to pick her and Cindy up on Fridays to clean their house.

Ethel decided to wallpaper the kitchen and Maxine told her, "I can wallpaper, I have done it before, I will do it for you." Ethel agreed to let her and said she would pay her for it. So Ethel and Maxine picked out the design of the wallpaper she wanted and Ethel said, "I have some wallpaper paste at home under the sink, so I won't need to buy any of that."

When they got back to Ethel's house Maxine got everything ready to do the job while Ethel was at work that day. Maxine looked under the sink for the wallpaper paste and all she could find was a bag of sizing. She hesitated about using this because Ethel said it was wallpaper paste, but she thought, "I guess this is what she wants me to use, so I will."

The paper went up easy enough and looked so nice after it was all done. When Ben got home from work he said, "Maxine you did a good job, it looks just fine."

Maxine told him about the sizing and he said, "I am sure it will be all right, don't worry about it."

So Maxine cleaned up the kitchen and put everything back in place and left to go home with Cindy. As they walked home Maxine kept thinking about that sizing and she couldn't get it out of her mind. She was tired that night so she went to bed early and was awakened by a dream she was having. She dreamed that the wallpaper peeled off the wall from the ceiling down to the floor, and then she couldn't get back to sleep. So in the morning she thought, "I will call Ethel and see if that really happened." Maxine waited until she knew Ethel was up and then called her.

"Hello, Ethel, is the wallpaper still pasted to the wall?"

"Why, yes it is, Maxine, why do you ask?"

Maxine told her about the dream she had and Ethel laughed and told her not to worry about it, it was there to stay.

Ethel's daughter, Sharon, was going to college in Adrian, Michigan. Once a month on a Friday night, Ethel would have Maxine drive her car to go get Sharon and bring her home for the weekend. Then when Ethel got out of work Maxine would go pick her up. Sometimes Sharon would bring a couple of her friend's home to stay with her and they were very friendly with Maxine. Her friends, Carolyn Hirschy and Kathy Knapp, lived in LaGrange, Indiana, and were all studying to be schoolteachers. When they got to Sharon's home they let loose and had fun all weekend. Ethel usually took them back to Adrian on Sunday after church and invited Maxine to go along and have dinner some-where if Ben didn't want to go with her. Maxine did this for Ethel most of the time Sharon was in college, so she and the girls were good friends. They said, "Maxine, you should come over and be our dorm mother, you would make a good one."

"I couldn't do that because I have the children, so that lets me out," Maxine replied.

Sometimes Ben and Ethel would go to Indiana to visit Carolyn's mother, sister and brothers and would invite Maxine and the children to go with them. It was good because Maxine didn't have a car and it seemed good to be able to go for a ride once in a while and visit. They would have a big dinner and invite another friend of Sharon's that at-tended the same college. It was nice to meet these people and have fellowship with them. Carolyn's boyfriend didn't live very far from her mother's home and he was a pig farmer with lots of pigs, from baby ones to huge ones ready to be slaughtered. He and his dad raised the feed for them also, so they were very productive farmers.

Maxine also continued to work for Mrs. Gertrude Robinson once a week and was able to take Cindy with her, also, because she was good and was able to entertain herself without interfering with Maxine's work. Thelma, Mrs. Robinson's secretary and bookkeeper, usually paid a lot of attention to her and so did Gert, as they both liked children. Thelma and her husband never had any children so she was always good to all children; she had a candy drawer and gave them candy whenever they came in the office. Mr. Robinson's business was oper-ated in their home and that is where the office was also; it was a big home and took all day to clean it. Gertrude had to pick Maxine up and take her home; that was the only way she was able to get to work and Gertrude liked the way Maxine did the housework.

Maxine had decided to go to the employment office to take a test to see what would be the best field she could train in for a job and it turned out to be for office work. They would get her a job she could train on as she earned a wage. So she told Gertrude, "I won't be able to work for you on Friday's anymore because I will be getting a job where I can earn while I learn on the job."

Well, Mrs. Robinson didn't want to lose Maxine as her housekeeper, so she had a meeting with Thelma, her secretary and book-keeper to ask her what to do, and Thelma said, "Why don't we send her to bookkeeping school and train her here in our office and pay her for four days a week here and one doing your housework?"

Mrs. Robinson agreed with that suggestion and asked her husband what he thought about it, and he agreed it would be all right with him because they needed another person in the office.

When Maxine went to work for Mrs. Robinson the next Friday, Thelma told her the plans they had for her if she wanted to accept them. Maxine was delighted to think that they would consider her for the job and told Thelma, "I will have to go to the employment office and let them know I am not going to take that other job. Thank you so much for thinking about me and giving me this chance."

Thelma made arrangements with the business school for Maxine to attend and made out a check for her to pay the tuition when she started. The joy that filled her heart was overwhelming as she drove home to tell the children. She thought, "Thank you Lord, you are my provider." She then realized that she would have to take evening classes because she couldn't afford a baby-sitter for Mark and Cindy. Mark was eleven and Cindy was four years old now.

Jack and Sharol were expecting a baby late in late November and there were showers planned for the new baby; it was exciting because this would be Maxine's first grandchild, just twenty years after she had married Jack in 1945. Maxine was thirty-seven years old now and what a joy she held in her heart for the coming of this child. Little Michelle Marie was born on November 29, 1965, soon after Thanksgiving and so much to be thankful for: a healthy beautiful baby girl, what a sweet bundle she was. She had many grandmas and grandpas still living on both sides of the family. On the paternal side there were six generations, and pictures were taken so that in the years to come there would be photographic records of this memorable occasion. On the maternal side there were five generations and photographs were also taken of all the proud grandparents, baby and mother.

This had been a very busy year for Maxine and she thought, "I am so happy and content with life the way it has been going now: a graduation, a marriage and a new baby all this year. God has been so good to me and blesses me and my family so much. I am so thankful to God and all He has done."

As she pondered in her heart the special events that had taken place previously, she realized it would be Christmas before long and another year would be here soon and God only knows what the New Year would bring to the family. Hope and anticipation filled her heart for the Christmas season coming soon and the family gatherings she loved to participate in with all the good food and fellowship it brings.

After inquiring, Thelma found out that it would be after the holidays before Maxine could enroll for the classes that would start in January. Maxine thought, "That's good, I can really concentrate on the holidays and don't have to think about schoolwork." She kept busy with all the shopping, wrapping gifts and planning the meal for Christmas. "So now I have something more to be thankful for, going to business school to learn so I may work in an office instead of doing housework all the time."

She thought on this for some time. Oh, how thankful she was for the entire blessing and for her *HOME SWEET HOME!*

My Home Sweet Home

A New Life of Commitment Brings Contentment

The story of Maxine continues, in a forthcoming book, to dramatically unfold throughout many years of trials and experiences of a young widow, raising her children alone, challenges to overcome one by one, continuing to keep her faith in God, no matter how hard the circumstances seem to be. Not knowing the outcome of some of these devastating experiences, her love for the Lord and her family continues to be the driving force to overcome them at all odds.

Daniel's marriage and more grandchildren gives Maxine a settled hope to realize more fully the blessings God continues to bestow upon her, and helps her to overcome the trials she has to endure with a grateful heart.

Mark has a very serious accident, not knowing if he will live or die, her faith sees her through this tragedy, along with the continued love of friends and relatives, even though the doctors didn't give her much hope of Mark ever living a normal life again, which he eventually does.

Young Jack divorces, not long after his second daughter was born. He marries Sue who has a son and a daughter from a previous marriage. This almost breaks Maxine's heart; she hates divorce so much because of what it does to the children, but she comes to accommodate and build a good friendship with Sue.

Cindy's teen years were defiant and rebellious, leading to a very young marriage and heartbreak, bearing two children, and then divorced which again broke Maxine's heart because of the children. A second marriage with two more children leads to betrayal and another divorce. Cindy's life is a complete novel in itself.

Maxine joins American Business Women's Association and works with others on projects and committees, raising money to give grants to help young women go to college. She travels to many places for conventions with the chapter she belongs to. Another dream came true.

Corresponding with cousins in Germany Maxine decides to take a trip to Europe to meet her father's family, whom she had always wanted to meet and get acquainted. Afterwards, Maxine visits her two sons in Alaska and while there she receives a job offer, so she decides to accept it and move to Alaska.

At fifty-five years of age, the courage to start a new life away from family and friends in Michigan is very strong. The decision to move to Alaska becomes one of the best choices she has ever made. Residing in Alaska for over twenty-one years, she retires at seventy-three years of age.

She learns to use the computer because she wants to write these books for others to read and learn from. She comes to realize that the life we live and the choices we make have a significant impact on the whole picture of our lives, from beginning to end. Lessons to be learned are not always easy and do affect many others along this road of life.

Maxine's next book, a continuation of her experiences into her later years will be action-packed, with true stories of Maxine's life, and her family's stories throughout many years until these books were written in her seventies. Praying some lost soul will read them and find hope and the everlasting love of God who gives to those who believe in His Son, Jesus Christ.

The new title is:

MY HOME SWEET HOME

A NEW LIFE OF COMMITMENT BRINGS CONTENTMENT

CHILD BE STILL, FEAR NO MORE

Fear will not last when peace abides within.
Turn on the light its magic will appear
after shadows have been lurking all around.
The heartbeats in rhythm as each foot
steps one in front of the other silently
moving toward the unknown listening with all ears,
reaching out and feeling the breeze
of waving arms upon my face.
A thought crossed my mind of Lillian Miller
back in Jackson Michigan—an extraordinary housewife,
Celebrating a Golden Anniversary with her husband.
What did that have to do with now, alone in the dark?
The light shines within me to show me the way,
happy am I to see the bright of day
and creation speaks loud and clear as darkness
is overcome by the light so fast.
Shadows seem to go yakity-yak as the breeze blows,
therefore, I am silent and can't say a word,
only fear, I can't see you, leave me this day
you're crowding my mind of the beauty around-
the vivid colors of reality and love
painted through my mind
overcomes fear like a joke being told.
On wings I soar to the highest delight
and float out of sight to be seen no more.
Ole' Mac come back down to earth once again,
to face each new day for
tomorrow will follow as long as I live,
and silver hairs that appear silently taking
o'er the crown and youth no more to be found.
The past forgotten yet I know where it has gone.
The heavens are waiting they call me to come
when fear disappears and its clasping arms
have finally released me and I can say with delight
Hallelujah! Hallelujah! Shalom!
Fear is gone to hold me no more and peace
like a river runs silently along the abiding shore
Child be still, fear no more.

Maxine E. Derr
September, 1995

FAMILY TREE

MAXINE (BOHL) DERR

Paternal	**Maternal**
Birth Place: Neustadt/Weinstrafe,	Birth Place: Whiting, Michigan
& Hiedleberg, Germany	& Clark Lake, Michigan
Vollweiler: Gottfried V. & Hanna Hiigli	Wheeler, Frank & Lucretia Bennett
Daughter Klara marries Henry Bohl, Sr.	Children: William, Hazel, Roy, Millie
Sons: Henry, Herman,	
Ludwig, Ernest	

Bohl, Henry **1889-1944**	**Wheeler, Hazelbelle Betty** **1903-1959**
Married 1919 Jackson, Michigan	

CHILDREN

BORN

1919	Bohl, Henry A. & Doris Myers
	Linda, Peggy, Henry A. Bohl Jr.
1921	" Herman Franklin & Gale Harrington
1923	" Harold Louis & Jeanne Shaw
	Carol Jean, Harold L. Jr. (Butch),Pamela
1926	" Clara Hazel & James R. Parr
	Richard, Sharon Kay, Laurie
*** 1928	" **Maxine Elisabeth & Jack Dean Derr**
	Jack D.; Daniel D.; Mark C.; Cynthia G.
1930	" Ernest Carlyle
1932	" Clark Zephaniah Potter

Maxine Elisabeth & Jack Dean Derr
MARRIED 1945

CHILDREN

BORN

1946	Jack Donald, & Sharol Conklin
	Michelle Marie; Misty Lynn
1947	Daniel Darwin & Cynthia Breton
1954	Mark Clark
1961	Cynthia Gale

FAMILY TREE

JACK DEAN DERR

Paternal
Birth Place: Clayton, Miichigan
& Adrian, Michigan

Derr, Alda (1885-1944) & MaeGerman
(1885-1965)
Sons: Donald J.
        Wilbur

Maternal
Ort, Charles & Matilda Mason
Floyd - 1883
Tatman, Charles & Hannah Bellis
Grace Elizabeth - 1894
Ort, Floyd & Grace
Daughter: Helen M

Derr, Donald J. 1910-1989	Ort, Helen M. 1910-1994
Married 1927 Jackson, Michigan	

CHILDREN
BORN

*** 1928   Jack Dean & Maxine E. Bohl

      1930   Marilyn & Larry Richardson

                JoAnna

      1936   Donald K.

1942 – Donald Derr married Vera M. Shaw
          Vera's children: Sharon & Gilbert Parker
                      Rose & Paul Thronton

1942 – Helen Derr married Love (Whitey) Williamson
          Whitey's children: Arleen, Vivian

(Note: Some dates are approximate)

New Bohl Clothing Store (1930)
Newstatdt/Weinstrafe, Germany
showing what Father (Henry) would have inherited
but instead chose to immigrate to America.

Father's (Henry) birthplace
and Grandfather Bohl's original store
Neustadt/Weinstrafe, Germany
1905

The Bohl Family – 1931
Maxine in Father's arms

254

Honorable Discharge from The United States Army

STATE OF MICHIGAN ss.
COUNTY OF JACKSON

Recorded in Soldiers
Discharge Liber _3_
on Page _416_
CURT E. BURNETT,
County Clerk

TO ALL WHOM IT MAY CONCERN:

This is to Certify, That *Henry Bohl*
†#1815722 Private 1st class Machine Gun Co Tenth Infantry
THE UNITED STATES ARMY, *as a* TESTIMONIAL OF HONEST AND FAITHFUL
SERVICE, *is hereby* HONORABLY DISCHARGED *from the military service of the*
UNITED STATES *by reason of* ‡ *Cir. No 77 W. D. Nov 21, 1918*
Said Henry Bohl was born
in Neustatt Bavaria, in the State of Germany
When enlisted he was 23 years of age and by occupation a Auto Mechanic
He had Blue eyes, Dark hair, Fair complexion, and
was 5 feet 4¼ inches in height.
Given under my hand at Camp Custer, Michigan this
15 day of May, one thousand nine hundred and Nineteen

W. E. Weilsch

Lieut. Colonel Infantry
Commanding.

Form No. 525, A. G. O.
Oct. 9-18.
*Insert name, Christian name first; e. g., "John Doe."
†Insert Army serial number, grade, company and regiment or arm or "corps or department; e. g., "1,620,302"; "Corporal, Company A, 1st Infantry"; "Sergeant, Quartermaster Corps"; "Sergeant, First Class, Medical Department."
‡If discharged prior to expiration of service, give number, date, and source of order or full description of authority therefor.

Father Heinie (Henry) Bohl's discharge papers from the U.S. Army at the conclusion of World War I. No mention of his "secret" missions in Germany that Maxine discovered he performed during the war.

255

Jack & Maxine
Wedding Day - 1945

l-r: Mark, Dan, Cindy,
Maxine, Young Jack
1962

Maxine
1951

Jack
1951

NAMES INCLUDED IN THIS BOOK

FRIENDS (OTHER THAN FAMILY)

A number of friends and acquaintenances have been a part of my life, some for a short time, others have been a continuious relationship through these years.

Aldridge, Dwight
Baraclough. Tom, Ester,
    Janice & Joan
Balch, Delores
Beers, Arahbell
Benn, Marjorie
Boss, Jackie (Johnson) Betty,
    Helen & Dottie, Jerry
Conklin, Mr. & Mrs. Chauncey
Cooper, Frances, Hank, Joan,
    Thomas, Nancy, Marsha
Consolino, Tony
Cummings, Roger & Josephine
Debolt, Marjorie
Dolan, Art
Donnelly, Dorene
Dunkel, Rev.'s Verdon, & Vernon
Ellis, Bud & Harold
Emerson, Sally
Fitzgerald, Orville
Furlong, Donald
Harrison, Thelma
Hemminger, Patty
Hess, Blain & family
Hudson, Charles, Elaine, Jim,
    Doug & Keith
Hunt, Stanley
Jordon, Clare, Mary, Sharon,
    Tom, Tim Pat,
    Mike & Jeanna
Kapp, Kathy
Lawarence, Pete & Anne

Lindsey, James, Martha & Mark
Lowe, Jack
Mumma, Slim, Marjorie & Bobbie.
Miller, Jerome
McCoy, Henry & Carolyn (Hirschy)
McMinn, Ethel, Melvin, Marlin
Meads, Jason B., Ph.D.
Miller, George, Lillian, Barbara, Mike,
    Susan, Patrick, Duane, Sherry
    & Roberta
Rainey, Virgina, Philip, Paul
Reed, Rosie, Homer, Jenny, Pat, Bill,
    & Robert
Rimers, Richard, Cleo, Burt, Brent
Robinson, Gertrude, Tom,
    Jim & Karleen
Robinson, Frances & Kenneth
Roller, Gilbert, Jerry & family
Sheldon, Gene, Betty,Shelly & Julie
Siefkin, Ben, Ethel, Sharon & Carol
Siefkin, Clarence, Loretta,
    Denny & Larry Abbott
Suggs, Eva, Len, Butch
    Tom, Lucille & Lonnie
VanBlarcom, Carl
Wagner, Robert
Webb, Phil & Don
Wieman, Elry, Beulah, Barbara,
    Marvin, Shirley & Marilyn
Wright, Carolyn, Wanda, David,
    Cheryl (Videto)
Zoreman, Jack & Betty

There may be other names I have not mentioned in this book. Please forgive me if I have left any names out of this list. I am writting a sequel to this story for the years after 1966 up to 2004; those years will include more names.

ORDER FORM

YES, I would like to have my own copy or more copies of the book, *Home Sweet Home* by Maxine Derr. Please send me:

_____ # books x $14.95 per copy =   _____

+ Postage & Handling: (shipping by U.S. Mail)
    Book Rate @ $2.75 per copy: _____

        (per book – four to five weeks)   *OR*

      First Class @ $4.50 *(up to 2 books)*:

        (one to two weeks)   _____

TOTAL ENCLOSED $ _____

We accept cash, check, or money order made out to Northbooks, or VISA/Mastercard. Prices subject to change without notice.

VISA/MC card # ☐☐☐☐ ☐☐☐☐ ☐☐☐☐ ☐☐☐☐

Exp. Date: ___/___   Amount Charged: $ _____

Signature: _____

(You may phone your VISA/MC order to Northbooks at 907-696-8973)

Please send my book (s) to:

Name: _____

Address: _____

City:_____ State:____ Zip:_____

Fill out this order form and send to:

ᑎORᴄᕼBOOKS
17050 N. Eagle River Loop Rd, #3
Eagle River, AK 99577-7804